THE
KIRTLAND
MASSACRE

THE
KIRTLAND
MASSACRE

by Cynthia Stalter Sassé
and Peggy Murphy Widder

DIF

DONALD I. FINE, INC.
New York

Library of Congress Cataloging-in-Publication Data

Sassé, Cynthia Stalter.
    The Kirtland massacre : the true and terrible story of the Mormon cult murders / by Cynthia Stalter Sassé and Peggy Murphy Widder.
        p.   cm.
    Includes index.
    ISBN 1-55611-309-9
    1. Murder—Ohio—Kirtland—Case studies.   2. Cults—Ohio—Kirtland —Case Studies.   3. Mormons—Ohio—Kirtland—Case studies.
    4. Lundgren, Jeffery.   5. Avery, Dennis.   6. Avery, Cheryl.
    I. Widder, Peggy Murphy.   II. Title.
    HV6533.O5S27   1991
    364.1'523'09771334—dc20   91-55182
                                                                          CIP

Manufactured in the United States of America

10   9   8   7   6   5   4   3   2   1

Designed by Irving Perkins Associates

ACKNOWLEDGMENTS

The sources for this book were widespread and numerous. In effect, the research consumed my life for a full year. All of my colleagues, the prosecutors, were very generous. Karen Lawson and Sandy Dray were particularly helpful. Patrolman Ron Andolsek of the Kirtland Police Department researched and compiled a nearly overwhelming amount of information. Chief Dennis Yarborough of the Kirtland Police Department was an invaluable resource, particularly for insight into the Reorganized Church of Jesus Christ of Latter Day Saints (RLDS) and church history. I also interviewed every witness who appeared for the State of Ohio and many who did not. But most of all, I cannot count the hours I spent with Jeff Lundgren's group—especially Sharon Bluntschly, Richard Brand, Greg Winship, Debbie Olivarez, Shar Olsen, Keith Johnson, Tonya and Dennis Patrick. All were honest, informative, and cooperative; I spent the most time with Debbie. I developed an affection and concern for these people that will last long after the world has forgotten about the Kirtland Massacre.

For historical background on the Mormon religion and Joseph Smith, Jr., I consulted a variety of books, including *A History of the Mormons,* by Douglas Tobler; *The Mormon Church: A Basic History,* by Dean Hughes; *The Mormon Murders,* by Steven Naifeh; *Mormonism in Transition,* by Thomas Alexander; *A Gathering of Saints,* by Robert Lindsey; *No Man Knows My History,* by Fawn M. Brodie; and *Early Mormonism and the Magic World View,* by Michael Quinn.

I am particularly indebted to my sister, Sara Niemeyer, and to Linda Evilsizer, who provided invaluable assistance; to my editor, Lisa Healy, for her patience, professionalism, and downright great ideas; to my agent, Faith Hamlin, for putting up with my insecurity; to my brother, Earl Stalter, and to my parents, Ruth and Roger Stalter, for their unfaltering support; and, most of all, to my husband, Greg, and my children, Ben, Meggan, and Jon, without whose love and sacrifice this book could never have been written, and to Peggy Widder for her patience and loving support.

—Cynthia Stalter Sassé

My sincere thanks goes to Faith Hamlin, Doug Stallings, Lisa Healy, Don Fine, Gary Swilik, Mike Sutila, John Kuntz, Claire Fenrich, Ken Cogburn and to the countless others who have helped with this project. Last, but not least, I thank my marvelous co-author and friend, Cynthia Stalter Sassé.

—Peggy Murphy Widder

To Greg, Ben, Meggan, and Jon.
You are my sunshine.
—Cynthia Stalter Sassé

Dedicated to my wonderful husband
John M. Widder
who always makes difficult things easy for me
and
to Andy and Nina
who were willing to put up with a distracted mother
while this book was being completed.
—Peggy Murphy Widder

CONTENTS

THE
KIRTLAND
MASSACRE

THE LUNDGREN GROUP

BLUNTSCHLY, SHARON JEAN

> Born August 18, 1958. Average height, heavy. Light brown hair, blue eyes. Shy, in a world of her own.

BRAND, RICHARD EUGENE

> Born April 11, 1963. Five feet, eleven inches tall. Blonde hair, blue eyes. Intelligent, witty, charming. Civil engineer.

JOHNSON, KATHRYN RENEE

> Born May 7, 1953. Dark brown hair, hazel eyes. Married to Larry Keith Johnson. Energetic, assertive, maternal.

JOHNSON, LARRY KEITH

> Born December 6, 1948. Dark brown, graying hair, brown eyes. Bachelor's degree in social work. Good old boy.

> JOSHUA JOHNSON—Born February 1979
> JEREMY JOHNSON—Born June 1982
> JUSTIN JOHNSON—Born June 1984
> JORDAN JOHNSON—Born July 1986

KRAFT, DANIEL DAVID, JR.

> Born September 29, 1964. Light brown hair, blue eyes, short, slender. Artistically and musically gifted. Gentle, humorous.

LUFF, RONALD BOYD

Born February 1960. Light brown, thinning hair, blue eyes. Short, muscular. Tight emotional control. Married to Susan Luff.

LUFF, SUSAN LOUISE

Born December 29, 1958. Medium brown hair, green eyes. Short, slender, attractive. Chatters constantly.

MATTHEW LUFF—Born July 1982
AMY LUFF—Born June 1985

LUNDGREN, ALICE ELIZABETH

Born January 21, 1951. Dark brown hair, blue eyes. Short, tends to extreme obesity. Plain. Soft-spoken, extremely manipulative.

LUNDGREN, DAMON PAUL

Born December 2, 1970. Light brown hair, blue eyes. Average height, slim. Delicate features. Son of Alice and Jeffrey Lundgren. Manipulative, violent.

LUNDGREN, JEFFREY DON

Born May 3, 1950. Light brown, receding hair, hazel eyes. Tall, muscular, tends toward obesity. Manipulative narcissist, thief, con man. Married to Alice Lundgren.

DAMON PAUL LUNDGREN—Born December 1970
JASON DON LUNDGREN—Born July 1974
KRISTEN MICHELLE LUNDGREN—Born June 1979
CALEB MATTHEW LUNDGREN—Born September 1980

OLIVAREZ, DEBORAH SUE

Born April 4, 1952. Dark brown hair, brown eyes. Average height, tends to be heavy. Attractive. Assertive, insightful. First cousin to Jeffrey Lundgren.

OLSEN, SHAR LEA

Born September 22, 1960. Blonde hair, blue eyes. Tall, very attractive. Charming, humorous.

PATRICK, DENNIS SIMS

Born August 21, 1954. Dark brown hair, mustache, green eyes. Tall, slender, attractive. Quiet, unassertive.

PATRICK, TONYA JEANNIE

Born July 25, 1956. Red hair, blue eyes. Average height, tends to be overweight. Warm, friendly. Married to Dennis Patrick.

MOLLY PATRICK—Born June 1980

WINSHIP, GREGORY SCOTT

Born September 24, 1960. Light brown hair, blue eyes. Tall, slim. Pleasant face. Warm, sensitive.

THE
VICTIMS

AVERY, CHERYL LYNN

Born May 27, 1947. Dark brown, graying hair. Short, plump. Plain, appealing face. Housewife.

AVERY, DENNIS LEROY

Born May 28, 1940. Graying dark brown hair, blue eyes. Short, average build. Regular features, receding chin. Meticulous. Married to Cheryl Avery.

AVERY, KAREN DIANE

Born August 3, 1982. Light brown hair, blue eyes. Appealing personality.

AVERY, REBECCA LYNN

Born January 23, 1976. Medium brown hair, blue eyes. Enjoyed crafts and sewing.

AVERY, TRINA DENISE

Born March 7, 1974. Long, dark brown hair, brown eyes. Good student.

THE LAW ENFORCEMENT OFFICERS

Cleveland Group II
Supervisor, Patti L. Galupo
Special Agent Roarke Wright
Special Agent Abigail A. Dickson
Special Agent Jean Stratman
Special Agent Bernie Teyssier

Kansas City, Missouri
Special Agent in Charge, George A. Rodriguez
Special Agent Richard Van Haelst
Special Agent Larry P. Scott
Special Agent Cynthia L. Grob
Special Agent Mark S. James
Special Agent Michael P. Schmitz
Special Agent Steven H. Frueh

San Diego District
Special Agent in Charge, James Stathes
Special Agent R. Scott Parkhurst
Special Agent Robert D. Lowery
Special Agent Lanny Royer
Special Agent James Allison

7

FEDERAL BUREAU OF INVESTIGATION

Special Agent Robert A. Alvord
Special Agent Lloyd N. Buck
Special Agent George W. Arruda
Special Agent Marshall L. Sullivan
Special Agent Gordon A. Hess, Jr.
Special Agent Gary W. Graff
Special Agent Joseph R. Haluscak
Special Agent J. Michael Ray
Special Agent Edward G. Bak
Special Agent John William Powers
Special Agent James A. Kennedy, Jr.
Special Agent John M. Hinkle

KIRTLAND POLICE DEPARTMENT

Chief Dennis Yarborough
Patrolman Ronald Andolsek

LAKE COUNTY SHERIFF'S DEPARTMENT

Sheriff Patrick Walsh
Lieutenant Daniel Dunlap
Deputy Ronald Walters

TUCKER COUNTY, WEST VIRGINIA

Sheriff Hank Thompson

THE
PROSECUTORS

STEVEN C. LATOURETTE, Lake County Prosecutor

KAREN LUTZ KOWALL, Chief Criminal Assistant Prosecutor

RICHARD COLLINS

SANDRA DRAY

JOSEPH DELGUYD

JOSEPH GURLEY

DAVID JOYCE, Geauga County Prosecuting Attorney

KAREN LAWSON

THOMAS LOBE

CYNTHIA SASSÉ

ARIANA TARIGHATI

THE DEFENSE ATTORNEYS

ROBERT LAFORCE: SHARON BLUNTSCHLY

CHARLES ATWELL:
JAMES KRIVOK: RICHARD BRAND

LEO COLLINS: KATHRYN JOHNSON

ELMER GIULIANI:
ROBERT TOBIK: DANIEL KRAFT

J. ROSS HAFFEY:
RICHARD MORRISSON: RONALD LUFF

LOUIS TURI: SUSAN LUFF

MARK ZICCARELLI:
JOSEPH GIBSON: ALICE LUNDGREN

ALBERT PUROLA:
CHARLES CICHOCKI: DAMON LUNDGREN

R. PAUL LAPLANTE:
CHARLES GRIESHAMMER: JEFFREY LUNDGREN

JOHN HURLEY: DEBORAH OLIVAREZ

JAMES KOERNER: DENNIS PATRICK

CLIFTON "PAT" JONES: TONYA PATRICK

GERALD GOLD: GREGORY WINSHIP

1

THE DEED— "BLOOD ATONEMENT"

On the evening of April 17, 1989, in Kirtland, Ohio, Jeffrey Don Lundgren, the leader of a tiny religious cult, executed five people. Lundgren had convinced the members of his group, a splinter group from the Mormon-derived Reorganized Church of Latter Day Saints, that the deaths were necessary in order for the group members to see God in the flesh on earth. For the executed, it was a Blood Atonement.

On that early spring evening, with the green of new leaves and the delicate pastels of blossoming trees and bushes barely beginning to soften the harsh browns left by the northeastern Ohio winter, the Avery family were invited to have dinner with the Lundgrens. Dinner was served in the old farmhouse on the outskirts of Kirtland, which Lundgren had rented for his family and several of his followers. The Averys were told that they would be accompanying the group on its planned trip to the wilderness, where Lundgren promised that God would appear if the group were free from sin.

After dinner, Alice Lundgren, Jeffrey's wife, abruptly left the farm, taking with her their three younger children, Jason, age fourteen, Kristen, age nine, and Caleb, age eight. Jeff and their oldest child, Damon, nineteen, remained behind, as did four other men, three women, two children, and the Avery family.

While the women, including Cheryl Avery, tidied the dining room and kitchen and washed the dishes after dinner, the other men, ex-

13

cept for Dennis Avery, went out to the barn located some distance behind the house. There, over the previous week, several of the men had dug a large pit, wide and deep enough to hold ten bodies, in the dirt floor of the building.

Then, each of the Averys, from the oldest, Dennis, to Karen, the youngest, was lured individually to the barn, bound and blindfolded, and dumped into the pit. Lundgren then executed the parents and their children one at a time, using his favorite pistol, a .45–caliber Colt Combat Elite.

After little Karen's death, Lundgren ordered his followers to cover the bodies with lime, then with rocks and dirt, and finally to pile the trash that filled the ground floor of the barn over the grave. Lundgren bathed, then accompanied his wife and his oldest son to the motel room he had rented for the Averys and removed any belongings they might have left behind.

After the Lundgrens returned to the farm, and the workers in the barn were finished, the group gathered in the farmhouse living room for a Scripture class. An hour later, class was dismissed and everyone went to bed.

2

IN THE BEGINNING

Jeffrey Don Lundgren was born May 3, 1950, in Independence, Missouri, the first of two sons born to Don and Lois Gadberry Lundgren. The new parents were proud of their first-born who, according to family accounts, was a handsome, bright little fellow.

The family was relatively prosperous. Don did well in the construction business, and Lois kept house and cared for her children, as was expected of a proper Mormon housewife. The family were active in their church, the "stake," or local congregation, of the Reorganized Church of Jesus Christ of Latter Day Saints (RLDS), an offshoot of the original Mormon Church, and spent much of their time at church functions.

The Lundgrens were concerned parents, although both sides of the family tended to feel that Don was perhaps a little too strict with his sons and that Lois tended to be rigid and remote, more concerned with keeping an immaculate house and clean children than with nurturing those children's immediate emotional needs. Lois was so intent upon preserving her antique furnishings that children were not permitted to enter the parlor unless they had just bathed and put on clean clothing. Even then, young bodies had to accept sitting still on the immaculate furniture.

Jeff has said that he was physically abused as a child, sometimes beaten for normal, childish mistakes or minor misbehavior. Don insisted that his children meet certain standards, and it sometimes seemed that the little boys were unable to live up to their father's expectations. Jeff has been described by his aunt, his father's sister, as a good child, eager to please, who despite his best efforts was con-

15

stantly being disciplined by his father for real or imagined infractions of the rules.

Jeff has said that when he was older he was punished by being thrown against a barbed-wire fence by his father. Jeff's claims of physical abuse have not been confirmed by any other family member. The neighbors, however, have spoken of acts of physical cruelty by Don and his elder son against neighborhood children and animals. On one occasion, according to a neighbor, Jeff nailed a rabbit to a slab of wood and then beat the animal to death.

In high school Jeff was a good-looking young man, but a loner, remote and arrogant. He was widely disliked for his manner and has been described as having had only one real friend, a young woman he had known since grade school.

As a teenager Jeff worked for his uncle, his mother's older brother, in the Gadberry furniture store. Jeff was a reliable employee, always on time and willing to work as many hours as required. He seemed so level-headed and reliable that his uncle sometimes left the young man in charge of the store all by himself.

School, the store and hunting with his father consumed most of Jeff's time. Don Lundgren was devoted to hunting and gun collecting, particularly black-powder weapons still made like those used at the time of the Revolutionary War, without the modern prepackaged neatness of self-contained rounds of ammunition. Jeff learned about firearms from his father, and hours were spent together discussing and cleaning the guns or using the weapons while hunting.

As a young adult Jeff stood about six feet with an average build, although he would later gain both muscle and fat to such an extent that he would be described as stocky. He had pleasant regular features, light-brown wavy hair that he wore average length and combed straight back, and a charming smile. The only flaws in his physical appearance were a somewhat receding chin and skin roughened by acne.

When Jeffrey, the first-born and the first to venture from the nest, went to college at Central Missouri State University, he carried his parents' expectations for success. But he had few real interests and no apparent focus. In his sophomore year at CMSU, majoring in electronics, Jeff spent much of his time at the student house sponsored by the RLDS, the Reorganized Church of Latter Day Saints, where he met Keith Johnson and Alice Keehler. Both would have a profound effect on his life and on the lifes—and sudden deaths—of five other human beings.

Alice Elizabeth Keehler was born January 21, 1951, the first-born of Ralph and Donna Keehler. Ralph Keehler was an ironworker at the time of his daughter's birth and had been a cook on a PT boat in World War II. Donna Keehler was a housewife and homemaker, rearing her children much as Lois Lundgren was doing. The Keehlers, however, were remote from the Lundgrens in every other way.

Money, which was plentiful in the Lundgren household, was a constant problem for the Keehlers. The Keehlers participated sporadically, if at all, in church functions and rarely attended their local congregation, whereas the Lundgrens were an active church family. Donna Keehler was a more nurturing parent than was Lois Lundgren, but Ralph Keehler was a remote father, as was Don Lundgren. The Lundgrens lived in a comfortable home in a prosperous suburb of Independence; from the time Alice Keehler was eleven the Keehlers crowded into a house trailer on a lot outside of Mack's Creek, some twenty miles from Independence and 150 miles from Ralph Keehler's job. Ralph would come home on weekends and on rare occasions would make the grueling round trip in the middle of the week. Alice Keehler was living a very different life from that of her future spouse, Jeffrey Lundgren. The families were alike in only one significant respect—both were severely dysfunctional. Communication of affection and mutual respect for each other was no more successful in the Keehler family than in the Lundgren household.

Alice was soon joined by a younger sister Sue, two years younger than Alice. Terri, five years Alice's junior, is married to her second husband, an oral surgeon who practices in Saudi Arabia. Alice's only brother Chuck is twelve years younger than she, has three children and is a recovering alcoholic and substance abuser.

Shortly after Chuck was born, Ralph Keehler was diagnosed with multiple sclerosis, and Alice's life became an inescapable misery. Because her husband was unable to work, Donna Keehler found a job as a secretary for the local welfare department. The job, while steady and dependable, provided little income to support a family of six, and the family's budget was much tighter than before.

Alice was frequently left in charge of providing care for her father and supervising her younger sisters and brother. Ralph Keehler's condition was being treated with cortisone and prednisone, and the drugs, combined with the frustrations of the illness and the helplessness it created, caused Alice's father to become physically violent.

Alice, as the child who was most often within easy reach, became the focus of her father's violence, particularly when she tried to intervene to protect one of the younger children. According to Alice, her mother was unaware of the violence; the children concealed their father's behavior to preserve family unity.

Alice says that she admires her mother, whom she characterizes as a very strong person. And it was true that Donna Keehler supported her young family when her husband became ill, earned a high-school equivalence certificate for her position as a secretary, and worked to provide for her children.

High school was a problem for Alice. She says she did not enjoy her high school years and wasn't popular with the other students. Alice, who had always been active in her church, continued with her church activities although her parents had little interest.

As a young adult, Alice had grown to five feet three inches. She had dark brown hair and large pretty blue eyes. Her nose was large, with a slight hook, her mouth wide and thin. Not a pretty woman, but her lively blue eyes and large engaging smile tended to draw others to her. She had a soft, thin, rather high-pitched voice.

It was at Central Missouri State University that Alice blossomed. She became active in the church youth group, where she met Jeff. The two began dating almost immediately, and shortly thereafter became sexually intimate. Alice was sexually naive, having had very few dates in high school, and Jeff may have exploited her inexperience. In any event, what may have started as a casual romance for the handsome young man quickly became almost an obsession. Jeff was always with Alice; he could not seem to pry himself away from her side. They ran as a team for president and vice-president of the church house and won easily. They were happier than ever before in their lives. There was only one cloud on their horizon. The Lundgrens did not approve of Alice. She was not of their social class, did not live up to their standards. They were certain that their bright handsome son could do much better, and were concerned that Jeff was failing all his courses because he insisted on spending his time with Alice rather than in class or studying.

Jeff, on the other hand, was determined to have Alice. When Don and Lois refused to consent to a wedding the young couple outflanked their elders—Alice became pregnant. Both dropped out of college, and at the wedding in the late spring of 1970 no member of Jeff's family was present at the church. Don and Lois refused to attend after having given their reluctant consent. Keith Johnson, a friend of the newlyweds whom they had met in the church house, was the only guest on Jeff's side of the church.

After the wedding Jeff found it was not as easy to support his soon-to-be-growing family as he had thought. Somehow his father had managed to make providing a more-than-adequate standard of living look easy. Jeff was ill-prepared for the new responsibilities and in desperation, some six months after the wedding, he enlisted in the Navy on November 9 and was shipped to San Diego for basic training. A few weeks later, on December 2, Jeff's first son, Damon Paul, was born.

The new mother, alone and feeling abandoned with a small baby and a husband so far away, moved in with the Lundgrens, who now appeared to have relented somewhat in their feelings toward their daughter-in-law. Alice has said her mother-in-law "polished the stone" in those months together when Lois Lundgren taught her son's wife social graces and gave her a taste for luxury.

But the young bride was not happy. She missed Jeff. She worried he might be sent to Vietnam and killed. Alice began writing letters to Jeff's commanding officers requesting that he be discharged because she couldn't live without him. The Keehlers and the Lundgrens were also recruited to beg the Navy to give Jeff up, and then Missouri Senator Stuart Symington was even prevailed upon to make an inquiry in the matter.

None of the requests was successful, possibly because Jeff apparently didn't cooperate with the campaign. In July Jeff was transferred to the USS *Sperry*, where he served until May of 1972, then was transferred to the USS *Shelton*. In June of 1973, Jeff was transferred again, to the USS *Schofield*, where he was serving when he was honorably discharged in July of 1974. In all of his assignments Jeff had served as a radio or electronics technician, impressing his superior officers with his knowledge and intelligence. He would advance rapidly in each command until, all unaccountably, he would begin to slough off and his work would suffer. The pattern recurred in each assignment.

* * *

For the last two years of Jeff's enlistment Alice lived in San Diego so that she and Jeff could be together when his ship was in port. Relatives of Jeff's mother were also living in southern California, so Alice had some family contacts while Jeff was away. In fact, the Lundgrens agreed to buy antique furniture from Jeff's family, to be paid back over time. The furniture was never paid for. This was the first time, but not the last, that the family knew Jeff and Alice to fail to pay their debts.

While they were in San Diego Alice and Jeff opened their home to Jeff's navy friends, particularly those Jeff was trying to convert to the RLDS faith.

Both the Mormon Church and the RLDS are evangelical, actively attempting to convert those who do not follow the Book of Mormon. Missionary work is considered to be holy work, and those who succeed in recruiting converts are generally rewarded with increased stature and respect in the church. As a young couple active in the church, the Lundgrens opened their home to the gentiles, hoping to prove through example the benefits of family life that flowed from RLDS membership. One of the young men who was particularly impressed with Jeff both on and off the ship, and consequently was attracted to the church, was Kevin Currie, who would later become the first to actually move into the Lundgren home while studying Jeff's teachings.

On July 24, 1974, just one week before his father was discharged, Alice's and Jeff's second son, Jason Don, was born. And a few weeks later the Lundgrens returned to the Independence area, where Jeff reenrolled at Central Missouri State University.

At CMSU Jeff and Alice Lundgren again became active in the church house where they had had so much success five years earlier. This time, though, as a married couple, their activities were necessarily more restricted. It was likely at this point that Jeff's later notorious roving eye first lit on someone of more than passing interest.

Twenty-two-year-old Tonya Patrick was a student at CSMU and also a frequent visitor to the church house. Tonya, with her vibrant manner and red hair and blue eyes, was a striking contrast to Alice, who had become strident and demanding as Jeff had tried to escape her smothering dependence. Jeff was smitten. According to Alice, Tonya was equally interested in Jeff, although Tonya denies that she was ever attracted to him.

It was also at this time that Jeff seems to have first constructed his intense dislike for Dennis Patrick, Tonya's husband. Dennis appeared to have everything that Jeff did not have, and to handle it with ease. Jeff could not comprehend why this should be, but it appeared that God was favoring Dennis, while Jeff had done more significant work on behalf of the church. Jeff believed himself to be both more intelligent and more devout than Dennis, qualities for which, according to his faith, he should have been rewarded by God with material comforts. But instead, Dennis Patrick seemed to prosper, while Jeff was saddled with a dependent, manipulative, demanding wife and an increasingly large family he could not seem to support.

Jeff also may have first practiced his embezzling skills at CMSU. It's certain that he did not remain to receive his degree, and the personnel records from the time Jeff was employed at the university have been destroyed, but the rumor persists that Jeff was asked to leave because of irregularities in funds or supplies entrusted to him. Alice says that she believed that Jeff had received his bachelor's degree and was working toward his master's.

From this period of 1976 or 1977 until at least 1981 Alice and Jeff struggled, Jeff having a string of jobs, frequently at hospitals or other public institutions, where he performed much as he had in the Navy. At first his employers were impressed with his ability and charm, then eventually he would be asked to leave because of some irregularity in the way he handled his job or because of his irresponsible attitude.

At one point during this time, Alice remembers, Jeff was arrested for passing bad checks. She was called to bail him out, shocked because she had known nothing of their financial straits and Jeff's way of handling the problem.

Also, according to Alice, at this time Jeff began to have affairs with other women. Debbie Olivarez, Jeff's cousin, says the family rumor was that the marriage was failing and that Alice deliberately became pregnant with Kristen to save her marriage. Kristen Michelle Lundgren was born June 21, 1979.

During this time Jeff and Alice carried on intermittent contact with Keith Johnson, their old friend from college. Keith and Jeff attempted to go into business together, raising a herd of beefalo, a cross between buffalo and cattle, which failed like Jeff's other schemes.

In 1980 Jeff worked in the maintenance department at Our Lady of the Ozarks Hospital in Blue Springs, Missouri. After he had been at the hospital for several months, two spare televisions and some other electrical equipment Jeff was responsible for were missing. Eventually the missing equipment was accidentally discovered in the Lundgren house. Jeff blustered that he had brought the items home to work on them, and because the hospital couldn't prove otherwise the matter was dropped, but Jeff was asked to resign.

Another incident occurred in Blue Springs that became the basis for much of Alice's folklore. Alice has told at least five different versions of the following story to different individuals, but this one, which she later told to Shar Olsen, seems to be the most credible because it most nearly conforms to the personalities of the principal players.

Caleb Matthew Lundgren was born September 13, 1980. While Alice was pregnant with Caleb (apparently another baby conceived to keep her husband by her side), she became certain that Jeff was having an affair with a woman he worked with. Alice suspected that Jeff was involved with several women at work but she was sure that this particular relationship was intense and of some duration.

One Friday payday, when the family was desperately in need of the groceries that were to be purchased with Jeff's paycheck, Jeff didn't return home at the end of the day. In fact, neither Jeff nor his paycheck appeared at all for the whole weekend. Alice became frantic and enraged that her husband was undoubtedly spending his family's money on a weekend with his girlfriend. When Jeff finally returned on Sunday evening, not at all repentant, Alice was furious. Standing at the top of the flight of steps leading to the front door, she lunged at Jeff, her hands raised and fingers flexed, ready to gouge at his neck. Jeff raised his arms to push his wife away, and in the process pushed her down the stairway. Alice ruptured her spleen and had to have emergency surgery.

Alice also claims that Jeff had taken to beating her regularly, and her mother has said that she observed unexplained bruises on her daughter's body. No one outside the immediate family ever saw any indication that Jeff beat Alice, although Alice has numerous times in conversations with numerous people blamed her ruptured spleen on a beating from Jeff.

Jeff's physical mistreatment of his son Damon has, however, been attested to by Dennis Patrick, who says he was on hand when Damon, then about ten years old, was knocked to the floor by his father's fists and kicked when he was down.

Finally, about 1981, Jeff and Alice returned to the Independence area and became involved in the Lundgren family's traditional church, the Slover Park Congregation. Jeff still felt the sting of the church's rejection despite what he felt were his best efforts to live a sin-free life and to bring new converts into the church. At the age of thirty-one he had not even been asked to join the RLDS lay priesthood, although most young men were called at about age nineteen or twenty.

According to Jeff's account, one day when the family was living in Independence he suddenly realized that the priesthood was a political organization, and he finally understood how to manipulate the church authorities. Jeff says that on that day he told Alice, "I've finally figured it out and I will bet you that within six months I can arrange to be invited to join the priesthood."

Jeff says that it took less than six months from that date to become a priest. But he also says that it was at this time that he finally lost all faith in the RLDS church, its traditions and its teachings. Even so, Jeff said, he realized that Scripture undoubtedly contained the truth, and it was now his challenge to find the answers for himself in Scripture.

He formed a study group, primarily from the congregation he and Alice attended, that met in the evenings in his home in Independence, much as his group in Kirtland would begin meeting in his home. There were two groups. The larger was taught in more general terms and less frequently, and the smaller group met more frequently and was taught difficult concepts.

Dennis and Tonya Patrick were part of the smaller group, as were Dennis and Cheryl Avery, who also attended Slover Park. A friend of Debbie Olivarez, Jeff's first cousin and later one of his followers, also attended the smaller sessions for a time, but the woman left because, she said, it seemed that Jeff was "making it up as he went along."

Even if so, Jeff appeared to attract a number of people who wholeheartedly believed that he had discovered the way to truth. Dennis and Cheryl Avery were among them. According to Debbie's friend, Cheryl Avery appeared to worship the ground that Jeff walked on, though Dennis was somewhat skeptical. Another devoted follower was a local professional man who largely supported the Lundgrens for the last two years that they lived in Independence with cash donations of several hundred dollars every month.

Jeff apparently was not satisfied with the amounts he was being given freely, and complained frequently and bitterly that he should be given half the incomes of all of his followers, it being their obligation to share equally with their teacher. At that point much of the freely given support abruptly disappeared.

It was time to move on to fresh and greener pastures. Jeff explained to his flock that he had discovered from the Scriptures that it would be necessary for him to relocate to Kirtland to discover the Truth and to receive power from God. Jeff's remaining followers had several fund-raising events to help the family accumulate sufficient assets to move, "sacrificing" their comfort for knowledge of God.

The Jeff and Alice Lundgren patent medicine show was taking to the road, moving to another location where the marks were untouched and where thousands of gullible souls, dedicated to the worship and knowledge of God, would appear every month. Kirtland, Ohio, appeared to be an ideal place to practice the scam the pair had come close to perfecting in Missouri.

3

CITY OF FAITH
AND BEAUTY

When the Book of Mormon was published in the spring of 1830, its youthful author could hardly have anticipated the eventual success of his "new gospel," or the widespread influence of the volume and its attendant church. Joseph Smith, Jr., only twenty-four at the founding of the Church of Jesus Christ of Latter Day Saints (also called the LDS and commonly referred to as the Mormon Church) on April 6, 1830, was, according to Joseph and to the official church history, a prophet of God who was called to locate and to translate the Book of Mormon through divine inspiration.

Although there are several different accounts of Joseph's initial encounter with God, some in Joseph's own handwriting, the official version has it that Joseph had a vision in the early summer of 1820 when he was not yet fifteen. According to the official account, Joseph reported that his vision occurred while he was searching the Scriptures for an answer to the dilemma he said had become foremost in his life.

Joseph and his family were at that time living in Palmyra, New York, an area that in common with much of frontier New England was experiencing an intense religious revival. Superstition and religious hysteria were common, with revival services being conducted by the Presbyterian, Methodist, and Baptist churches, as well as by itinerant preachers and self-proclaimed prophets. Joseph later claimed that he had become confused by the public disagreement among the leaders of these churches and, in his uncertainty, had searched for guidance in the Bible. He said his search was rewarded with the verse from James 1:5: "If any of you lack wisdom, let him ask of God, that giveth to all men liberally, and upbraideth not; and it shall be given him." Further prayer was followed by a vision in which Joseph was warned that none of the currently existing churches was correct.

The church history relates that Joseph experienced another vision on September 21, 1823, when he was informed by an angel called Moroni that God was calling upon Joseph to translate a gospel of Jesus Christ engraved upon thin gold plates in the language of a civilization that had once existed on the American continent. Moroni also revealed that the gold plates were concealed in a hill near Joseph's home, and that two stones, the Urim and Thummim, which could be used to translate the plates, were concealed with them. Joseph, however, was not permitted to locate the plates until several years later. There is little credible evidence that Joseph mentioned these early experiences to anyone until after he claimed to have located the plates and to have begun translating them. The translation was published in March of 1830 as the Book of Mormon.

According to Joseph Smith, Jr., the LDS was structurally a return to the original church founded by the disciples of Christ. The structure and teachings were based on the text of the Book of Mormon and revelations received by the prophet, Joseph Smith, Jr. In several significant areas the teaching of the LDS is unique. Alone of all contemporary Christian churches, the LDS was founded on the basic concept of an unchanging God who, because His nature is the same now as it was in the time of Adam and as it will be at the end of time, speaks to mankind now as He did in the time of the prophets recorded in the Bible. Joseph Smith, Jr., the prophet-president of the church, claimed to have spoken to God frequently on a wide variety of subjects. Each of these revelations delivered to Joseph was, according to LDS doctrine, the word of God communicated through direct conversation, and was to be followed explicitly. The revelations delivered to Joseph were later published in a volume called *The Doctrine and Covenants*, which is one of the three holy books recognized by his followers.

The Saints of Joseph's church became accustomed to the intervention of God in their everyday lives as Joseph received revelations on a variety of topics from the mundane to the divine. In response to the command of God, the Saints picked themselves up from western New York State and moved to Kirtland, Ohio, where the church missionary efforts had been unusually successful. During the several years that they were in Kirtland, the Saints, again at divine command, built a Temple at great personal sacrifice. However, in Kirtland, as in New York and later in Missouri and Illinois, the church members seemed to antagonize their neighbors. In the spring of 1839, after having been violently expelled from Kirtland and from the Independence, Missouri, area the Saints established their own city, Nauvoo, on the Illinois shore of the Mississippi.

Radical new doctrines began to develop among the Saints in Nauvoo. For the first time polygamy reared its head, although the Reorganized Church denies that polygamy ever became an accepted doctrine of the church during Joseph Smith's lifetime. The evidence, though, seems clear that Joseph not only practiced polygamy personally but that he also encouraged the upper hierarchy of the church to do likewise. It was also at this time that Joseph introduced his radical community-planning concepts and other startling ideas about the plural nature of God and the progression of man to eventual godhood. At that time Joseph was ordained prophet and president of the church, trustee in trust for all the church property, editor of the church newsletter, supervisor of the building of the Temple in Nauvoo, mayor of the city, chief justice of the municipal court, commanding officer of the Nauvoo Legion (a city-run militia), and proprietor of the general store. He also had himself crowned king of the Kingdom of God.

In the early 1840s Nauvoo became the largest city in Illinois, with the consequent balance of political power in the state falling to the Saints. The Saints, not being entirely unworldly, attempted to wield that power and were once again subjected to mob violence. On June 27, 1844, Joseph Smith, Jr., and his brother Hyrum were shot to death by a mob in Carthage, Illinois.

Following the unexpected death of the prophet, various claimants to power rose in the LDS church. The largest group of Saints followed Brigham Young, former head of the Council of Twelve, who led his congregation to the Great Salt Lake Valley of Utah. This group became the organization today commonly called Mormons.

The second-largest group of Saints believed that Joseph Smith III, son of Joseph Smith, Jr., had been designated by previous divine appointment to be the prophet-president of the church. At the time of his father's death, Joseph Smith III was not yet twelve, so this group was without its spiritual leader at a time of historical crisis. However, in 1852 some of this group began a process of "reorganization" according to their understanding of the "pattern" of the church established by Joseph Smith, Jr. In 1860 Joseph Smith III was formally ordained as prophet-president of the newly established church, the Reorganized Church of Jesus Christ of Latter Day Saints, or RLDS.

The LDS and RLDS churches continue to disagree about many doctrinal concepts in addition to that of the origin of the doctrine of "spiritual wives," or polygamy, including the nature of God, the proper approach to tithing, and the proper procedure for succession to the office of the prophet-president of the church. But upon the fundamental belief that God today speaks directly to man as He did in Biblical times, both churches agree. In both churches worshippers are taught that anyone may receive a personal communication from God, although only those who are ordained as "prophet, seer, and revelator" speak from God to the congregation.

Jeff Lundgren taught a third approach to the doctrines of Joseph Smith. His followers were told that Joseph Smith was not really a prophet. Jeff said that Joseph had had a divine mission to reveal the Book of Mormon to the world and to build the Kirtland Temple, but that Joseph exceeded his authority when he attempted to found a church. According to Jeff, it was clear that the organization and development of the early church were not divinely inspired; Joseph was just making things up as he went along.

One of the things the two Mormon churches have quarreled about over the past century is the ownership of the Kirtland Temple, which was in question from the death of Joseph Smith, Jr., in 1844 until 1880. At the time of his death Smith was trustee of all church property, but a question of the correct succession of the trusteeship and the consequent ownership of the Temple and the land on which it stood came up at the time of the prophet's death. The question was never completely resolved until 1880 when the RLDS sued Joseph Smith III in Common Pleas Court in Painesville, Ohio, to resolve the question of ownership. Judge L. S. Sherman heard legal arguments. Both churches claimed to be the true doctrinal successor to the church established by Joseph Smith, Jr., and both thereby claimed ownership of the Temple. On February 23, 1880, Judge Sherman found that the RLDS was more clearly the doctrinal lineal descendant of Joseph Smith's church and so was entitled to ownership of the Temple. The Kirtland Temple has been owned by the Reorganized Church ever since.

When the Saints moved to Kirtland in 1831 it was a small farming community of about a thousand people. There were some shops, a grist mill, a post office, one hotel, and a few other buildings and homes. Kirtland was, in effect, the Latter Day Saints headquarters from 1831 to 1833, and by the end of 1831 the LDS boasted an Ohio membership of some 1500.

On December 27, 1832, Joseph Smith, Jr., announced that he had received a revelation from God regarding a Temple to be constructed in Kirtland. The revelation contained explicit instructions about the construction of the Temple, but also instructed the faithful simply to prepare to build, not to start construction.

Their first concern was to obtain the proper site for the building. They agreed that the land had to have elevation, as it was traditional at the time to build houses of worship on a high point of ground so that worshippers' struggle to the summit might remind them of the difficult way to Heaven. The land also had to be within one mile of Kirtland for convenience and be inexpensive. The acquisition committee eventually settled on land at the crest of a bluff overlooking the Kirtland Flats and purchased a parcel of 156 acres for $5,000.

The Temple was built in 1830 at a cost of $45,000 to $70,000, most of which was donated by well-to-do members. Joseph Smith was forced, however, to borrow the final $14,000 to complete the structure. The building was built according to Joseph's revelation: It is fifty-five feet long and sixty-five feet wide in the inner court. The exterior walls are composed of local sandstone taken from a quarry now located in Chapin Forest, a park some five miles south of the Temple. The interior is built from local hardwoods, white poplar, oak and walnut painted a pristine white. The first floor of the Temple contains a vestibule and sanctuary, with matching pulpits on either end of the sanctuary for the Melchisedec and Aaronic priesthoods. The second floor is similar to the first but simpler in design. It was intended for classes. The third floor is an attic containing five small meeting rooms. The exterior walls at the base are four feet thick, tapering to a width of one foot at the top. The walls are composed of crushed stone rubble mortared together and covered with stucco. The stucco contains crushed dishes and glassware contributed by the LDS housewives, which makes the walls glisten and sparkle in the sunlight. The Temple was dedicated on March 27, 1836.

The RLDS maintains the Temple as a church historical site and conducts special services in the building on holidays and at other times. The church provides free guided tours of the Temple, which are a favorite holiday pilgrimage activity for both RLDS and LDS members. Tiny Kirtland attracts at least twenty thousand visitors every year to tour the Temple and other historical buildings important to both churches.

During the summers the Kirtland Temple guide service is augmented by temporary guides, usually students, who are given free housing and paid $125 a week. The permanent guide service is primarily composed of couples who volunteer their services as a tithe to the church. These couples are generally retired and don't need a salary. The church does provide free housing in various structures located near the Temple.

This is the guide service that Jeff and Alice Lundgren joined. When they arrived in Kirtland on August 19, 1984, they found a tiny, tight-knit community largely invisible to the casual traveler. The main street of Kirtland, Chillicothe Road, has become Ohio State Route 306 since the time of Joseph Smith, and one of the few direct arteries from north to south in Lake County. Modern Kirtland lies just over one mile south of Interstate Route 90, where it follows the Lake Erie shoreline after having swung north from the Ohio Turnpike through Cleveland and before it sweeps on north and east through Erie, Pennsylvania, to Buffalo, New York. Lakeland Community College, one of Ohio's many publicly funded two-year colleges, lies just south of the intersection of I–90 and Route 306. Lakeland also houses the summer training camp for the Cleveland Browns and has attracted a number of small motels to the intersection, including the Red Roof Inn, located almost in the shadow of the freeway.

Just south of the College, Chillicothe Road falls steeply away to the flood plain on either side of the Chagrin River. The red brick church building built by the Kirtland Stake of the LDS church in 1981 lies on the north side of the Chagrin River. On the south side of the river but still on the flats are several historic buildings, important to the RLDS and LDS churches, including the Sidney Rigdon General Store, once the property of one of Joseph's chief disciples and, according to church tradition, the first building Joseph Smith, Jr., set foot in in Kirtland.

Past the Sidney Rigdon Store, Route 306 swings around a curve and up the bluff to the south of the flood plain. At the top of the bluff stands the Temple, just east of the road and across the street from the Kirtland RLDS church. The Temple is surrounded by neatly kept gardens that serve to separate the building from the surrounding town. Just south of the gardens sits the Kirtland Temple Visitors' Center, a small, single-story dark gray building trimmed in white. The Visitors' Center assists pilgrims in knowing more about the Temple's history and houses the offices of the guide service and the Temple book store. Behind the Visitors' Center are several small, two-bedroom apartments maintained by the RLDS as free housing for the temporary guides who live on the site during the summers.

On the other side of the Visitors' Center from the Temple gardens is a modest white-framed two-story house also maintained by the church as housing for Temple guides, and across the street, next to the RLDS church, are two larger white-framed houses, also intended for guide families. The house next to the Visitors' Center was the house occupied by the Lundgren family while Jeff was employed as a guide at the Temple.

Just a short distance south of the Lundgren house is the Kirtland Town Hall, located in an antiquated fire station. The Kirtland Fire Department no longer occupies the building, but it is home to the six-man Kirtland Police Department and contains other city offices, including the mayor's office and the city council chambers. Next to City Hall are the Kirtland schools, and across the street are the Hilltop Apartments, a rather grim collection of buildings containing two-story townhouse units. The Patricks lived in the Hilltop Apartments during their entire stay in Kirtland. Just north of the Hilltop Apartments is the Gallup studio, where Danny Kraft was employed for more than three years.

The village is primarily a bedroom suburb, but the tiny downtown area is all that is generally seen by tourists in Kirtland to visit the Temple, as Greg Winship and Richard Brand and a group of church friends did on Memorial Day weekend in 1984. This was the first of three annual pilgrimages made by the two young men to the Temple. Jeff and Alice Lundgren had not yet arrived. Greg and Richard would become members of the Lundgren group.

On August 19, 1984, Jeff and Alice Lundgren and their four children arrived in Kirtland. Jeff and Alice officially became members of the guide service on that day. According to Jeff's statement, he and Alice went for a drive through Kirtland after their arrival, surprised that the pocket-sized village was the home of the Temple. They drove south on Chillicothe Road to Chapin Forest, a county park located five miles south of the Temple that contains a quarry. In his statement Jeff claimed that on that day he located a holy spot in the park where the Book of Mormon plates were buried, and according to Keith Johnson and Kevin Currie, that spot was in the quarry. Jeff denied that the holy spot was in the quarry but admitted he had told his followers, as a test of their faith in him, that the plates and the Sword of Laban—a sword that according to the Book of Mormon had been brought to the New World from the Holy Land in prehistoric times—were stored in the quarry. The group members failed the test when, one by one, they went to the quarry to check for themselves whether the plates were actually there.

Damon, Jason, and Kristen Lundgren were enrolled in the Kirtland schools on August 24—Kristen in kindergarten, Jason in fifth grade, and Damon in the eighth.

Jeff and Alice had the nest egg contributed by the group in Independence that they could use to meet their basic needs for a while in Kirtland but it was urgent that the family develop some other income if they were to survive. Full-time employment as guides at the Temple left little extra time in which to earn an outside income, even if Jeff had been inclined to do so. There were, however, two sources of untraceable cash Jeff quickly located.

From his earlier visit to the Temple, Jeff was aware that many Temple visitors gave cash donations to the guides, to be turned over to the church for Temple maintenance. He could also observe that receipts weren't usually given for such gifts. It was not a reach for him to conclude that the church had no knowledge of the amount of donations except as reported by the guides. Jeff was further pleased to learn that no accounts were kept of sales at the Visitors' Center book store— he began skimming from the receipts. God was providing. He further provided, by Jeff's lights, when Kevin Currie made a pilgrimage to the Temple in October of 1984.

At Jeff's trial Kevin described his shock at seeing his old friend from the Navy after ten years when Jeff opened the door of the Temple for him. After the Temple tour conducted by Jeff, Kevin went back with Jeff to the Lundgren home, where he noted that the house was in bad repair and the children's clothing was ragtag. Eventually the conversation led to money, and Kevin was shocked to hear that the family was forced to live on the charity of strangers, since the church did not provide a salary for the guides. When Kevin left, he too donated—two hundred dollars.

Kevin Currie was not the first nor the last visitor to be presented with the little drama of the starving Lundgren family. According to Currie, Jeff would strike up conversations with as many people as possible during a tour. After the tour Jeff would invite those seeming particularly susceptible to his home, where, as with Currie, they were exposed to the Lundgren children dressed in their most ragged, most ill-fitting clothing, and to Jeff's and Alice's talk about the difficulty of feeding four growing children, and so forth. Many left hundreds of dollars for the saintly Lundgrens.

According to Bishop Kenneth Stobaugh of the RLDS church, who was Director of Historical Sites when Jeff was a tour guide, the church has since calculated that Jeff made off with between $17,000 and $21,000 from the book store and visitor donations during his three years of service as a tour guide. It is a conservative figure, based as it is on the average amounts realized from the store and donations and not taking into account the active pitch being made for gifts. Nobody is sure how much tax-free income Jeff realized from the Kirtland Temple.

4

COMING TOGETHER

Somehow, whether through his study of Joseph Smith, or through his trial-and-error studies of human nature in the groups he attracted, or through other reading, Jeff Lundgren, the one-time loner and arrogant teen disliked by his contemporaries, was developing the ability to charm and confound—when it suited him. Those not the objects of his attention continued to be repelled by his arrogance and self-centeredness.

Alice was a real asset. She, too, had developed an unusually keen insight into the needs and weaknesses of others that she would use to manipulate them. The sensitive antennae that the abused child had developed as a defense now became weapons on behalf of herself and her husband.

The Lundgrens had a nice arrangement at the Temple, but Jeff was beginning to miss the adulation of his group in Independence. In Kirtland he was just another guide, no matter how often or how successfully he scammed the tourists with the tale of his great personal sacrifice in dedicating his life to the Temple.

When Kevin Currie arrived on a priesthood retreat in October, 1984, Jeff told his old friend the same story that had been so effective with other tourists, but added an explanation for relocating from Missouri that was a more polished version than he had fed to the group there. This was the first time Kevin had heard anyone assert the contemporary relevance of the command in the *Doctrine and Covenants* to "come to the Ohio, for there ye shall receive power." Even so, after some eight hours of conversation and "study" with Jeff and Alice, Kevin was convinced.

A few months later in February, 1985, Kevin Currie moved in with the Lundgren family in the house next to the Visitors' Center, took a job with the Veterans' Administration Hospital in Brecksville, and soon turned over his paycheck to Jeff to help with household expenses. While Alice wasn't exactly pleased to have another full-timer in the home, Jeff used Kevin as babysitter and, better, decided how much of Kevin's paychecks should be allocated to Kevin's needs. Jeff would divide his earnings as he saw fit, feeling he'd already been unfairly deprived of his rightful half by people who thought their needs were more important than his.

Kevin did not complain, apparently feeling that he owed his religious faith to Jeff and Alice—it was as a result of his contact with them in San Diego that he had joined the RLDS—and that he *owed* them this opportunity to reach for a new understanding of God, with himself, after all, a spiritual beneficiary. He would be an ingrate and fool to complain.

During this time, Jeff studied the symbols used to decorate the Temple, and began to weave chiasm, a concept he had discovered in an obscure scholarly paper several years before, and his own explanation of the significance of the Temple decorations into his tours. Chiasm was the notion that all things created by God were created according to a pattern. All things in nature, said Jeff, including the human body, had two identical halves. Such a pattern had to be divine and the mark of God. Jeff taught that anything not chiastic, not divinely symmetrical, had to be manmade, and that Scripture and anything else, including the Temple, could be tested for its divine origin by determining whether or not it was chiastic. The Temple was purely chiastic as it was, according to Jeff, identical not only from right to left but from front to back. And so the Temple was clearly divinely inspired and truly the House of the Lord.

Jeff later claimed to have had a vision in the Temple during this period. He would report this experience to his followers many times. According to Jeff, one evening he was going about his duties in the Temple when a "personage" entered. He immediately knew that this personage was an angel in the image of a man dressed in white robes and radiating a brilliant light. The angel walked up the stairs to the third floor, but Jeff didn't immediately follow, he didn't feel welcome. Finally he felt he was being summoned and went upstairs and there fell on his face, overcome by knowledge of his own unworthiness.

All but one of the people Jeff recruited into his group in Kirtland had been reared in the RLDS church. Danny Kraft, a convert, was baptized by Jeff in Kirtland.

Daniel David Kraft, Jr., was born in 1964 in Keokuk, Iowa, an unusually gifted young man. When he was seventeen he was playing seven instruments in addition to the guitar. He was equally precocious in representational art. The rest of Danny's life was not so rewarding.

His parents divorced when he was ten, and Danny would later tell friends that he had been physically abused by his parents. He felt isolated from his parents, he said, and it was clear—and understandable—to his friends in Kirtland that Danny came to believe that in Jeff and Alice Lundgren he had found the loving parents he'd been searching for. The Lundgrens gave the appearance of being in agreement about all of the important things in life, as Danny's parents were not. The Lundgrens provided guidance and attention, as his parents had not, and the Lundgrens often reminded him that they were his loving parents, appointed by God and always acting in his best interests. (Danny has still not been able to accept that his substitute parents might have cared for him even less than his original mother and father.)

As part of his fascination with representational art Danny enjoyed the study of architecture, and was particularly interested in the architectural history of the Mormon church, mostly because he had been raised in Nauvoo, Illinois, a major historical center of the church. During high-school years he'd participated in Mormon-related archeological projects in Nauvoo, and finally, as part of his interest in the history of Mormonism, had applied for a job as a summer guide at the Kirtland Temple, one of the major religious centers for both the Mormon and RLDS churches. It was this summer of 1985 when Danny first met Jeff Lundgren and was baptized into the RLDS church. He gave up his long-term goal of becoming a commercial artist and settled in Kirtland to search for God, supporting himself and providing his portion of the support for the Lundgren family by his employment at Gallup's Art Gallery, where he made miniature models of Shaker furniture.

A thin young man with delicate but sharp, well-balanced features, hair sandy-brown and curly, Danny's blue eyes danced with good humor and mischief, seeking the beauty in the pictures his mind made of the scenes around him. His jolly wit and sense of fun made him a favorite wherever he went.

Danny arrived in Kirtland to take up the guide job just days after

Sharon Bluntschly. Sharon Jean Bluntschly, born in August of 1958 in Bay City, Michigan, the third of five children, moved with her family to Beaverton, Michigan, a small farming community, when she was four. She insists her childhood in Beaverton was idyllic and that her family were perfect. Actually, Sharon was the odd one out in most any gathering, a tag-along with her siblings, not accepted by her peers.

She had always been overweight and self-conscious about it, didn't date in high school or college. Her farm family converted to the RLDS faith when she was eight, and from then on her activities outside the family centered around either the church or the school. Sharon attended Graceland College, an RLDS school in Lamoni, Iowa, in 1977 and 1978 and from 1980 through 1983. During her absence from Graceland to help care for an ill family member she attended classes at Mid-Michigan Community College and had several boring jobs. She left school in the second semester of her senior year, after changing her major four times.

It was after she left college that Sharon became a tour guide at the RLDS auditorium at the church world headquarters in Independence, Missouri. Some years earlier she had been a guide at several church historic sites in Nauvoo, Illinois, and wanted to be a guide in all three major church historical centers. The only place she hadn't been able to serve was the Kirtland Temple in Kirtland, Ohio. She'd applied but wasn't accepted until the spring of 1985. She arrived in Kirtland in May, 1985.

Sharon has always been more or less overweight, depending on her dieting. She seems to have no self-esteem. Because Jeff and Alice were affiliated with the RLDS, which she revered, any guard Sharon was capable of mounting against manipulation was completely down. When Jeff and Alice convinced Sharon that with them she was accepted and loved, she was theirs. She never really understood the doctrine that Jeff preached. All she knew and believed was that if she was a good girl, as Alice and Jeff told her to be, she would be loved and accepted and provided a special place in Zion. Never mind overweight, the Lundgrens made her feel she was special. Sharon was ready-made to be attracted to a handsome, charming man like Richard Brand, only to suffer an unrequited love in silence. Sharon was not, unfortunately, the sort of person Richard would find attractive.

By the time Danny Kraft and Sharon Bluntschly arrived in Kirtland to begin their guide service in May of 1985, Jeff's primary spiel was altogether in place. Within a few days after Sharon's arrival he began teaching "classes" in the Visitors' Center auditorium about chiasm, the Temple and the Book of Mormon. The classes became very popular, since Jeff was teaching things that none of his listeners had heard before, things that allayed the confusion generated by the recent radical changes in the church—just as these doctrines had done in the classes in Independence. In Kirtland, however, the classes grew more quickly than they had in Missouri, and Jeff was soon asked to teach a Sunday school Book of Mormon class in the RLDS church across the street. But as he had done in Missouri, Jeff also taught more intense, more radical classes to a small select group that had begun as the class of guides in the Visitors' Center and continued to meet separately from the larger class. Sharon and Danny were charter members of that smaller group.

Sharon first met Jeff on May 18, the day she moved into the apartments behind the Visitors' Center. Jeff and Caleb were vacuuming the apartment next door, getting it ready for its summer tenant. Sharon offered to help. Later she reported that at first the Lundgrens were a bit standoffish and seemed to prefer that she not spend time in their home, but she soon became very comfortable with the family, feeling that Jeff and Alice seemed like a second set of parents. Sharon's parents eventually met the Lundgrens and said they liked them very much. The Bluntschlys were particularly grateful that the Lundgrens would be so *kind* to an insecure stranger so far from home.

Beneath the surface something sinister was forming. By the time Sharon had been in Kirtland for two weeks she had been persuaded by Jeff's teachings that she must remain in Ohio. At about that time she also had the first of many experiences with Jeff and Alice that would lead to her belief in Jeff as a prophet—and her participation in murder.

Two weeks after her arrival in Kirtland Sharon and Alice were on the couch in the Lundgren living room. Alice had taken Sharon under her wing in an apparently motherly way, even though she was only a dozen years Sharon's senior. As they were talking, Alice suddenly began to tell Sharon things that Sharon found so amazing she could barely believe what she was hearing. Alice told her that Joseph Smith, Jr., was alive and well and that Jeff had *seen* him. She said that Jeff had special powers, that he was a prophet, that he had had a vision in which he had seen Christ on Calvary and had seen all things through Christ's eyes. While Sharon listened to such outlandish statements made by her apparently sane, matronly, down-to-earth companion, she became so upset that she couldn't listen. She felt, she said later, "like the top of my head was going to come off." Then, just at the moment when she felt she could take no more, Jeff walked into the room.

Jeff had been at the Visitors' Center, he said, when he had felt that something was wrong at home. He came right home. Walking into the living room, Jeff snapped at Alice, "What's going on here?" When Alice explained what she and Sharon were talking about, Jeff chastised her, said no one was supposed to know about these things.

Sharon, of course, was convinced by that that Jeff really did have special powers. (Now, she says, she feels that the whole thing was a set-up, intended to have just the effect that it did have.)

By the end of the summer Sharon spent all her waking hours at the Lundgrens', as did Danny. Sharon was usually with Alice, virtually a maid for the family, coming to the house after work at the Temple, preparing meals, cleaning up after meals and doing the housework. Danny and Kevin spent most of their free time in the basement studying the Scriptures—the Bible, the Book of Mormon, the *Doctrine and Covenants*. All three rotated babysitting duty when Alice and Jeff went out. For the first time in her life Sharon felt necessary, valuable. She believed Alice genuinely liked her, as few people ever seemed to. Kevin and Danny felt that their lives had taken on new meaning, and Danny had found the seemingly secure, loving family he'd never had.

Alice has said that during this time she was very proud of her husband and was happy. Jeff was a respected member of the church and the community, the family was free of the anxiety of financial crises. Alice also claims to have had no knowledge of the source of the family's income, that Jeff excluded her from such matters.

When the summer guides' season ended, Danny left for a semester, much to Jeff's displeasure, to go back to art school in Portland, Maine. By this time Sharon was taking all her meals with the Lundgrens, and Jeff had suggested she turn over her paychecks to him. It was cheaper, he said, to buy for one household than two and the money could be better managed if one person were doing it. Sharon, no longer employed at the Temple, was required to pay rent for her apartment, which Jeff promised to pay as well as to provide whatever money Sharon needed for necessities.

So Jeff was now collecting paychecks from Kevin and Sharon, and skimming funds from the Temple.

Enter Richard Brand.

Born in 1963 into a comfortable middle-class family—father an air controller, mother a housewife and secretary at the RLDS headquarters in Independence, Missouri—Richard remembers his childhood as happy and stable. In high school he was popular, an A student graduating eleventh in a class of 430, a member of the National Honor Society and the school yearbook staff, a baseball and basketball player.

Raised in the RLDS church, Richard stopped attending in high school in spite of, or maybe because of, pressure from his parents, who always were very active in the church. He returned to a serious study of the Scriptures in 1983 although he had a strong skepticism about the doctrines and functions of the RLDS church. By the time of his graduation with a degree in civil engineering from the University of Missouri in Kansas City, Richard had come to believe that the modern church was misguided and that many of the prophet-president's revelations were false.

Just under six feet, slim and well-muscled, Richard has blonde hair, blue eyes and sometimes a mustache. He was and is charming, witty, likeable, but also immature and in some ways a perpetual adolescent.

When he showed up in Kirtland with friends on Memorial Day weekend in 1985 to take the Temple tour, Richard was prime material for Jeff Lundgren. A college graduate and engaged to be married, he suddenly was facing the need to grow up and shoulder the burdens of an adult. He felt that he was abruptly being pushed into a world for which he was little prepared.

After taking Jeff's tour he was subjected to the Lundgren family theater, as were most other visitors, and responded to the advertised need of this valiant family sacrificing its all in God's service. Joining this family would be like a safety net for Richard, a cushion against the on-rushing burdens of adulthood with its attendant responsibilities. Here all uncertainties were answered. Here Richard could revert to the role of the good boy who mostly conformed, a part he'd played comfortably for more than ten years.

By the time of this trip to Kirtland Richard had inherited fifteen thousand dollars from his grandmother. He had already begun to question the doctrines of the RLDS church and had decided that the church did not deserve his tithes. The Lundgrens did. Eventually he would give Jeff most of the inheritance, beginning with fairly large amounts shortly after the Memorial Day weekend was over. Richard had also been impressed by Jeff's apparent conviction that it was necessary to come to Ohio to see God, but he believed he could not come until he was specifically invited to do so by Jeff.

Not everyone who came into close contact with Jeff and Alice in Kirtland succumbed to their siren song. Jim Fincham, a huge, hearty, red-haired agronomist from Independence, toured the Temple with a friend in September, 1985, and at first was so taken by Jeff's tour and his interpretation of the importance of the Temple that he took a year off from his business. He and his wife moved to Kirtland with their two children to become Temple guides.

But the next spring, Fincham caught Jeff stealing from the Visitors' Center. He reported it to the Temple authorities, but to his knowledge the authorities did nothing. Fincham left the guide service after a year and he and his family severed their ties with the RLDS.

Another non-fan was Dale Luffman, the new Stake president who arrived in Kirtland in January of 1986. He and Jeff clashed immediately, Luffman finding Jeff stiff-necked and heretical and unwilling to take direction. Jeff in turn opposed the relatively liberal views of the new Stake president, and undoubtedly felt that his own brilliance was not sufficiently appreciated by this Luffman, whom he saw as an interloper. After all, by this time the response to Jeff's teaching had been just about all that this hugely egocentric man could have prayed for. His knowledge of the Scriptures was widely admired among both the local RLDS and LDS congregations, and visitors to the Temple who had heard of Jeff in Missouri or Utah often requested his tours and a private audience with him.

Jeff's admirers would even tell him that, particularly in profile, he remarkably resembled Joseph Smith, Jr., with the implication that such resemblance was more than coincidence. Indeed, the local LDS church, although the officials now deny it, actively tried to recruit Jeff. According to Richard Brand's account, the LDS offered Jeff a position on the Council of Twelve, the church governing council, with powers second only to the Prophet himself, if he would switch his allegiance. At one time, after the Lundgren group had moved to the farm, the LDS sent some forty of its members to the Lundgren home to prune the apple orchard, apparently to show Jeff what the church could do on his behalf.

*   *   *

In the spring of 1986 Jeff returned to Independence to invite Richard Brand to Kirtland. Jeff's reasons for electing to recruit Richard were obvious: Richard had already demonstrated an unusual willingness to accept Jeff's teachings and interpretations of Scripture; Richard still had a substantial amount of his inheritance in his possession; and Richard had excellent earning potential as a civil engineer.

On Memorial Day weekend, 1986, Richard again came for a visit, and within the first two weeks of June he returned to Kirtland to stay. Danny Kraft had also returned in May to be a part of the guide service for the summer. So by the end of the summer of 1986 Jeff's first recruits were firmly entrenched.

A sour note came in September of 1986 when Kevin Currie, an early recruit, left the group, unable to tolerate the violence that was beginning to permeate Jeff's teachings.

At first Jeff just talked about a defense of the Temple. He taught that Zion, the City of God where Christ would walk the earth in the flesh with men, would occur in Kirtland. According to the RLDS church, Zion would happen in Independence, but Jeff derided that. God was sure to come to earth at the site of his House, and that House was located in Kirtland, not in Independence. He then went on to say that there would be a great earthquake, a mountain would be made, and the Temple, the House of the Lord, would be on top of that mountain. All current churches were in error, there was no church that was the true church of God, and therefore the House of the Lord was in the hands of Satan. Jeff and his followers, he said, would be called on to occupy the Temple both during and after the earthquake, and then to defend it against all possible invaders until God Himself should arrive.

Meanwhile, Sharon continued to live in the summer guides' apartments and work full-time as a supermarket clerk. Danny was a Temple guide during the summer of 1986 but when fall came and the season ended he began working at Gallup's Art Gallery across Chillicothe Road from the Lundgren house, where he built his miniature furniture with skill and a distinct flair.

Richard lived in the Lundgrens' basement during that summer, studied Scripture four to eight hours every day, worked out with Jeff's weights and helped with chores around the house, including helping to weed Jeff's garden. By the time Richard had been in Kirtland for two months he was convinced that Jeff was a prophet.

Sharon was very attracted to Richard, but as usual for her it was unrequited. Not easily discouraged when she set her mind on something, Sharon began to spend time with Richard, just talking, either in the basement of the Lundgren home or in her own apartment. For her, the time the two spent together was exciting, even magical; Richard enjoyed the friendship of someone who shared his interest in and opinion of Jeff Lundgren. That was it for Richard, who had a fiancée with whom he was still in love. Sharon, overweight, wasn't in the running.

In any event none of the young people living in the Lundgren household had much free time to spend in anything not supervised or required by Jeff or Alice. Followers had to be of one heart and one mind with God, which, of course, meant of one heart and one mind with Jeff, which further translated into doing exactly what Jeff wanted done, exactly as Jeff would have done it, exactly when Jeff wanted it done.

Jeff and Alice were in control. The reasons given for the control were always benevolent and mostly religiously centered, although later Debbie Olivarez would say that the only two topics of conversation were Scripture and sex, with Scripture explaining and excusing all. The women, for example, were taught to be "carnal, sensual, and devilish." In the Book of Mormon, the state of being that is described as carnal, sensual, and devilish is characterized as evil, but in Jeff Lundgren's group the women were expected to bear children and were required to be sexual, sensual, and submissive, which Jeff called "carnal, sensual, and devilish."

Sharon, self-conscious about her physical appearance and her unworldly upbringing, resisted the idea of displaying her sexuality. In this, as in many other matters, Alice took Sharon under her wing. Whenever the group rented and watched movies, which was often, Alice would point out to Sharon the behavior and mannerisms of any actress Alice considered seductive. This instruction was done both privately and in front of the group. Jeff also required that Sharon diet in order to be more attractive, and Alice rented Tina Turner videos, which she would watch with Sharon to try to teach her to imitate the rock star's sensuality. Somehow Sharon was never able to get it right, which kept her in a state of sin.

Richard, Sharon and Danny were never allowed to make any decision for themselves, no matter how insignificant. Jeff decided what should be prepared for each meal, even how it should be prepared. Jeff decided whether the television would be watched, who was allowed to watch, what programs were watched. No one was permitted to choose anything without asking approval from Jeff or Alice, and above all, *no one was allowed to question Jeff.* And Jeff was able to manage this degree of control without having claimed to be a prophet.

5

PROPHET, SEER, AND REVELATOR

"Jeff as prophet"—developing that concept was Alice's job. Alice had planted the notion that Jeff might be more than a mere man to Sharon just two weeks after Sharon had arrived in Kirtland. As each member of the forming group arrived at the Temple, or had contact with other group members, Jeff's status as a prophet was never discussed with a new convert by Jeff himself—Alice or other group members were always the advance guard.

Those who eventually became Jeff's closest followers were convinced of his status as a prophet incrementally and through signs that some might find trivial to unlikely. Common to all these people was an early belief instigated by their church heritage that God provides prophets for man and that a prophet currently exists on earth as God's messenger, sent by God to tell the faithful how to live their lives and to help prepare the way for the coming of Zion. Jeff exploited the unquestioning faith of good people steeped in the doctrines of Joseph Smith, Jr., and the RLDS church. Many have claimed that Jeff "brainwashed" his followers. If that is so, then it is fair to suggest that these people were "prewashed" by the church.

Even prosaics such as going to the movies were used by Jeff and Alice. Both enjoyed movies, would frequently spend an evening out at a movie theater and more frequently rent videocassettes. Early in 1986, on one of his rare nights out, Kevin saw *The Highlander*, starring Sean Connery. He recommended it to Jeff, and Jeff and Alice later saw and liked it so much that they returned to see it a dozen times and later, when the movie was released on videocassette, bought a copy. *The Highlander* became a training film that Alice used for recruits.

The film tells the story of a race of immortal beings born hundreds of years ago in many different countries. The hero was born in Scotland, therefore the title. The villain was born in an obscure part of Russia and is known as the Kurgan. The immortals are moving through time to a confrontation during which all but one of them will be killed. The survivor will receive special supernatural powers, including the power to read the minds of others. The immortals can be killed only by beheading.

Jeff found a kinship with the film. Qualities claimed by the immortals and/or by the hero were the same ones he himself claimed, including having the power to read minds and having seen all things in the past and the future, just like the Highlander. Jeff now claimed to be immortal. He said that his skin could never be pierced by man, and that beheading was the manner of death mandated for sinners by the Bible and the Book of Mormon.

The Highlander was also Alice's special movie; Jeff emphasized to the group that Alice, as the perfect woman, wife, and mother, combined the qualities of the three women loved at various times by the hero. Alice was proud of her portrayal in the film and used it at times as another vehicle for teaching Sharon the proper behavior for a woman. Alice did feel, however, that *her* parts in the film weren't played by actresses who could do her justice. She believed that when she was slim, as she was not now, she looked most like the actress Lynda Carter, Wonder Woman.

Full Metal Jacket was another favorite. Jeff liked it for its illustration of military tactics and the military life. Jeff had, after all, decided that his small group would be the army of the Lord, and that he would be its general.

During 1986 Jeff spoke more and more about the Temple and that it was in the hands of Satan's forces. The purely defensive action he had originally preached, meant to hold the Temple for Christ in the Last Days, now turned offensive, designed to wrest the Temple from the godless gentiles and to bring about the coming of Zion when those who were without sin would see God in the flesh.

The taking of the Temple was based on the Parable of the Vineyard in *Doctrine and Covenants*, chapter 38. Jeff referred to the area of several blocks surrounding the Temple and its gardens as the Vineyard, and explained that the Vineyard had to be cleansed of sin now, just as the Vineyard of the parable had been purged of its wild olive trees. The area Jeff labeled the Vineyard contained the residences of the Temple guides, the Fishers, and the Luffmans. Ken Fisher was the local RLDS bishop.

To prepare for the assault on the Temple, Jeff instructed Danny Kraft to create a detailed diagram of the Vineyard to be used by Jeff in planning the attack and in instructing various members of the group in their roles. He also organized military games after dark in the Temple gardens between his home, the Visitors' Center, and the Temple. The games were to enable the participants to become familiar with the immediate area of the Temple at night, and for the group members to learn to recognize each other's silhouettes after dark.

A favorite game was Capture the Flag, with the flag located at the side door of the Temple. Danny was particularly proud of himself the night he was on the team assigned to take the flag, when he dressed himself as a woman and walked right past Jeff and took the flag unrecognized by anyone.

The next recruit, Greg Winship, came to Jeff's group via Richard Brand. The two had been childhood friends since age five, and their friendship not only stayed strong but built with the years. Like Richard, Greg was a college graduate—Graceland College in Independence, Missouri, B.A. in business administration—and before that had gone to Truman High School in Independence. Greg went a step farther than Richard and married his college sweetheart, but it didn't last. It was in the backwash of the divorce that Greg visited Richard in Kirtland in August of 1986, and became impressed with the Lundgrens not only because Richard was but also because Richard said he was convinced Jeff was indeed a prophet and that it was necessary to come to Kirtland to learn God's message and fulfill it.

Sensitive and articulate, Greg, built slim with blue eyes and brown hair, was easy to like. When he came to visit that August he also watched *The Highlander* with Alice, even taking detailed notes as Alice provided a running commentary about the powers of the central characters and the proper method of beheading evil human beings. He would watch this "indoctrination-and-training film" with her again the next year when he came to stay and be a part of what seemed God's plan.

A few years later he and Richard, disenchanted, would risk their lives by leaving the flock.

On September 9, 1986, Jeff Lundgren received an Ohio driver's license. The lives of all involved with Jeff were irretrievably altered when that permit was obtained. Regulations of the Federal Bureau of Alcohol, Tobacco and Firearms require that the identity of the purchaser of a firearm be verified by the seller through a driver's license. The driver's license number is recorded by the seller on an ATF form along with the buyer's name, description, address, and other identifying information. Jeff could not buy guns legally without a driver's license.

On September 27 Jeff purchased a pistol and two rifles, and on September 29 he bought a .38–caliber pistol. Accumulation of the arsenal intended for the assault on the Temple had begun.

In August of 1986 Dennis and Tonya Patrick and their daughter Molly moved into church property until they were able to locate housing in Kirtland. Tonya Jeannie Patrick was born in July of 1956 in Independence, Missouri, and her husband some two years earlier in August in Biloxi, Mississippi. Both had been active for most of their lives in the RLDS church, and had, in fact, met at the RLDS house at Central Missouri State University, where they also met Jeff and Alice. From almost the first, the young couple seems to have been fascinated by the older couple, who apparently had an ideal sort of RLDS married life that they were gracious enough to allow younger friends to be part of.

Like many of the others, Tonya and Dennis seemed an intelligent, even outgoing couple, made friends easily and moved up in the social hierarchy of the church as a young married couple. Once again, church conditioning along with intelligence and vulnerability seemed the common thread among the burgeoning group. Over time the Patricks kept up sporadic contact with the Lundgrens, but also came to be somewhat put off by what they saw of Jeff's abusive treatment of his oldest, Damon; his harsh, perfectionist demands on Jason; and his irresponsibility as a husband. On the other hand, Jeff impressed them as a knowledgeable and informative student of the Scriptures, and eventually they found themselves deeply involved in the Scripture classes Jeff taught in his home in Independence. They also contributed to the support of their old friends so Jeff could go on with his study of the Scriptures, which, after all, benefited his students. And they keenly felt a loss when the Lundgrens decided to move to Kirtland.

Not surprisingly, then, they were pleased when Jeff and Alice contacted them and suggested they too relocate in Kirtland, since it was only there that they could receive true power and the opportunity to help bring about Zion and the living presence of God on earth. The invitation hardly seems to jibe with Jeff's already expressed distrust of Dennis Patrick, until one takes into account his attraction to Tonya, who was a somewhat heavy-set woman with a distinctly pretty face, a head of beautiful red hair and a redhead's typical coloring, not to mention being personable and popular. Mustachioed Dennis, on the other hand, was hesitant in his speech and manner, seemingly indecisive, finding it difficult to assert himself. To some his timidity was distinctly unappealing.

Dennis was more than unappealing to Jeff. Jeff was deeply jealous of Dennis over Tonya, to the extent of a secretly expressed conviction that Dennis would have to die at some point during the search for God.

Jeff prepared the way with this account to the group of a vision he said he had had even before he left Missouri: He was searching for the plates on which the Book of Mormon was inscribed. He said he'd found himself following a path in a dark thick fog toward where he knew the plates were concealed. Somehow he knew that Dennis Patrick was following him and intended to take the plates for his own selfish benefit. Then and there he knew he would have to fight Dennis for the plates and ultimately be forced to kill Dennis to preserve the precious plates.

In his original version, Jeff said at the end of his vision he saw himself taking the plates to the RLDS church conference, where he would be praised for his efforts and his closeness to God. In Kirtland he did not reveal that the plates were to be turned over to the church leadership, instead claiming that the plates were intended to be shown and interpreted by him as the prophet of the Last Days. In both versions, Dennis Patrick was described as a usurper who plotted to supplant Jeff in his rightful place, even though, according to Jeff, Dennis at that time was not consciously aware that that was his evil plan.

The manner in which the story about Dennis Patrick became a part of the group mythology was typical of Jeff's manipulation of the group. Dennis was not to be told the story, Jeff emphasized. The vision made it clear that Dennis was not truly a member of the group. Jeff taught that a man was the head of his family, and that as the head of the household the man was responsible for the sins of his wife and children and, conversely, that a man who sinned damned his entire family. Therefore Tonya and Molly Patrick were also sinners in spite of any efforts they might have made to the contrary. Dennis damned them all.

The gospel according to Jeff also held that anyone not a member of the group, and thereby one of God's chosen, was an enemy. Any person who was an enemy was an agent of evil, and Jeff's group not only was permitted to lie to enemies, but such lying was actively encouraged.

Furthermore, Jeff could and did lie to those who were in a state of sin, including sinful group members. This set up nervous currents and cross-currents—members suspected that Jeff had lied to them although they couldn't prove it. Each did know, or assumed, that others were told things about him or her that Jeff did not share with the particular person under discussion. And so nobody could trust anybody. Anxiety ran rampant, which of course provided an atmosphere conducive to Jeff's control of all.

None of the group members was permitted to discuss Jeff's teaching with others out of Jeff's presence. Such discussion was called "murmuring," and was considered sinful. No one was permitted to disagree with Jeff in any way. Disagreement, too, was sinful.

Deviation, they believed, could not be concealed from Jeff. He was able to devine when one of his disciples was rebelling even internally against a new teaching or against a directive requiring obedience to some new rule. Jeff appeared to be capable of reading the thoughts of discontent that they tried not to reveal to anyone—indeed, that they tried not even to *think*. Everyone was continually accused of both overt and covert sins, making certain that at least an occasional accusation would prove out. The members tended to overlook Jeff's extensive knowledge of the exploitable side of human nature, his ability to read faces and body language, and Alice's experience and insight.

They needed to attribute Jeff's understanding of their thoughts and feelings to the supernatural powers they became convinced he possessed—as he wanted them to. They were not difficult to convince. Richard's faith in Jeff's special powers was confirmed when he saw Jeff's strength on the weights increase considerably over a relatively short period of time during which Richard believed that Jeff had not been working out because he hadn't seen Jeff do so at the house. In fact, Jeff had been working out regularly with a friend from the Temple at that friend's house. Richard did not investigate, he naively accepted that Jeff had received increased physical strength from God because Jeff's faith and knowledge of God had increased. Small faiths grew into all-encompassing ones. They could, of course, be unsettled and even broken by long, persistent redeemable evidence to the contrary—which eventually did happen with Richard.

Jeff also prophesied freely, and even more freely interpreted the fulfillment of those prophecies. One particularly egregious example would occur years later during Jeff's trial for murder. When Richard had eventually lost faith in Jeff and left the group, Jeff had insisted that one day Richard would return and would be on his knees before Jeff, the prophet. During Richard's testimony at Jeff's trial the prosecutor had Richard assume the positions on the courtroom floor in which the Averys had been placed in the pit. Richard knelt on the floor as the father, Dennis Avery, had knelt in the pit. Later Jeff claimed to the jury that Richard's posture on the floor had fulfilled his prophecy!

Nonetheless, in spite of the intimidation and overt manipulation of the followers by Jeff and Alice, the single most effective and cohesive force holding the group together was the deep faith and hope that had brought each individual member there in the first place. Each *sincerely* wanted to see God and to be part of bringing about the second coming of Christ. Each believed that the church of miracles and prophets in which he or she had been reared had gone astray and was no longer responsive to God's will. Each, in trying to do right, eventually did tragic wrong.

When Jeff's teachings grew increasingly violent in the summer of 1986, the group began to take on a military tenor. Shooting and killing were discussed more frequently in classes, at first as something that would happen when the group defended the Temple from those who would attempt to take it from them after the predicted earthquake. Jeff began to encourage and then to order the men to buy guns for their protection and the protection of their families. Jeff and the other men began regular trips to local firing ranges to practice shooting. The atmosphere within the group became more intense, more isolated. Non-group members were called "gentiles." Gentiles could not be trusted and would not be saved during the earthquake—they had had the opportunity for salvation through faith in Jeff's teachings and had rejected it.

Even with the violence in the classes and the fear Jeff and Alice inspired in the members, to outsiders the group's members appeared to be content and even happy. Most who came in contact with any of them found them to be unpleasantly cocky and arrogant, but no one, other than members' families, appeared to doubt that the members were happy to be living as they were. After all, no one was permitted to appear sullen or discontented, depressed, or unhappy. Any such appearance was interpreted as questioning Jeff and was quickly squelched. Jeff's followers spent most of their days trying to behave as Jeff required, to think as Jeff required, to avoid any action that could be interpreted as a mistake, *and* to appear happy and contented. All of which helped to deflect any serious contemplation of the *consequences* of the violence that was gradually taking centerstage in class.

6

CLEANSING THE VINEYARD

January, 1987: Greg Winship, Richard's long-time friend, applied for a job as a full-time tour guide at the Kirtland Temple. And Dana Edson, Richard's fiancée, came to visit him. Dana, independent, self-willed, and in love, followed Richard to Kirtland to investigate the situation with Jeff and to make Richard's devotion hers as well. However, Dana's family was both well-connected within the RLDS and distinctly unenthusiastic about Jeff Lundgren.

Rumors were rampant in the upper echelons of the RLDS that Jeff's so-called ministry at Kirtland was very far, indeed, from orthodox, and that Jeff was essentially a clever and slippery con-man and thief who had an unhealthy influence over the young people drawn to his teachings. So Dana's parents were most unhappy that she was visiting Richard, given his belief that Jeff was some kind of prophet. On his part, Jeff felt that Dana's presence in Kirtland was raising some inconvenient questions in Independence about him and his activities, in turn jeopardizing his livelihood. Jeff proceeded to tell Richard that Dana was not destined by God to be his wife and that he must break off his engagement with her.

At this time—before it suited him to teach and act otherwise—Jeff taught that for each man God had created one and only one woman. All of the souls of all the people who had ever existed, did now exist, or would in the future exist had been created at the beginning, and each man's soul had been made complete by the creation of a woman's soul just for him. Therefore, one of the tasks of each man and woman was to find the person especially created to be his or her spouse. Jeff followed the premise with the injunction that among the many things

God had revealed exclusively to him were the identities of those uniquely created for each other. Dana, according to Jeff, was not created for Richard. Richard, who loved Dana, was torn between Dana and Jeff. Within a few weeks he decided that if he believed Jeff in some things he must believe him in all things, and he ended the engagement in February. Upset and heartbroken, he did not dare to show his feelings, as any such display would have been reported to Jeff and he would have been chastised for questioning God's will by an apparent questioning of Jeff.

Not long after, Sharon approached Alice and Jeff and said she'd been thinking a lot about Jeff's teachings regarding the eternal nature of the relationship between men and women and had been wondering who *her* man might be. In particular, Sharon wondered if perhaps Richard might be the man for her. Alice said she and Jeff had been wondering the same thing. Sharon, a sure convert, would be useful for holding Richard against backsliding. Jeff said he would consult the Scriptures to determine whether or not Richard was the one, and within days told Sharon that, indeed, she and Richard were created for each other and that they would eventually be married.

Sharon was ecstatic. Richard was not. It was no wonder that Sharon, a lonely, inexperienced girl, found herself quickly drawn to the attractive young man. But so long as Richard was engaged she had no hopes. When Richard broke off his engagement at Jeff's direction, she thought she saw her opportunity and took it. Otherwise, she had no idea that her desire for Richard coincided with the interests of Jeff and Alice.

When Richard was told of the arrangement, he was considerably less enthused than Sharon. In fact, even though the two were told to begin immediately to get to "know" each other and to begin their courtship, they were not "married" until more than two years later.

In February of 1987 Dennis and Tonya Patrick applied for residency at the Hilltop Apartments, the complex of two-story townhouse apartments on Chillicothe Road in Kirtland across the street from the police department and the schools. Jeff instructed the Patricks to locate in the Hilltop Apartments so that they could keep an eye on the police. The Patricks moved into the Hilltop Apartments the day before Greg Winship began his guide service at the Temple.

*   *   *

In April of 1987 Dennis and Cheryl Avery and their three young daughters moved to Kirtland from Independence. Cheryl Lynn Bailey Avery was born in 1947 in Washington State, a diminutive woman with a strong personality. Although trained as a schoolteacher, she elected to stay in the home and made many of the decisions about the family. Rather plain with a pleasant face and cheerful smile, she tended to favor hooded sweatshirts with the drawstring of the hood pulled tight about her face. She married Dennis Leroy Avery, some seven years older than she, in 1970. Slender with dark brown graying hair and blue eyes, he was an unambitious man with a timid if rather dogmatic manner, given to being argumentative and meticulous. He was a likely mate for the stronger and more authoritative Cheryl. Neither in their fashion fitted the image of the authoritarian male and passive, serving mate that Jeff Lundgren ordained. The Averys may have seemed a less than desirable couple to the prophet, but they produced three lovely daughters: Trina Denise, born March 7, 1974; Rebecca Lynn, born January 23, 1976; and Karen Diane, born August 3, 1982. At the time of their deaths, on April 17, 1989, at the hand of Jeff Lundgren they were, respectively, fifteen, thirteen, and six. In the executioner's eyes, the sins of the parents were the sins of their children. Trina and Rebecca's real problems at the time were those pretty much common to teenage girls. Karen was simply a warm and friendly six-year-old.

Cheryl and Dennis, like most of the others, became involved with the Lundgrens in Independence, where they joined Jeff's Scripture-study classes. The Averys were something less than popular in the class, especially with Jeff, but they persisted—especially Cheryl, who became a particularly enthusiastic participant. And after the Lundgrens moved to Kirtland she kept up an intermittent contact with them by phone and letter, contact that Alice and Jeff found increasingly annoying.

Indeed, members of Jeff's group had been hearing Jeff and Alice complain for some time about the Averys. Cheryl had been pushing her husband to move to Kirtland in Jeff's wake, to absorb some of Jeff's perceived knowledge and the power that came from it. Dennis, less convinced, was reluctant to move but gave in and eventually agreed to come to Kirtland, even though Jeff had told the Averys not to come.

Dennis resigned from the Centerre Bank in Kansas City, Missouri, on February 19, and the die, so to speak, was cast. Jeff and Alice, though, were distinctly not pleased. They ridiculed the couple and their children. Dennis Avery, they said, was stupid, lazy, couldn't hold a good job. Cheryl was unwomanly, since she wore the pants in the family, and Dennis was unmanly to allow it. As for the children, the two older girls were rebellious and rude—even though someone less judgmental would call them typical teenagers.

The Averys proceeded to appease the Lundgrens. They chose the route of material goods—which was known to influence Jeff. They gave the Lundgrens a car, although Jeff and Alice complained about it and eventually would hand it down to their oldest, Damon. Still, once it became clear to the Lundgrens that the Averys were moving to Kirtland, Jeff or Alice gave them the name of a realtor who on the weekend of April 18–19 showed the Averys a house for rent on Chillicothe Road immediately south of Kirtland. Jeff went along when they checked out the house and approved it for them. The owner, Stanley Skrbis, mentioned at the time that he also just happened to own a fifteen-acre farm with a house at 8671 Kirtland–Chardon Road south of Kirtland that he was considering renting. Nothing more was said about the farm property at that time, though, of course, it would figure prominently later.

On April 24 the Averys sold their house in Independence, netting a profit of $19,000 that they intended to use as seed money to support their family in Kirtland until the Last Days arrived or Dennis could find a good job—whichever came first. Neither event ever took place.

A few weeks after the Averys moved to Kirtland, Sharon overheard part of a typical exchange between Jeff and Alice about the Averys. Cheryl, though dominant within her own family, apparently had a need for someone outside it to be dependent on, to submit to, and that someone was Alice, to the extent, according to Alice, of relentlessly depending on her for direction and guidance in so many matters that Alice resented it and wanted to be rid of it. Why, she asked Jeff, were the Averys in Kirtland anyway? And Jeff told her: "So I can get their money."

The Averys, however, were putting that plan at risk by the way they were going through their money. By June, Jeff was conducting a special class to pressure Dennis to hand over the $10,000 left from the house sale. In return, Jeff promised, he would take care of the Avery family, including paying all their bills. Apparently persuaded, on June

26 Dennis brought a check made out to cash for $10,000 to the Lundgrens' home. He asked for Jeff, and when he found out Jeff wasn't home refused to leave the check with Alice. (He came back later to give it to Jeff.) Alice, of course, was furious, which in turn earned Dennis a chastisement session. As for Jeff, the day after he received the check he went on a shopping spree, buying, among other things, the .45 Colt Combat Elite pistol that he would use some two years later to execute Dennis, Cheryl, Trina, Becky, and Karen Avery.

The group classes were by this time meeting several evenings a week for three to four hours per session in the living room of the Lundgrens' home. Each class was mostly a lecture by Jeff, who was now openly acknowledged within the group to be God's prophet who would bring about the Last Days, but his true status was not revealed to the gentiles, since they weren't sufficiently accepting of Jeff's exalted status. Because of Jeff's role, no one else was allowed to speak or teach in class unless invited to do so by Jeff.

Frequently Jeff couldn't make a point as effectively as he wanted, so he would request Alice to amplify for the prophet, which she did enthusiastically. Alice always sat at Jeff's left hand during classes, a sign of her unique status, and was always alert for any sign of rebellion.

According to Bishop Stobaugh, the RLDS had been hearing for some time from returning pilgrims about Jeff's unorthodox teachings in the Temple and in the Book of Mormon class. Also, the church in general and Bishop Stobaugh in particular were increasingly disturbed by the growing indications that Jeff was stealing from the Visitors' Center and soliciting donations from pilgrims to the Temple. On one occasion Bishop Stobaugh confronted Jeff about the shortages in the Visitors' Center receipts and asked to compare the accounts kept by Jeff with the cash-register tapes from the same period. Jeff claimed that the register tapes had been stored in the Temple basement and had been destroyed by water seepage during a recent flood. There was no sign of water damage to the Temple basement but the tapes had, indeed, vanished. As for Jeff's unorthodox teachings and his cash solicitation, the bishop had not been able to find anyone who would go on record about what he or she had heard. The bishop felt that his hands were tied, but he was deeply uneasy and wanted to separate Jeff from the Visitors' Center, from the Book of Mormon class, and from the Temple as soon as possible.

Jeff's teachings in the Temple and in the Book of Mormon class were indeed unorthodox. And some of the rationale for them came from his use of a recent decision of the World Conference of the RLDS that permitted women to be ordained as priests of the church. Many of the more traditionally oriented church members had for some time been discontented with the current prophet, Wallace B. Smith, some even going so far as to say that the prophet was a false prophet or that the church had no prophet. Into such an atmosphere, a revelation reversing more than one hundred fifty years of church tradition fell like a lighted match on a powder keg. A conservative minority threatened secession and ultimately formed the Restoration branch of the church.

Jeff preached and taught that the admission of women to the priesthood was a sacrilege and was simply one more indication that the church had fallen into the hands of Satan. The latter revelation was, of course, saved for the ears of his closest followers, but Jeff did not hesitate to speak against the prophet and the church in milder terms in his Book of Mormon class and in the Temple. Eventually, Stake President Dale Luffman withdrew permission for Jeff to lead the class.

This rejection by the church increased Jeff's contempt and hatred for it. His grandiose notions of his own importance, coupled with his narcissism, led him to fantasize ever more elaborate, more violent methods of retaliation. And the habitual, unquestioning obedience of Jeff's followers allowed him not only to indulge his fantasies but to take steps toward carrying them out. Classes concentrating on the Temple takeover were now held several times a week.

Greg Winship was an exception to the true believers. In the summer of 1987 he left the area against Jeff's direct command to participate in a volleyball tournament and refused to milk his father for money for Jeff.

Jeff then proceeded to separate best friends Richard and Greg. He casually mentioned to Richard one day during a ping-pong game that he had had a dream that foretold that one day Richard would be required to kill Greg. He said that in his dream Greg was hiding in a house. Jeff came to the front door of the house to kill Greg but Greg ran out the back. Richard was waiting for Greg in the back yard with a crossbow and shot and killed Greg.

Richard understood the dream to have the force of prophecy. He believed the dream to be literally true and to mean that at some time Greg would be so far removed from the grace of God that he would be killed. So Richard, dedicated to doing God's will, could not trust Greg. Jeff had effectively separated two men who had been friends for years.

Even then, though, Greg was not altogether chastened. When he left the apartment behind the Visitors' Center in September, he moved in with friends in a nearby town, against Jeff's explicit instructions.

But Greg did not use his reservations about Jeff to warn off his old friend Shar Olsen.

Shar Lea Olsen was born in September 1960, in the same hospital where Greg was born—their mothers were roommates. Greg and Shar had known each other all their lives, and had been friends for as long as they could remember.

A tall, attractive blue-eyed blonde, Shar is warm and witty with an offbeat sense of humor. She had taken some college courses in early childhood education, but has never received a degree. She is an articulate person who speaks rapidly and freely, laughs heartily and frequently and her good humor tends to be contagious.

Shar was reared in the Independence, Missouri, area, where she, like so many of the others, was active in the RLDS church youth groups. It was through the church that Shar came to know Debbie Olivarez. After that she made several church pilgrimages to Kirtland in 1985, 1986, and 1987. On Labor Day weekend of 1987, Shar came to Kirtland to visit her friends Greg and Richard. On their recommendation, she especially requested a Temple tour led by Jeff, talked with him afterward, and was so favorably impressed with Jeff and his teachings, and particularly with the command to come to Ohio, that when she returned to Missouri she immediately began to make arrangements to move to Kirtland.

Shar arrived in Kirtland just before the Lundgrens also began to make a substantial change in their lifestyle. Bishop Stobaugh had finally found someone who was willing to make an official statement to the church about Jeff's teachings in the Temple. The bishop quickly moved to remove Jeff and Alice from the guide service, effective October 1, and they were told to vacate the church-provided house they were living in by the end of October.

Jeff had already prepared the group for his expulsion from the Temple by telling them in August that church funds had been stolen from his car when he was taking them to the bank and that the church unfairly suspected he had stolen the money. Apparently Jeff had felt sufficiently threatened when confronted by the bishop about the cash shortages from the Visitors' Center that he arranged a cover story.

When Jeff was given his vacate order by the church he contacted Stan Skrbis about the farm property that had been available for rent six months earlier. The property included a large house, a very large red barn and fifteen acres with an apple orchard, a pond, and a gas well. The property was still available, probably because the house was old and in poor repair. Jeff arranged with Stan that work would be done to maintain the property in exchange for rent, and told his followers that the situation presented an ideal opportunity to fit their lives closer to God's plan.

Jeff directed that his unmarried followers should move into the farmhouse with his family. In that way, he said, the group could function as a family, as it should, with him as the father for all and Alice as the mother. It had been revealed to him, he said, that all the members of his group were, in God's eyes, actually a family and that they had been a family at some time in the past. Of course, it was also true, according to Jeff, that the children who had been born to him in this lifetime—Damon, Jason, Kristen and Caleb—were of a superior status in the family, even though they were now required to sacrifice the attention of their parents and to share their parents' love with adult strangers. Group members were required to call Jeff and Alice Mom and Dad. Shar nicknamed the Lundgren children "the naturals," and the others "the unnaturals." The nicknames stuck.

Kevin Currie returned to the Lundgren home in August. In the year he had been gone he had managed to talk himself into believing both that the violence that had so alarmed him in class in 1986 would not be so bad since it would only be defensive, and that his memories of what was being taught were exaggerated. Even though he had kept in some contact with Jeff and Alice during his absence, he was hardly prepared for the changes in Jeff's ideas. As Jeff's fantasies had grown, so had his plans and his arsenal. On the day that the group had moved to the farmhouse, Shar walked into the dining room to see the table, which could comfortably seat twelve, completely covered with semi-automatic rifles, pistols, revolvers, and ammunition in clips and belts.

7

IN THE PROPHET'S HOUSE

When Shar, startled by the arsenal casually spread across the table, gasped and stepping backward, accidentally striking her head on the doorjamb, Jeff looked up at her, shrugged, and said, "They're just for hunting."

With Shar the lie was a mistake. As she would say later, "Common sense tells you that all those handguns and semi-automatic weapons aren't used for hunting." And from that time on, Shar kept some reservations about Jeff's claims and teachings.

The others, however, had abdicated critical thought about even Jeff's most outrageous claims. They subscribed by now to Jeff's siege mentality and truly believed that it was, as he said, "us or them." Jeff had, it seemed, convinced them that everyone outside the group was an agent of the devil, bent on destroying Jeff and, by extension, his followers. This mindset led to behavior these previously law-abiding people would never have been capable of imagining, not to mention condoning. But now, as a matter of course, they could routinely lie about all aspects of their lives to those they came into contact with on the "outside." They stole from employers and/or stores in the area; and later, just weeks before the murder of the Averys, all who were eligible obtained whatever credit accounts they could, intending to charge purchases to the maximum and to then be unavailable to pay for the charges. All the result of Jeff's teaching that it was appropriate to lie to the gentiles, who had rejected God's message and so were condemned to eternal death. It was a message Jeff had gleaned from some of the teachings of Joseph Smith, Jr., as promulgated by the Mormon church. According to the Mormons, a misstatement was not a lie if told to further God's greater purpose. As Jeff and his group equated Jeff's thoughts and teachings with those of God, antisocial acts that furthered Jeff's well-being were not only justified but were performed in a holy purpose and thus were the fulfillment of God's law. Man's law in such a belief system was irrelevant.

Of course, none could be counted on to be as diligent in the Lord's service as Jeff himself, so Jeff was forced to keep a tight rein on the whole group. Jeff answered the telephone; if he were home nobody else could touch the phone without permission. If Jeff was gone Alice was in charge of answering the telephone. If neither Jeff nor Alice was at the house, Jeff would appoint a "house sheriff," one of whose primary duties was to answer the telephone. The other duty, as Debbie Olivarez would later describe it, was to keep the Lundgren children "from killing each other." There was to be no disciplining of the naturals by the unnaturals.

Only Jeff was allowed to get mail from the mailbox. No exceptions, not even Alice. Sometimes Jeff would pass on mail to the addressee, sometimes not. Particularly if the recipient was being informed that bills were delinquent, Jeff would often withhold the mail. Shar, for instance, did not discover that many of her bill payments were late or unpaid until she was contacted at work by her creditors. Jeff would then explain that money owed outside the family was simply not important; the Last Days were coming and he didn't intend to be constrained by obligations to Babylon anyway.

At the time the family moved to the farm, Richard, Sharon, Danny, Shar and Kevin were working outside the home and turning their paychecks, and any other funds they received, over to Jeff. The Patricks, the Averys and Greg Winship, who were not living at the farm, were setting aside a portion of their monthly budgets to turn over to Jeff, who often complained that the family wasn't receiving sufficient support from those living on the outside. Family members were frequently encouraged to write to their former families (who, of course, were now considered gentiles) to ask for money on some pretext or other.

The only adults living at the farm who were not employed at outside jobs were Jeff and Alice. Jeff, the self-proclaimed Lord of the group, had a single job—to be the prophet. His only physical exertion involved working out with the weights to stay fit. His survival was crucial.

Indeed, Jeff's considerable physical strength was interpreted as a gift from God. Richard relates that on one occasion he observed Jeff lifting a much heavier weight than he'd been able to hoist just a few days earlier—so he said. Richard, as expected, interpreted this increase in physical power as an increase in spiritual strength as well—further indication that Jeff was the superhuman he claimed to be. Such indications were important to someone like Richard, who needed to continue to believe in Jeff in the face of Jeff's actions that were not easy to reconcile with his status as the man God had chosen as prophet.

For example, Jeff was neglecting to take care of the Averys as he had promised to do when he talked Dennis Avery into turning over his $10,000. At that time Jeff had said he would pay the rent for Dennis and Cheryl. Frequently the Averys' rent was not paid, and Dennis would have to beg Jeff to live up to his promise. This "harassment" substantially irritated Jeff, who considered it to be the worst form of "murmuring." Dennis and Cheryl were severely and frequently chastised for such presumption. The stricture against murmuring within the group became so severe that none of the family members were permitted to discuss Jeff's teachings among themselves outside of class. The only exception was that husbands were required to interpret the teachings for their wives, husbands being responsible for the spiritual enlightenment of their families.

In the gospel according to Jeff, women weren't really capable of understanding the word of God without a good man's—husband's—help. Women were intended by God to satisfy their husbands sexually, to bear children, to keep the home, to comfort and nurture their men. Alice was the perfect woman, all being required to look on her as a role model. In theory, that is. Alice in the home hardly seemed to have conformed to the model. She did virtually no physical work, which according to Jeff was proper since Alice's primary function was to be the prophet's wife, a role that carried its own weighty responsibilities. The other women in the family, who were employed in full-time jobs outside the home, had no such exalted responsibilities and were expected to do all the housekeeping as well.

Actually Alice was known to lie about the house in a semi-stupor as a consequence of consuming quantities of Miller Lite and Excedrin for her "headaches." She would be up until long after midnight watching television, drinking, and talking with Jeff, then would sleep until noon or early afternoon the next day. On many days Alice's primary interaction with her children was to leave her bed in time to sit in front of the television watching "Duck Tales".

Another of Alice's favorite pastimes was to have Jeff order up a Red Lobster party tray for her, at thirty or forty dollars apiece, three to four times a week. They would take it to the bedroom, no members usually allowed. Peeled shrimp was her particular favorite. Small wonder that at the time of her arrest Alice Lundgren weighed some two hundred twenty pounds.

Alice was also in charge of the house; all work was done at her direction and to her satisfaction. During spring cleaning the women who did not live at the farm were required to come to the Lundgren home to help out. Alice was partial to antiques. She and Jeff would make frequent antiquing trips to shops and flea markets throughout Ohio, during which Alice would indulge her passion for antiques and Jeff would purchase additions to his arsenal. Such trips most often occurred after Jeff had managed to tap some significant new financial resource.

Alice did seem to get whatever Alice wanted. Though she would later claim to have been a battered woman and to have been battered during the time that the group lived together, none of the other adults recalls seeing Jeff actually strike her.

As described by group members, life with Jeff and Alice would proceed reasonably calmly for a while, then Alice would become angry about Jeff's behavior or the behavior of some other group member or would be criticized by Jeff for something. She and Jeff would retreat to their bedroom and the group would hear arguing, sometimes for hours. Generally the arguing consisted of a great deal of screaming and yelling by Alice and low-toned inaudible replies from Jeff. Alice later said that during such times she was threatened with death by Jeff and a pistol was held to her head.

Alice would later claim that much of the battering she was subjected to was because of difficulty in submitting to Jeff's bizarre sexual demands. Alice told several people that Jeff's sexual practices including eating feces and rubbing fecal matter on various parts of the bodies of each partner. No one in the group ever noticed any evidence of such practices, although Richard did discover some objects in an abandoned truck parked behind the barn. According to him, in the truck's bed he found a large dildo and a glossy male homosexual magazine that carried a cover price of $40. Richard is certain the items belonged to the prophet. It's also true that Jeff taught that there was no sexual act that was wrong, that any act between spouses was approved by God and that it was the duty of husband and wife to satisfy each other. He also complained that Alice was infrequently available to him sexually. Whatever the truth, after the argument was over Alice would apologize to the group for her unwomanly behavior, and Jeff would give her whatever she wanted.

Shar recalls one time when she was severely chastised because she had offended Alice. It was Mother's Day, 1988, and Shar asked to call her mother, although she knew she was supposed to have broken all emotional ties to her original parents and to look on Jeff and Alice as her real parents. Jeff, apparently in a generous mood, granted Shar permission to call her mother, and she placed a brief call home. Alice, however, took to her bed for several days, saying she was devastated by Shar's lack of consideration for her feelings. Shar was severely reprimanded for her sin during the entire period that Alice chose to stay in bed. Shar remembers at one point rapping on Alice's bedroom door and, when she was allowed to enter, apologizing for having caused Alice such distress. Alice weakly replied, "That's all right, dear. These are things we mothers just have to go through."

If Alice hadn't been in bed it's likely she would have been one of the primary chastisers, since this was a duty she relished. "Sessions" were conducted by Jeff, by Jeff and Alice, and sometimes with Ron's participation, by Alice alone, and were generally held in the "rabbitry" in the barn. There, in the room Jeff used as an office, the offending family member would be told to take a seat facing both Jeff and Alice. Generally, that family member's "spouse," whether actual or assigned, was also required to attend the session. Jeff and Alice would then talk with the miscreant, nonstop for forty-five minutes to an hour, sometimes shouting. The content of the session was always the same, although the specific sin sometimes varied. Jeff and Alice would remind the person being sessioned that any conduct not of one heart and one mind with Jeff was sinful. Then the sinner would be told in painful, lengthy detail just how sinful his or her conduct was, how it was harmful to the group as a whole, since no one would be able to see God until the whole group was sin-free, and how painful the conduct was to Jeff and Alice, whose burden and responsibility was to bring the entire group to God, and each additional sin, whether deliberate or from negligence, simply made that task more difficult and prolonged. No one in the group was indifferent to the importance of being sessioned, since by this time it was being made abundantly clear in class that the ultimate wage of sin was death. Everyone felt directly threatened with the knowledge of his or her sinfulness. Although Alice has stated that she also felt her life was threatened, it's difficult to believe that statement—she was the only woman in the group to be armed; she carried a 9–mm automatic in her purse.

There's no doubt that Alice was Jeff's cheerleader. She supported his claims to extraordinary powers, even saying she had herself witnessed manifestations of his special gifts from God. Alice, though, was the queen bee in the day-to-day life of the family, her word second only to her husband's, and in some ways may have superseded his, since many times he seemed to have acted mostly to please her. No question, her status was exalted beyond any other woman's in the family; the men were not permitted to touch her, not even accidentally.

Son Damon, on the other hand, had the status of being the prophet's heir apparent but had little power and little was required of him. Jeff had declared that Damon would be the next prophet. Of course, there was no indication that Jeff intended to retire at any time in the near future. No one except Jeff himself was permitted to give Damon orders.

Damon, a high-school wrestler, was in charge of the physical training of the men, getting them fit for the assault on the Temple with calisthenics and a run through the orchard. He was also allowed to be excluded from many of the group's meetings. Such special privileges went to him not only as one of the naturals but the first-born of the naturals.

All the Lundgren children received special treatment and more privileges than any other members of the group. None of them was an angel at home—actually unruly—with the exception of Caleb. Like their super-privileged parents, though, all the children had learned by their parents' example to conform to normal social expectations in public in the community outside the farm. Which helps explain why many beyond the farm had little or no idea what went on there.

As a tension release, the group members laughed and joked frequently. One of their favorite jests highlighted their isolation. When local people referred to the group as a cult, some member was likely to remind the others that they should never drink Kool-Aid, a reference to Jim Jones and the Jonestown massacre. Mostly, as ordered, group members each desperately tried not to have forbidden, discontented thoughts, and concealed from others what discontent they couldn't deny to themselves, putting on a false face of cheer and contentment. It was this facade that helped to beguile Deborah Sue Kroesen Olivarez.

Deborah Olivarez was born in April of 1952 in Independence, Missouri. Her mother, Bonnie Gadberry Kroesen, is Lois Gadberry Lundgren's younger sister. The two have had a strained relationship for years because in Bonnie's view Lois disapproved of Carlos Kroesen and claimed that he had never been able to provide as well for his family as Don Lundgren. So the blood relationship to Jeff carried early tensions as well.

Debbie is the second of six children. Gregory, three years older, has been a member of the Sikh faith for twenty years and has taken a Sikh name. He is married to his third wife. There is one other brother, six years younger than she, and three sisters, four, ten, and twelve years younger than Debbie.

Debbie still thinks of her childhood as being happy, although she was required to assume many household responsibilities at an early age. She started to learn to cook at the age of seven (and later became the Lundgren group's cook). By the time she was ten or eleven she was doing all the cooking for the family, and at twelve, the cleaning and laundry as well.

Debbie was very much the glue that held her family together. She volunteered her services, and her help was accepted to a degree she found nearly overwhelming. But she never asked for relief or help.

Debbie's father owned and operated several family businesses during her childhood—sold storm windows, drove a bakery delivery truck. Then, when Debbie was in fifth grade, he learned about a small grocery store for sale in Odessa, Missouri. With backers from the family's RLDS congregation, Carlos Kroesen bought the grocery store and the family moved to Odessa.

In Odessa Debbie's father not only operated the grocery store but was also the pastor for the local RLDS congregation. Debbie met Alice Keehler—later Lundgren—for the first time in Odessa. The girls attended the same school, although Alice was older and did not belong to the popular crowd of which Debbie was a part.

Suddenly, when Debbie was fifteen and a sophomore in high school, her world came crashing down. Her father's backers sold the store out from under him, absorbing every penny and even raiding the checking account. As a result her father was disgraced because he could not meet his obligations, and was removed as pastor and silenced by the church. A peculiar reward, and one hardly calculated to endear the RLDS to the family, including Debbie.

The family was now forced to leave their comfortable home in Odessa and relocate in Harrisonville, Missouri where they bought a doughnut shop and lived in a two-bedroom duplex. The children shared one bedroom, where the girls slept in a double bed and the boys slept on mattresses on the floor. When the shop failed in the middle of Debbie's junior year of high school, the family returned to Independence, where her father became an insurance salesman. Debbie was furious with the church, with her father's backers, with her parents, with her life. Then, shortly after the move, Debbie was raped by her boyfriend. She never was able to tell anyone about the incident, but it seemed to undermine her self-respect; she felt used, was certain that no one else would ever want her.

So when she met John Olivarez, a high-school senior, at Zion's League, the RLDS youth group, and he began to press her for dates, Debbie became sexually involved with him and they were married at the end of her junior year. Debbie returned to school in the fall, but by now she was pregnant with her first child and was forced by school officials to leave at the end of the first semester, because she was "setting a bad example." they said. Even so, Debbie had accumulated two and one-half credits more than she needed for graduation, so she asked for permission to be graduated with her class. Permission was denied. John Carlos Olivarez was born in March of 1970.

John Olivarez, a department manager for a local Sears department store, believed that it was his wife's duty to work outside the home to help support the family, so Debbie went to work when her son was only a few weeks old in the office at an auto dealership where her mother-in-law was also employed. When after a while Debbie could no longer tolerate the job and left, she became a school bus driver while pregnant with her second son. Jared Olivarez was born in April 1974. After Jared's birth Debbie became a part-time nurse's aide at night, which exhausted her when combined with caring for her children. Still, Debbie enjoyed nursing, began to think seriously about attending nursing school. In August of 1976 Bonnie Jo Olivarez was born. Debbie was still determined to become a registered nurse, although with a catering business she was running from her home, the PTA (she was president of her chapter for a year), church missionary activities, and the demands of being a working wife and mother, she hardly knew where the time would come from. Being Supermom was exhausting.

Finally, when Bonnie was three, Debbie felt capable of taking on the course work for her degree. Her husband and his parents had other plans. With his parents' backing, John put his money *and* Debbie's into the purchase of a restaurant that he expected her to manage. She went along, with some protest, agreed to manage the restaurant for a year but did insist that at the end of that time she would leave the restaurant and enroll in nursing courses. Good as her word, she attended Penn Valley Community College, where she was president of her graduating class, and graduated in 1984 with an associate's degree in applied science.

Now, finally, Debbie expected her life to be better. But somehow, even though she was making more money and was working at a job she enjoyed, two years after she graduated she found that she felt depressed, even suicidal. It took a long time, but she finally pinpointed her marriage as the source of her problem and became even more convinced that the relationship had to change when she discovered that John had been having an affair. She tried to talk with him about it but he refused.

Debbie filed for divorce in late 1986, and it was granted in early 1987. Debbie and John shared custody of their children, but the boys were to live with their father while Bonnie, whom Debbie describes as being much like her, would live with her mother. In May, 1987, Debbie changed jobs to become a surgical nurse, which she enjoyed, but just two months after that she injured her back moving a patient and had to have surgery in September. In October, she had more surgery, this time for a gall-bladder problem. If there were a female Job, Debbie might well qualify for the role.

With the divorce and her employment problems, Debbie was now having severe financial difficulties. What to do? Where to go? She sought the support of the church and her family, but felt that her pleas for help were rejected on all sides. By November of 1987, Debbie Olivarez was at the end of her rope.

Next step—her cousin, Jeff Lundgren.

8

THE ARMY
OF THE LORD

Jeff and Alice and their extended family had barely settled in at the farm when a distraught Debbie Olivarez, along with her mother and her grandparents (who were Jeff Lundgren's grandparents, as well), came to visit for several days in mid-November of 1987. Debbie's grandparents wanted to investigate the rumors they had heard about their grandson's living situation and the matters he was teaching.

When they arrived from Independence, they found most of the adults working outside. The weather was mild, the house trim and clean, the group seemingly prosperous and contented. The newcomers were impressed by the cohesiveness of the group, a unity apparently drawn from mutual affection for each other and devotion to a higher calling outside themselves.

During the few days Debbie and her family stayed with the Lundgren family they were taken to local tourist attractions, including the Kirtland Temple. There the group was treated to a demonstration of Jeff's continuing influence at the Temple; the assigned guide simply turned the tour over to Jeff. This tour was the first time Debbie had heard Jeff's teaching about the significance of the chiastic construction of the Temple.

That evening after dinner, while the group was still seated around the dining room table, Jeff and his grandfather began arguing about the probable current location of the gold tablets on which the Book of Mormon was inscribed. It was pretty much the same discussion common among scholars and lay members of both the RLDS and Mormon churches. The source of the conflict was and is that it seems highly unlikely, if not impossible, that golden tablets buried in a hillside in Central America during a prehistoric war should mysteriously have relocated some fifteen hundred years later in a hillside in northern New York State. The subsequent disappearance of those records rendered the debate apparently insoluble.

However, during this discussion at the farm, the subject of the debate was not as important as that Jeff's grandfather became very upset. He'd had a stroke, so his wife and daughter interrupted the exchange to take Mr. Gadberry to bed; the two women also retired for the night, which left Debbie with her friend Shar and her cousin Jeff and his wife Alice. Whereupon Debbie was subjected to an hours-long course on the Scriptures according to Jeffrey Lundgren, including God's plan for the world, and Jeff's prophecy of the coming earthquake and the reestablishment of Zion. Shar and Alice told Debbie about Jeff's role and the role of his family in the Last Days, and the eternal death that awaited those who had been offered the truth and who rejected it. By the time Debbie had slept on her new knowledge, she was almost convinced that she must settle in Kirtland.

Jeff and Alice told Debbie that when she moved to Kirtland she should live with them in their house. It would be improper for her to live on her own as an unmarried woman, they explained, and since Jeff was her true father in God's plan it was correct that she should live in Jeff's house until she was married. Jeff also revealed that John Olivarez had not been Debbie's true husband and that she would have to come to Kirtland to find her true husband. Jeff and Alice said that the adults who lived with them all had jobs outside the home and that they turned their paychecks over to Jeff, who then paid the family expenses and the bills for the entire family out of the accumulated funds. Everyone was provided for as he or she needed. The Lundgrens neglected to mention that while cash would be provided for anyone in the family who asked, such requests were discouraged, and too many requests earned a "session."

The reason, Jeff and Alice said, that they were not working outside the home was because they were trying to establish an antique shop in the barn, to be called Kristen's Cupboard. Antiques and miniatures contributed by Dan Kraft would be sold, and the combined incomes from the antique shop, sale of fruit from the orchard and sale of rabbits to be reared in the barn would be sufficient for the family to become financially independent. Eventually, all members of the group would be able to leave their outside jobs and concentrate on the family enterprises.

The whole plan sounded pretty wonderful to Debbie. Here, it seemed, were people who, unlike John and the church that had deserted her father, were warm and caring, who already accepted her as if she were one of them, who would love her for herself and who were willing to take on all her responsibilities. No more financial worries, she would be emotionally supported instead of drained. And more, the group was working to establish the divine kingdom on earth. They, more than anyone else she had ever known, were struggling to bring about the events her church had once taught her could come to pass only when mankind was sinless enough to receive them. The notion of violence in connection with the coming of the Lord bothered her, but somehow it did not seem real to her. Not at that time. Besides, Jeff, her own flesh and blood, assured her that a degree of violence was part of God's plan, and that she and her loved ones would be safe because she was part of Jeff's family. All she needed to do to gain entry and be a part of this family that promised no stress and divine salvation, that would give her the emotional and physical relief and protection she so badly needed, was to turn over her paycheck to Jeff and do exactly as he said. At this time it hardly seemed too much to ask.

And yet Debbie still had not *finally* committed herself to returning permanently to Jeff by the time she and her family left Kirtland before Thanksgiving. She arranged, though, to return for another visit at Christmas, to give herself the chance to decide for certain whether or not the apparent tranquility at the farm was real. Apparently it was pretty much a formality in her mind, though, for when she returned to Independence she put her house on the market.

At about this time when Debbie was visiting, another family of recruits arrived in the Kirtland area. On November 17 Ron and Susie Luff and their two children moved into an apartment in Wickliffe, a nearby Cleveland suburb.

Susan Louise Edson Luff was born in December, 1958, in Independence, Missouri. The second of four children born to Robert and Milda Edson, she has a brother two years older than she, a brother six years her junior, and a sister fourteen years younger. She earned a degree in business education from Jacksonville University in Jacksonville, Florida, was a substitute teacher and taught night classes in accounting, typing, shorthand, word processing, and office machines.

In 1981 Susie married Ronald Boyd Luff, a navy petty officer who had been born in Independence. Both the Luffs had been raised in the RLDS church and had met at a church picnic. Their son Matthew was born in July of 1982 in Florida, where his father was stationed. Ron was discharged from the navy in 1984 after serving six years, during which he was regularly commended for his ambition and efficiency as an engine room technician. After his discharge he returned to Missouri and took a job in the maintenance department of a utility company. Amy Luff was born the year after Ron's discharge. Ron was resentful that in spite of his efforts and his intelligence, he couldn't find a job that would provide a better living for his family.

A prime candidate for Jeff Lundgren.

In December of 1986 Ron and Susie went with Ron's parents to Kirtland to tour the Temple. Ron, of course, met Jeffrey Lundgren during the tour and was approached by him with the concept that it was necessary to come to Kirtland to receive the true word of God. After that encounter the Luffs kept up contact with the Lundgrens until in late summer of 1987 Ron decided he could wait no longer. It was time to make the commitment to living according to God's will— man's hadn't worked out and Jeff was persuasive. The Luffs moved to the Kirtland area in October, 1987.

Ron Luff is muscular, balding, with light brown hair, a mustache, and blue eyes. His delicate features are obscured by heavy, horn-rimmed glasses. A taciturn man, slow and precise in his speech, his emotions always seem under tight control. He has a permanent hearing loss in both ears as a result of a firecracker explosion when he was fourteen years old. He is tough, persistent, dedicated to achieving what he has committed himself to.

Susie Luff is a slender woman with green eyes and brown hair who tends to wear a rather severe expression. She talks rapidly and at length on any topic that happens to cross her mind, in contrast to her reined-in husband.

The Luffs' new neighbors would later remember that the young couple were warm and friendly. Shortly before, Ron had gotten a job at the Cleveland Electric Illuminating Company, a local utility, as a fork-lift operator.

At first Ron was the only member of the Luff family to attend classes, which were now four or five nights per week, with more than half the time spent on military planning and training directed toward the capture of the Kirtland Temple. Jeff taught that there was no difference between military strategy and religious training; after all, many of the prophets in ancient times had been great military leaders, and Joseph Smith, Jr., had been that kind of leader. Conquest and destruction of those who were not godly had always been part of God's plan.

The men were required to train with the weapons assigned to them, the women were required to learn their husbands' weapon, including how to clean and reload it. None of the women had a weapon except Alice. The women had to learn to identify different types of ammunition in the dark by touch, preparing them to reload for their men in the dark, which was when the assault on the Temple would occur. May 1 was D-Day. God would appear at the Temple on May 3, which happened to be Jeff's birthday. Jeff said he arrived at this date by deciphering the meaning of the symbols on the front doors of the Temple.

The Temple doors are, in fact, decorated with a pattern of ovals in which three upright ovals on the top of the door are supported by two identical horizontal ovals laid end to end; the horizontal ovals are in turn supported by three upright ovals above two horizontal ovals. According to Jeff, the patterns of the ovals represented the third day of the second month of the Hebrew calendar, which, he declared, was May third. Of course, in teaching this exegesis of the door decorations, Jeff omitted mention of the fact that he had assigned to Danny Kraft the task of finding a repetitive 3/2 pattern somewhere in the Temple. Jeff also made much of the fact that the pattern appeared on the doors of the Temple. The entrance, he told the group, was where people posted their office hours. Only natural, then, that God should cause the date of his return to appear upon the doors of His House; a sort of down-to-earth logic for the divinity.

In the Temple takeover battle plan designed by Jeff code names were assigned to all the participants. Jeff was Eagle I; Damon was Eagle II; Richard was Talon I; Kevin was Talon II; Danny was Eagle Eye; Ron was Falcon I; Greg was Falcon II. The farm was Eagle's Nest; the barn was Red Eagle. Locations around the Temple were also coded, from Vineyard I, the alcove behind the stake office, to Vineyard IX, the Lundgrens' former house near the Visitors' Center. The Temple was Mount VI. Richard and Damon were Team I; Danny and Dennis Patrick were Team II. The entire family was to congregate at Eagle's Nest on the night of April 30.

In some versions of the plan, the Averys were not to be included and not to be informed, but were simply to be left in their home to be destroyed in the resultant earthquake with the gentiles. Jeff frequently said, in discussing this version of the plan, that the Averys were so stupid that they would never know what was happening even if they were told. In other versions of the plan the Averys were to come to the farm but would be killed by some members of the group at some time during the assault on the Temple (which was closer to what finally happened). One plan, talked about during at least one class, was for Alice to execute Cheryl and the girls as soon as she was informed that the Temple had been taken.

The women were to stay at the farm with the children. At approximately 1:00 A.M. the men were to leave the farm, equipped with firearms, knives, and a crossbow. The crossbow was intended to eliminate silently any unsuspecting individual who might have been out at that hour. Apparently Jeff was particularly concerned about Kirtland Police Chief Yarborough, an insomniac who patrolled his village on foot when he couldn't sleep. The back of the men's camouflage gear was to be marked with luminescent tape so that they would be able to follow each other without communication in the dark. They were to go to the corner of Chillicothe Road and Kirtland–Chardon Road, where they were to set a fire at the self-service GasTown station, causing an explosion and creating a diversion.

After starting the fire the men were to proceed single file behind Jeff through the underbrush and small trees along the ravine beside the Chagrin River for three or four miles to a point behind the RLDS church, which is across the street from the Temple. Once behind and below the church, they were to climb the bank as silently as possible. When they reached the top they would enter the buildings and residences surrounding the Temple one at a time and kill whomever they found there. Jeff would lead Team I into the buildings, and Jeff would do the actual killing. People were to be beheaded—a silent method of killing frequently mentioned in Scriptures as a manner of execution for those who opposed God's armies.

Jeff talked often about the reason for killing those he expected to find in the houses near the Temple. He also related the details of the deaths he'd planned for the inhabitants of the vineyard. Those in authority in the church were targeted for the most extreme measures.

For instance, Jeff planned that Dale Luffman would be bound and gagged and forced to watch the execution of his wife and children by beheading or gutting before he himself would be killed.

After the buildings surrounding the Temple were secured, the men were to occupy the House itself, then Jeff would notify Alice by walkie-talkie and she and the other women would come to the Temple with the children.

The most commonly discussed version of the plan included the execution of Dennis, Tonya, and Molly Patrick. Jeff preached that the Patricks were irredeemable because Dennis had resisted the truth of Jeff's path to Zion. The Patricks would have to die before God could arrive, their deaths thereby serving the common purpose. The Patricks would be killed after the Temple was taken, their bodies thrown outside to convince the police that the group had hostages and that they were serious enough to execute the hostages.

After the taking of the Temple they were to hold it for three days. If they were successful, at the end of that time the earthquake would occur, God would appear, and Zion would be created. Jeff created elaborate plans for holding the Temple, including assigning positions on the roof and in the tower to be occupied by gunmen whose fire would cover the areas surrounding the building. Jeff's position was to be in the steeple. Food and other supplies actually were stored in the basement of the Temple in preparation for the assault.

In all of the later versions of the plan Alice and Debbie were the only women who had specific assigned roles—Alice, leader of the women and children, to execute some people if necessary; Debbie, medical officer. As medical officer she was to steal from the hospitals where she worked whatever medical supplies she could and to be available to treat wounds. Jeff explained that it would not be a particularly serious matter if any of the group was killed in the takeover—he would be able to raise them from the dead. The bodies would simply be stacked in an out-of-the-way corner of the Temple until Jeff could attend to them.

Jeff repeated time after time that the assault on the Temple could be successful *only* if the entire group was free of sin, just as he was. And those obstinate in their sin were dead in God's sight, and the wages of continued rejection of Jeff's truth was physical and spiritual death. During class discussion of military tactics and drills, violent death in many forms was frequently, graphically described by Jeff. On many occasions Jeff swore that he intended to see God in the flesh and that he would not let anyone stop him. If necessary he would kill any member of the group who refused to eliminate sin from his life and thoughts. And he could read their thoughts. He convinced them that he had that ability by the artful use of a combination of set-ups, coincidence, and subterfuge. But why did they believe? Most importantly because they *wanted* to believe, they wanted to see God and were afraid even to consider that Jeff might be a fraud. To doubt was to self-destruct—and education, intelligence, and such mundane defenses had little power in the face of such need and desire.

Except for Shar, who was able to resist Jeff's spell, at least to a certain extent. Shar believed and did not believe. Shar wanted Jeff to be a prophet, she wanted to believe that Zion was possible, she wanted to believe she could be a part of creating Heaven on earth, but at the same time she was still able to see clearly that much of what Jeff taught and advocated was a concoction.

Jeff and Alice had informed Danny and Shar that they were intended for each other and that they would eventually be married, just as Richard and Sharon were destined to marry. Shar resisted the idea. She liked Danny, but felt no romantic attraction to him. As a delaying action Shar would deliberately pick arguments with Danny so she wouldn't be expected to spend time with him. At first, like the others, she was afraid Jeff would read her intentions in her thoughts and she would be punished. When that didn't happen, her faith in Jeff's abilities tended to be further undermined. But Jeff's most serious shortcoming in Shar's eyes was his plain failure to pay her bills and those of others in the group, as well as his tendency to dissemble about whether or not the bills had been paid. When she had agreed to join the family and surrender her paychecks to Jeff, he had promised to take care of all her obligations so that she would have nothing outside the family to worry about or to distract her from Zion. When she was contacted at work by collection agencies it was embarrassing and distracting. Jeff's answer was that nothing outsiders did could touch her, that he would protect her from Babylon. Shar had trouble squaring this with Jeff's image of a holy man and prophet. *But even so, a part of her still believed, and like the others could not prove him wrong through the Scriptures.* That last was tremendously important, because of early indoctrination, for Shar and the others.

*   *   *

It was this belief that helped persuade Debbie Olivarez to join the group, because Shar's friendship was very much a consideration for Debbie when she made up her mind to move to Kirtland. After Debbie put her house up for sale in December of 1987 in preparation for her move, she also at Jeff's instruction made lists of her household goods and of her debts. On Christmas she returned to the farm for one last visit, to make sure that the peace and contentment she believed she had seen at the farm were real.

Jeff and Alice picked her up at Cleveland Hopkins International Airport, and during the hour-long drive to the farm Alice told Debbie that the group had a surprise for her. When the trio pulled in to the farm, Debbie learned that the surprise was a play, written and directed by Richard especially for Debbie.

The play was in two parts. In the first each member of the family did a short skit or monologue mocking himself or herself as he or she used to be. In the second each performed a skit showing what he or she would be in the future. (Later Debbie would remember that six-year-old Caleb Lundgren was called "Caleb, the Destroyer of Ten Thousand Gentiles." Debbie thought at the time that that was a joke. She would learn it was not.)

While in Kirtland Debbie reviewed her lists of household goods and debts with Jeff and Alice, and was told which of her furnishings to keep and which to sell and what to do with the proceeds. Like Shar and the others, she was also told that when she came to Kirtland Jeff would pay all her debts from the funds he controlled as the head of the household. All she needed to do was turn over her paychecks to him.

Debbie agreed. She could no longer bear her burdens alone.

When Debbie returned to Independence a few days before the new year she had irrevocably decided to move to Kirtland. She told her children what she was going to do and told them that while she hoped they would choose to come with her, they could decide. Of course she had some anxiety, but she also concentrated on Cousin Jeff's persuasive assurance that if she were a loyal and sin-free member of his group her children would be saved in the final cataclysm because they were her children.

Debbie, however, was secretive in her contacts with her friends. She told them that she was moving to Kirtland but nothing more. She did not tell them she would be living with Jeff and Alice, and she certainly did not tell them about Jeff's prophecy of a great earthquake and that a mountain would be made and God would come to earth. She regretted the need for secrecy, but by now believed that these people were outsiders, gentiles who had rejected the truth and were therefore beyond redemption.

She kept her secrets, packed her things and sent out job applications to the Cleveland area.

9

THE TIME IS AT HAND

As Debbie Olivarez was preparing to move to the farm in January of 1988, Richard Brand was being hired as a civil engineer in the city of Mentor, a Cleveland suburb north-northeast of Kirtland, and thereby making Jeff Lundgren very pleased—Brand's salary would now be considerably higher than his previous one as a laborer in nurseries. And, exemplifying Jeff's prescribed show of loyalty and trust by a group member, Richard made Jeff the beneficiary of the insurance policy provided by the city, some $12,000.

Not all were so compliant—Kevin Currie in particular. Through his job at the local Veterans' Administration hospital processing veterans needing psychiatric treatment, he picked up some knowledge of obsessive behavior that surfaced in various forms of mental illness. As Kevin would attest, Jeff seemed to be removed from a sense of the reality of the violence he preached, while at the same time being obsessed with notions of sin and punishment unto death. The Scriptures Jeff was immersed in seemed more real to him than the world outside the holy books. Kevin also felt that Jeff was becoming suspicious of him, to the point that his life was in danger.

One evening in February a cake was being served—a rarity except for someone's birthday—and Jeff's daughter Kristen asked him what the occasion was. He told her it was Kevin's going-away cake. Kevin thought he got the message; Jeff intended to kill him. The next morning he left for work as usual, got a ride to the bus station, and went on to Buffalo.

Jeff, of course, was furious. Knowing Kevin as he did, he was sure that his former old friend had gone to Buffalo. However, he pretended that it was his power to read minds and thoughts that made it possible for him to know where Kevin had gone. At first he threatened to go to Buffalo to kill Kevin himself, then said he would cause Kevin to be struck by a fatal illness or die in an accident. Whatever and however, he assured all, Kevin was a dead man.

Kevin thought so too, and tried hard to leave no trail. He never stopped worrying about the master plan to cleanse the vineyard.

Debbie Olivarez, of course, was unaware of the reasons for Kevin Currie's departure and continued to make plans for her move to Kirtland. She had wanted to wait until Bonnie finished the school year in Independence, but Jeff was saying that the mountain would be made before that—probably by May 3, and he wanted Debbie in Kirtland by April 1 to prepare. In spite of some misgivings, Debbie went along and arrived at the farm with her daughter Bonnie on April 1, 1988. Almost immediately after her arrival her household furnishings were sold, at Jeff's instructions, at a garage sale, Jeff pocketing the proceeds. And Debbie went to work for the family as a surgical nurse at a Cleveland hospital.

John Olivarez protested when he found out where Debbie had taken Bonnie and filed for a change of custody, which Debbie first fought and then agreed to after Jeff assured her that if she stayed faithful Bonnie would be safe even in Independence. He also promised Debbie that when the earthquake arrived he would go to Independence and kill John, pinning the custody papers to his chest with a Bowie knife. Debbie, who had no reason to have any love or concern for John, drew a floor plan of John's house.

Meanwhile Shar, in contrast with Debbie's growing confidence in Jeff, his works and teachings, was becoming increasingly disenchanted. She would later remember in particular a time when Jeff claimed he was going to speak with God. He had announced his impending dialogue with the Almighty at a class held the evening before the morning it was to take place. He said he would go to the top of the hill that was the highest point in Ohio, which also happened to be just down the road from the farm. The wondrous morning, he said, getting carried away, would be cloudless, and a beam of light would shine about him as he spoke to God from the hilltop.

Shar stayed awake all night—if Jeff's divine communion took place it would silence her doubts; if it didn't, which she suspected, well, then she would know that. In the morning, just before dawn, she heard Jeff stirring about downstairs. She moved quietly down the stairs to find him seated at the kitchen table, not acting as though he were about to have a divine exchange.

When Jeff asked her what she was doing, she said she had just wanted to be on hand to lend him support for this momentous moment in his life. He thanked her for being a dutiful daughter, put on his shoes, and ambled out the door. Watching him leave through one of the front windows, she noted that the sky, contrary to Jeff's forecast, was cloudy. She also failed to discern any shaft of light falling in the direction of the hill. After Jeff returned he made no mention of what God may have said to him. At the end of the class that night he reported vaguely about an insight he had had that day from God. When Shar asked about the discrepancy in the weather prediction, he at first ignored her, then said he'd consult the Scriptures and get back to her. He never did.

On the twenty-fifth of April the Kirtland Police Department was contacted by a concerned neighbor, the mother of a child about Caleb Lundgren's age, reporting that her child had been playing with Caleb when the boy suddenly announced that on May 3 "the earth would open up and demons would come out." The police told her, not unreasonably, not to allow her child to play with the Lundgren children. Still, the beginning of a suggestion of something peculiar at the farm had taken place.

Another and more meaningful alarm was sounded by Kevin in Buffalo, still very worried about Jeff's plans to take over the Temple and that people, including his friends, could die. Kevin, from his hiding place in Buffalo, called the FBI.

Agents at the Buffalo office thought they had another nut on their hands but forwarded the information to Kirtland just in case. The man who received the initial information from "Confidential Informant Number I" was Kirtland Police Chief Dennis Yarborough. Yarborough, forty-nine, had been chief of the six-man force for a dozen years, after being in police and undercover work all his adult life. Yarborough began his career in the armed forces, leaving only when he felt he had found a job in police work that offered him the same satisfaction of matching wits with and eventually outwitting anyone who chose to live outside the law.

A taciturn man, Yarborough's often grim, tight-lipped expression hides an offbeat sense of humor. A country Columbo, his intelligence masking his down-home manner, he is something of a loner who relies on his own judgment and evaluation of a situation. Only his wife of almost a quarter-century has a significant impact on Yarborough's opinions. And to Dennis Yarborough, no matter what the FBI in Buffalo thought, Jeff Lundgren and his group constituted a substantial potential threat. Yarborough, himself a member of the local RLDS stake, had become acquainted with Jeff's peculiar reputation through the church.

The chief first spoke with Kevin Currie on April 28, when Kevin provided details of the assault known to him. He had one caveat— Yarborough could not reveal to *anyone,* and particularly not to anyone with whom Jeff might have had contact, that he knew anything about the plot. Yarborough was immediately faced with a dilemma. Should he take everything Kevin was saying at face value and immediately proceed to neutralize whatever threat the group represented, or should he delay and investigate further, hoping somehow to confirm some of Kevin's accusations? He decided to do both.

Yarborough assigned thirty-five-year-old Ron Andolsek to investigate the people living at the farm—names, ages, occupations, backgrounds. Andolsek, a high-strung man with deep-set, intense dark eyes and high, prominent cheekbones, is an honors graduate of Kent State University with a degree in law enforcement. Being a policeman was all he has ever wanted to do. An investigation of the Lundgren group was precisely the type of demanding, detail-oriented task he thrived on. And meanwhile Yarborough established surveillance of the farm and the Temple and scheduled a twenty-four-hour patrol of the area surrounding the Temple.

Time was apparently short. The two police officers, with responsibility for dozens of lives weighing on their thoughts, discussed the best way to handle the threat. Andolsek was confident that the assigned patrols would be able to take out a few amateur soldiers if they were foolish enough to follow through with Lundgren's plan. He wanted to lie low and to find out as much as possible about the group before Jeff or anyone else was aware that the police knew anything about them.

Yarborough, on the other hand, while confident that he and his officers could handle Lundgren and his group should it become necessary, wanted to prevent even the slightest possibility that anyone would be hurt. He was in favor of letting Jeff know that the police were on to him, hoping that the assault would then be cancelled. Andolsek strongly disagreed. Disclosure, he felt, would greatly reduce whatever intelligence the police would be able to get about the group, and so would have a long-term negative effect on any efforts to contain whatever damage the group might do.

Yarborough finally decided on a compromise approach. He would not reveal to Jeff that the department knew anything about his plan for the Temple, but he *would* let Jeff know that the police were keeping an eye on him. Yarborough asked Jeff to stop by the station, where he told him that there had been complaints from the farm's neighbors about gunshots from the area of the farm. He took care to tell Lundgren that he didn't suspect anyone at the farm of firing the shots but wanted Lundgren to know that the police would be keeping a watch on the area in case there were any problems.

Shortly after his visit to the station, Jeff informed the group that God was displeased with them. There was too much sin in the group for them to be able to take and hold the Temple. Jeff could also be a realist, it seemed. But what next?

Now that the police were aware of the potential threat posed by Jeff's family, the relationship between the two groups settled into a game of cat and mouse. The police continued to investigate the group members and their backgrounds, taking advantage of whatever excuse available to go onto the farm or into the house.

One time, Andolsek used the neighbors' complaints about the flock of geese that ran loose on the farm property to investigate the cars parked behind the barn. In spite of Jeff's statements that the cars had been abandoned by the owner Stan Skrbis, Andolsek established that they actually belonged to Debbie Olivarez, Danny Kraft, and the Averys. Another time, Jason witnessed a fight at school and Andolsek questioned him about the incident at home. He didn't manage to get a glimpse of the weapons he was hoping to see inside the farmhouse. For his part Jeff told the group he thought their phone was being tapped and ordered them never to discuss anything sensitive over the telephone. He also had the number changed. In late May Jeff called the police station to report gunfire in the area, apparently trying to divert attention from the farm.

Jeff had other problems besides the police and, as he saw it, the likely treachery of Kevin Currie. Sometime in May, Shar told him that she wanted to leave. It had, after all, been building for a long time. Jeff and Alice talked with Shar, assured her she had their love as her true parents, told her that to leave meant her death, whether by bullet, knife, accident, or disease—it was all the same because Jeff would have caused it. They told her that *wherever* she went Jeff would be able to find her, just as he could find Kevin. After all, he could read her mind. Eventually, in the face of the threats and promises, Shar said she would stay.

In a few weeks, though, she changed her mind and had accumulated money for her leaving, money she could conceal from Jeff. The restaurant where she worked as a waitress had made a mistake in the payroll and given her an incorrect check. Management promised to have the check recut but since the restaurant was part of a chain the replacement check would have to be cut at the regional office, which might take time. Shar could honestly tell Jeff, who asked her about it, that the check had not arrived. Finally the assistant manager handed Shar the replacement check. She said nothing to Jeff about it when he picked her up that evening to drive her home. She was terrified, though, when for the first time in weeks he asked her if anyone at work had said anything to her about the check. She said no, but at that moment wondered if, indeed, Jeff could read her mind—it was weeks since he'd mentioned the check yet this day he had. Even so, she said nothing.

A few days later Shar again told Jeff and Alice that she intended to leave, but not that she had the money to do so. This time the Lundgrens took her and Danny to Jeff's office in the barn, where he and Alice and Danny lectured, talked, screamed for hours about her folly in leaving the group. Finally, Shar remembers, toward the end of the session, Alice looked her in the eye and said, "I know what it is. You just want to get screwed."

That was enough. Shar got up and walked out of the barn. She was afraid, but as she would say later, she knew she had to leave because she was sure that anyone who stayed would end up dead or in prison.

*   *   *

Over the next few months, Jeff pressured Greg to move into the farm-house. Greg was continuing to withhold part of his salary because of personal living expenses, and with the departure of Shar, Jeff was looking for as much additional income as he could find. Greg finally moved in in September. It was also at about this time that Jeff and Alice revealed to Debbie and Greg that God had intended them for each other. Debbie was very happy; Greg was not.

During the summer, annoyance with the Avery family continued to build. The fate of those "ripened in iniquity" was death, and in classes it was made clear that Dennis and Cheryl were ripened in iniquity.

Ever since the Averys had arrived, Alice had complained about Cheryl's dependence on her. It seemed that Cheryl couldn't make a decision about how to handle *any* family problem without coming to Alice, and after Debbie arrived would repeatedly call wanting advice from Alice and Debbie about her children's problems. At first Alice had been annoyed by Dennis and Cheryl but had spoken well of their children. But soon that tolerance waned. Eventually Alice complained that Trina was fat and lazy and disrespectful and that Becky was disobedient. Almost no one had anything bad to say about little Karen.

Everyone would remember Karen's large brown eyes and endearing smile. When the group members were telling law officers and prosecutors about the killings, all broke down when they talked about Karen's death. In fact, her sisters were no worse behaved than most children their age, and were surely better tempered and behaved than the Lundgren children. But the Avery children were condemned by the prophet to suffer for the "sins" of their parents.

10

THE SWORD OF LABAN

Dennis Avery was no more popular with the Lundgrens than his wife. Jeff required that each member of the group who did not live on the farm prepare a budget and that any amount left over after essentials should be given to Jeff. Greg Winship was the least diligent; Jeff believed that Dennis Patrick was concealing some of his income; Ron Luff contributed the largest amount. But Dennis Avery not only claimed that he could not contribute anything at all but went so far as to demand the return of the $10,000 he had given Jeff a year earlier.

Dennis repeatedly told Jeff that he hadn't fulfilled his end of the bargain. Jeff was not paying the Averys' rent as he had promised, and Stan Skrbis was harassing Dennis. Jeff blamed Dennis for not being ambitious enough to land a job that met his family's needs.

Finally, on July 15, the group moved the Averys in the middle of the night to a house Jeff had rented for them in Madison, about fifteen miles from Kirtland. The move was done at night and secretly so that Skrbis wouldn't be able to locate the family and demand the several months of unpaid rent. Stan Skrbis never saw any of the Avery family again.

Dennis Avery was different from the rest of the group in other ways as well. He never pictured himself as a man capable of murdering gentiles in the service of Jeff the prophet or anybody else. He felt like a tired old man with physical problems. Even eating, he said, made him tired. At the same time he didn't respect or fear Jeff. During classes he would argue with some point that Jeff had made. A favorite phrase was, "Yes, but . . ." None of the others dared disagree with Jeff, dared refuse to fit into the mold of an ideal man dictated by Jeff, dared to question Jeff's distribution of the group's assets. Jeff called Dennis too stupid to understand the opportunity he was being given.

Stupidity was not the problem. Dennis, in his criticism of Jeff, really appeared to envy Jeff's power, that Jeff was supported as he was by the others. Dennis would say that he couldn't wait until the mountain was made so that he, too, could be a teacher of the truth like Jeff and could have others work for him and wait on him like Jeff.

The others in the group were amazed that Dennis did not seem to comprehend the possibly lethal consequences of his behavior. Perhaps because Dennis and Cheryl were rarely invited to classes, the threat that Jeff had come to represent to the lives of those inside the group did not appear real to the Averys. Dennis and Cheryl were never privy to *all* the group's intentions, although they were informed about the plot to take over the Temple. Surely the Averys never were aware that Jeff had openly discussed the time, place, and even manner of their deaths during classes.

That the Averys were in a state of sin and would die was a common topic of discussion by the time Shar left the group. The subject of violent death was one the group had become very familiar with through class discussion, everyday conversation, and the movies Jeff loved to watch. At first, though, the proposed takeover was not taken seriously. It was sort of a child's game of war for adults. Like Capture the Flag, a favorite, after all, of summer campers such as the Boy Scouts. Eventually, though, the fact that Jeff actually intended that people should die horribly began to impress itself upon their minds. No one can say when it was that they began to believe that something would really happen, but whenever it was, by June of 1988 the threat was real and palpable at every meeting. By June everyone except Dennis and Cheryl Avery understood that the price of disobedience to Jeff in thought, word, or deed was death. Everyone also believed that he or she had little or no option for life outside the group. Their destinies were entwined with Jeff's. God had selected them to follow His last prophet. To forsake this divine calling was physical and spiritual death. It did not matter, according to Jeff's teaching, whether that death occurred immediately or at a later time. As God was eternal and all things existed simultaneously in Him, anyone who was destined to betray the truth had, in God's eyes, already betrayed that truth and, as the wages of that betrayal were physical and spiritual death, anyone who would at any time betray God was already dead to Him. So, according to Jeff, it was not significant whether that person died as a child or lived to an extended age, the soul of that person was doomed and the time on earth could not alter that fact—thereby setting the rationalization for the Avery children's demise.

Since Jeff, by means of his special relationship with God, was able to tell whether or not any particular person was doomed, logically Jeff was judge, jury, and executioner. When Jeff said that the Averys would have to die, no one questioned the judgment.

Non-group members have continued to find it surprising that more questioning did not take place. Jeff's teachings could change over a period of weeks. Jeff was also preoccupied with sex, as mentioned. "There are only two things we talk about around here—Scripture and sex." Jeff would frequently come up behind Debbie, she has reported, and say such things as, "I'm going to run my tongue all over your body." God approved of any kind of sexual behavior, Jeff taught.

Jeff prophesied events that did not occur, though he always had an excuse. In hindsight, all but Danny Kraft and Kathy Johnson have said they can see the deception, but at the time each individual was isolated with his or her own thoughts and doubts, which each was frantically denying and suppressing. Critical thinking processes were jammed. The static of externally imposed and internally monitored terror was too effective to permit analytical thought or objective observation. The questioning process was short-circuited.

Even though Jeff's power was supreme within the group, and they believed he spoke in God's stead, Jeff was aware that Yarborough and Andolsek were keeping an eye on him and his activities, though, given his tendency to paranoia, he at first exaggerated the extent of the investigation.

Jeff began to worry that the Kirtland police or the FBI or some other federal agency would raid the farmhouse and find the weapons cached there. Some months before he had had Danny build a secret extension from the closet in Jason and Caleb's bedroom into the attic, but now he came to feel that not even that hiding place was safe enough. For one thing, Shar knew about the closet. Also, Jeff realized that such a hiding place was just the sort of thing a cop might search for.

Finally Jeff decided he would move the weapons to the Luffs' apartment, where they could easily be concealed in a closet. The plan had numerous advantages. First, it would be a test of Ron's loyalty, as Susie was almost certain to resist the idea. Second, the plan would demonstrate the extent of Ron's control over Susie. And the weapons would be accessible to Jeff from the Luffs' apartment within an hour but would not, in his estimation, be discovered by the police since they were in another jurisdiction.

Sometime in August, the guns were wrapped in blankets and carried in duffel bags from the farm to the Luffs' home. They were stored in a closet under the stairs for several months, then gradually were returned to the farm a few at a time as Jeff regained his confidence that a raid was not imminent.

Shar, though, was still terrified, still afraid to let others know what she knew, out of fear that her friends might be hurt as a result, but also afraid not to tell what she knew because she was almost certain that innocent people would be harmed or even killed if someone didn't stop Jeff. And she knew that Jeff was watching her—she had been confronted once by Jeff at the place where she was working. Jeff had told her and the others that she would not be able to make it on her own and would come crawling back to the group. When Shar bounced a check at a local discount store patronized by the group it seemed he might be right. The overdraft had occurred as the result of confusion about when deposits were available to be drawn on, and so was soon covered, but meanwhile Jeff and Alice, aware of the situation, had paid the store the face amount of the check and taken the original check home, where they showed it to the others as proof that Shar couldn't cope on her own. Shar, in turn, was feeling nearly paranoid as it seemed Jeff had resources to know what had happened to her.

She decided to contact someone she trusted, to warn him of the imminent danger to him and his family and to seek his advice about how to proceed about the others in danger. On September 20 she called Dale Luffman. Dale promised not to reveal anything she told him until the two had agreed on what should be done. Shar then told Dale everything she knew about the plot to take over the Temple, and Dale drove from his meeting with Shar to the Kirtland police station and told them what Shar had said. He had no doubt that Jeff Lundgren was capable of every act that Shar said the prophet planned. The next day Ron Andolsek contacted Shar and asked to meet with her.

Shar was upset, angry, and afraid but agreed to meet with Andolsek in a local restaurant where Shar agreed to cooperate with the police and the FBI. She became "Confidential Informant Number II."

*   *   *

Meanwhile, in mid-August Debbie's back was once again injured on the job; she quit working and from then on stayed home and did housework and all the cooking for the family. In September her house in Independence was finally sold. The $22,000 check she cleared on the deal was intercepted by Jeff in the mail, Alice endorsed it, Jeff deposited it, and the Lundgrens went on an antiquing spree. A few weeks later an $11,000 settlement check from Debbie's Worker's Compensation claim arrived. That check, too, was handed over to Jeff.

Beginning with the disclosures of C.I. I, Kevin Currie, in May, Yarborough had been talking with the Lake County office of the Federal Bureau of Investigation, located in Painesville, the county seat, trying to persuade the Bureau that an FBI investigation of Jeff's family was justified. But to the Bureau, the report of a single individual who may well have been either unbalanced or vengeful hardly merited the mobilization of the Bureau's resources to dog the activities of a self-proclaimed prophet with a handful of followers.

Agents were only willing to provide Yarborough and Andolsek with surveillance tips and advice to help them get more information about the Lundgrens. But with the emergence of C.I. II (Shar), who both confirmed the information provided by C.I. I and was willing to work with local law-enforcement to prevent any violence on the part of Lundgren's group, the FBI did officially open an investigation. Surveillance was maintained through a van parked across and just down the street from the farmhouse, and at least two surveillance flights were taken over the farm and Temple.

Also, as summer passed into fall, Jeff began pressuring group members to resign their memberships in the RLDS church. All of them eventually did so, although Sharon's departure was complicated by the fact that the church also had an on-going dispute with her about rent she still owed on the apartment she had occupied until the group moved to the farm in October of 1987. Eventually Jeff paid the few hundred dollars of Sharon's debt to the church.

The RLDS also continued to be alarmed about the growing radicalism of Jeff's teachings. Finally Shar's revelations to Dale Luffman about the plans to assault the Temple became the final straw, and the decision was made to excommunicate Jeff, Alice, Damon, and Jason. On October 10, 1988, Dale Luffman and Bishop Stobaugh called on Jeff at the farm. Jeff talked with them on the porch and informed the others that he had resigned from the church. According to Luffman and the bishop, Jeff and his family were officially expelled during that visit.

Later that same day the Kirtland area was struck by a violent thunderstorm, followed by a double rainbow. Jeff promptly searched the Scriptures to see if the rainbow had a special significance. Later he convened the group in an impromptu class that became the first step on the road leading to the deaths of the Averys some six months later.

In that class Jeff referred the group to the Book of Revelation, chapter 6, verses 1 and 2:

1. And I saw when the Lamb opened one of the seals, and I heard, as it were the noise of thunder, one of the four beasts saying, Come and see. 2. And I saw, and behold a white horse: and he that sat on him had a bow; and a crown was given unto him: and he went forth conquering, and to conquer.

Jeff declared that the double rainbow they had just seen had been the bow referred to in verse 2 and that the storm had been the "breaking of the first seal" of the seven seals on the book, which only the Lamb that was slain may open. Therefore, according to Jeff, not only was the end of the world, the Apocalypse, at hand, but it was clear that Jeff was being acknowledged as the prophet who would bring about the end, that Jeff was He who would go forth conquering and to conquer.

Shortly thereafter Jeff began to teach that it was his responsibility, and thus his household's, to bring about the breaking of the remaining six seals. According to Revelation 6:4, upon the breaking of the second seal, "there went out another horse that was red: and power was given to him that sat thereon to take peace from the earth, and that they should kill one another: and there was given unto him a great sword."

Jeff interpreted the breaking of the second seal to mean that people should die. Within weeks he began teaching that according to a chiastic interpretation of the Book of Mormon, Moroni lost ten followers in preserving the gold plates. Thus, said Jeff, it was necessary for him to lose ten followers to retrieve the plates, and these ten followers were the people who must die with the breaking of the second seal. And Jeff knew, of course, just which ten people should die: first, foremost, and inevitably, the Averys were doomed. Richard and Sharon and the Patricks, including Molly, were also on God's hit list.

The group had been long conditioned to accept that these individuals should be selected to be eliminated as a part of God's plan. Jeff and Alice had always disliked and resented Dennis and Cheryl and their family and for months had talked about the fact that the Averys did not fit into God's plan for the Temple takeover. Also Jeff taught that the sins of the father were visited on the children, and thus the children of evil parents are also evil and must be eliminated with their parents.

Dennis Patrick had also been a thorn in Jeff's side. For years Jeff had perceived in Dennis the man that he himself wanted to be and had, in effect, wanted to take Dennis's place and take over Dennis's life. The group was unaware of the source of Jeff's attitude toward Dennis, but they did know the strength of his feelings and they knew that Jeff believed that Dennis wanted to supplant him. In what appears a near-classic role reversal, Jeff had projected his own feelings onto Dennis. Dennis, of course, did not understand why, in Jeff's view, he was unable to do anything right. Molly and Tonya Patrick were slated to die because of Jeff's jealousy of Dennis.

Richard was just a pain in the neck. He constantly questioned. His questions were not hostile and weren't necessarily rebellious, but were frequent and distracting and forced Jeff to devise answers consistent with each other and with what had been taught before. Richard was also resisting Jeff's plan for his life. So far he had refused to marry Sharon and showed no inclination to change. Sharon, on the other hand, was an inconvenience. She was extremely dependent on Jeff and Alice for approval, running to them with any comment Richard might make to her in confidence that might be interpreted as "murmuring" or questioning. Sharon was often in a world of her own, and in spite of her best efforts, she continued to be very overweight. Sharon's personality and her appearance displeased the prophet. She was dead weight.

These were the ten scheduled to be executed in order that God's wrath could be vented elsewhere than on the group as a whole. They were to be "fuel for the fiery furnace," consumed to begin the conflagration that would eventually envelop all who did not believe in Jeff. The names of the ten, except for the Averys, were never discussed in class, but were made known in out-of-class impromptu conversations.

The Patricks and Richard and Sharon, of course, were never told that their deaths were imminent.

The group members, in spite of conditioning, were frightened. They all knew that Jeff was capable of at least considering random violence, and his brutality to animals indicated a callousness about the value of life in general.

Beginning in early January of 1989, the meetings took place every night, lasting until well into the early hours of the morning. The Patricks and the Luffs brought their children to the farm, where they were put to bed to be awakened and returned home by their parents whenever the class adjourned. The Averys, as usual, were almost never invited.

It was also at this time that Jeff began to bring his favorite pistol to class. The .45–caliber Colt Combat Elite, which he had bought the day Dennis Avery had given him the $10,000, was ready at hand on the table or desk in front of Jeff. No one else brought a weapon to class. No one complained or contested Jeff's edict that people would be killed. All were clearly afraid, but apparently stronger than the fear was the faith that Jeff would lead them to God.

11

FUEL FOR THE FURNACE

By January of 1989, everyone was on edge and exhausted, except Alice, who had no outside job and no household responsibilities. Jeff's .45 was as usual on the table at the long nightly meetings. Attention was very much on that handgun.

Damon was now required to attend more often than before but continued to be excused more often than any members except the Averys—though, of course, not for the same reason. Damon was being prepared to be the prophet's successor. Damon would later be described by teachers and friends as a nice guy who was more of a follower than a leader, and Jeff would have preferred that his son be athletically gifted. Damon's prime talent appears to have been success at concealing the nature and extent of his father's plans and of his own involvement in them. His friends believed he was a kind if socially inept young man very much controlled by his father. The truth appears to have been that Damon entered into all the planning and training with relish, as long as he wasn't required to work too long or too hard.

Damon was put in charge of the men's physical training, Jeff believing that the physical training Damon had had as a short-term member of the Kirtland High School wrestling team would help him devise a program for keeping the men in good physical condition for taking over the Temple and then living in the wilderness. He devised a simple program of calisthenics and appeared to enjoy leading the other men. Occasionally he required them to run or jog through the orchard. He bullied them too, sometimes requiring Richard to kiss his feet.

96

Damon appeared to know about everything happening around the farm, resented the idea that anything might happen without his knowledge. As first among the "natural" offspring, he was rarely disciplined by his father or mother. And, of course, they would allow no criticism of the naturals.

In late January, apparently worried that the execution of at least four of his productive followers would leave the group with too few members, Jeff contacted his old friend Larry Keith Johnson and asked him to come to Kirtland to visit and learn about all the marvelous things he and his group were doing.

Keith arrived in Kirtland on February 16, to be welcomed with open arms by Jeff and Alice. In fact, according to Keith, the Lundgrens reimbursed him for the cost of his plane ticket. Keith was then given an opportunity to observe the group at home and had a short course in Jeff's teachings, much as Debbie Olivarez had had fifteen months before. On February 18 an invitation was extended to Keith and his immediate family to move to Kirtland as soon as possible and to accompany the group on its coming wilderness experience. Keith went back to Missouri on February 19, where he and his wife Kathy immediately began to prepare to come to Kirtland. In mid-March the Johnsons arrived in Kirtland and were housed at Jeff's direction with the Patricks. The two families could keep an eye on each other.

Kathryn Renee (Hubbard) Johnson was born in May of 1953 in Denison, Iowa, and grew up on a farm near Woodbine, Iowa. An honor-roll student in high school, she participated in extracurricular sports, particularly track. For her freshman year in college, she attended the by-now familiar Central Missouri State University, where she majored in nursing. After her freshman year she transferred to Northeast Louisiana State University in Monroe, Louisiana, where her fiancé also was, and at the end of her sophomore year the two married. They returned to Woodbine, where both had grown up, and where Kathy worked in a nursing home as a cook and manager of the kitchen. Kathy's marriage deteriorated and she was divorced in 1976. She moved to Council Bluffs, Iowa, and worked for a dentist, and six months later married Larry Keith Johnson, some four years older than she. Actually Kathy and Keith had met at Central Missouri State University when Kathy was a freshman, and since then Keith too had had a failed marriage. Keith took his new bride home to Latour, Missouri, where Kathy again worked as a dental assistant, until Joshua Johnson was born in February, 1979. After Joshua's birth Kathy went to work for her in-laws in the insurance business, eventually operating her own insurance agency until her third son, Justin, was born in June of 1984. The second, Jeremy, had arrived in June of 1982. A fourth child, Jordan, was born in July, 1986. The Johnson children never attended public school, were home-schooled by their mother and other adults in the schooling cooperative.

Kathy has since complained that Keith was physically and verbally abusive to her, which he denies. The two are unquestionably very different people—Kathy vigorous, assertive, intellectually ambitious; Keith content to hold a factory job in spite of having graduated from Central Missouri State with a degree in social work.

For years, Keith and Kathy were good friends of Jeff and Alice Lundgren. Keith had known Alice since high school, and had met Jeff at college. The two couples would visit together, and for a time Alice and Kathy were best friends. Even after the Lundgrens moved to Kirtland the two families kept in regular contact, so Keith was not particularly surprised when in January of 1989 Jeff contacted him and urged him to come to Kirtland with his family. Jeff said he needed Keith to complete his group and that the Johnsons must move to Ohio immediately. The Johnsons quickly responded and moved to Kirtland in March, 1989.

Kathy Johnson is tall and solidly built, with hazel eyes and brown hair. Her features somewhat resemble Alice's, although Kathy's face is rounder and flatter and she is by far the more attractive of the two. Keith Johnson has dark-brown, graying hair and dark brown eyes. His features are small, somewhat pinched, and he is developing jowls. He has been described as a typical "good ol' boy."

In late February of 1989 Jeff pondered the ways the Averys should be killed. He told the classes—the Averys absent—he had searched the Scriptures to find the answer and had discovered a partial solution:

Men were to be cut in two, so, he concluded, Dennis Avery would be beheaded. Dennis's death would occur last so that he could watch the deaths of his children and his wife. Women were to be slit across the lower abdomen with a sword, either horizontally or vertically, so that their organs would spill out. So this was the death for Cheryl and Trina Avery. Children should be swung by their heels and their heads smashed against a wall so that their skulls split and their brains spilled out. This was how little Karen would be killed. Becky posed a conundrum—should she be executed as a woman or as a child? Jeff and Alice discussed the matter at lunch, and Alice suggested that Becky's manner of death should depend on whether the thirteen-year-old had begun her menstrual periods.

Jeff made it clear that the group would have to withdraw to the wilderness to see God and that the deaths of the Averys would occur before the wilderness trip. He also ordered that Richard and Greg should stop resisting the will of God and consent to be married to, respectively, Sharon and Debbie. The two men had resisted long enough and were not surprised when in early April Jeff announced that he would tolerate no more delay. They were required to come to him one at a time, like a Mafia godfather, to ask for the hands of their assigned brides in marriage.

Greg and Debbie were married on April 4, 1989, in a ceremony written and performed by Danny Kraft. Jeff united the couple himself with seven words indicating that he gave the woman in marriage. Richard and Sharon were married the following day in an identical ceremony, the only difference being when Jeff asked Richard during the rites why he was marrying Sharon and Richard honestly replied, "Because you want me to."

After the ceremonies Jeff prophesied that each couple would soon produce a child. All four believed, in spite of Debbie's partial hysterectomy. Sharon had the prediction come true when she became pregnant within two months of her wedding day.

During the first quarter of 1989, Jeff was directing that the group make additional preparations for leaving for the wilderness, including purchasing what, in his mind, was proper armament. He felt the special need for a weapon that could be effective against the sophisticated armaments that could and would be brought against them. Where, he wondered, could he lay hands on a .50–caliber rifle?

Coincidentally, Ron Luff's brother had made guns and was in the process of making a .50–caliber rifle fitted with a machine-gun barrel. Jeff told Ron to contact his brother and offer to buy the weapon, and a deal was struck for nearly $3,000. Ron and Susie drove to Missouri over a long weekend to pick up the rifle, leaving their children Matthew and Amy at the farm. When they returned, the forty-eight-pound rifle became a part of the group's arsenal, Jeff saying it could be used to shoot helicopters out of the sky or to destroy tanks from the steeple of the Temple.

Group members were instructed to keep six sets of warm-weather clothing and six sets of cold-weather clothing. Anyone who did not have enough appropriate clothing was to let Jeff and Alice know. Alice would go shopping and select the clothing to be taken. Each person was instructed to get as many credit accounts as possible, both at department stores and from banks. Each account was to be charged to the maximum with supplies for the wilderness and was never to be paid since the group would not be able to be located by their creditors. Jeff called the plan "spoiling Babylon." It wasn't really stealing, the system and those who ran it were evil, so they were just using the tools of the devil to do the work of God.

Jeff's campaign to take advantage of untapped credit sources may have delayed Dennis Avery's execution by a day. Jeff learned on Saturday, April 15, that Dennis Avery had managed to qualify for a Mastercard with a $1,000 limit on which he had made no purchases and about which he had not informed the prophet. When Jeff found out about the asset he said, "I'm going to take that boy shopping!" They proceeded to buy several guns on Sunday, April 16, charging the card to the limit. Previously, Jeff had told several group members that the Averys were to be killed on the sixteenth.

In early spring of 1989 group members were also told to inform employers and relatives of their impending departures but were told not to tell the truth about where they were going or with whom they were going. Richard and Sharon each wrote to their families, copying sample letters written by Alice, to tell them they were eloping and going to Disneyland on their honeymoon. It was the story they told their employers when Richard asked for two weeks' vacation in mid-April and Sharon quit. Danny told his boss he was going to an antique-and-miniatures show in California. Damon told friends that the family was taking a vacation in California. Greg Winship and Dennis Patrick also asked for vacation time. Ron resigned, telling his supervisor that his grandfather had died and left him a family business that he was going back to Missouri to run. The Averys were instructed to tell their families that they were moving to Wyoming.

By early April the group was ready to leave Kirtland to head into a wilderness—most had no idea where they were going, but Jeff and Alice had been scouting sites in southern Ohio for several weeks. Sometimes the Lundgrens took Danny or Greg along. Finally Jeff had selected a location he felt would be ideal but kept it a secret.

Jeff also had Debbie and Greg researching psychological studies of police in general and SWAT teams in particular; he wanted to know about unsolved crimes and how the criminals had gotten away with them; he wanted to know how hot a fire needed to be to cremate a human body; he wanted to know about explosives. When Debbie wasn't able to find the information on cremation, Jeff decided to abandon his original half-formed plan to kill the Averys at their home in Madison, then set the house on fire. Eventually Damon was assigned to read the books on explosives and produce some homemade bombs.

Where to kill the Averys was a major decision. For some time Jeff, as mentioned, considered carrying out the executions in their Madison home, and one time threatened Sharon that if she didn't eliminate her sins she would be required to come along and watch. She would later say she was sure that Jeff intended she never return if she were taken to watch the Averys being killed.

The second week in April ushered in a pleasant early spring in northeastern Ohio. Grass was sprouting, the trees were budding, flowers were again decorating the landscape. And Jeff Lundgren had finally decided how and where the Averys were to die.

He had earlier named the western end of the barn the Red Sea, based on the color of the barn and the fact that the low-lying, dirt-floored barn tended to flood. Now he had decided that the Averys— and, so far as the group knew, maybe the Patricks and Sharon and Richard—would be buried in the barn. For three weeks Jeff had been spending most of his waking hours with Keith Johnson, bringing him up to speed on his teachings and plans. Beginning on April 10, Jeff set Keith and Ron to work digging a pit in the barn large enough to hold ten people.

At noon when the men came in for lunch and at the end of the day

Jeff and Alice would review the progress of the pit with Ron and Keith. At first there was some difficulty in eliminating a drain to make the pit large enough, but eventually they got it under control and the bottom of the pit was simply somewhat muddy.

The men were told to be finished and out of the barn each day before Richard returned home from work. Damon and Greg and Danny were assigned to collect rocks from around the pond some forty feet behind the barn. The rocks were loaded on a trailer behind the tractor and hauled to the back wall of the barn, where they were thrown into the barn through a small window located directly above the pit. The rocks were intended to weight down the bodies when the pit flooded. Susie, who was at the farm with her children while Ron worked on the pit, took lemonade out to the men working on the rocks, and out of boredom even helped them for a little while.

One evening that week the Averys invited Jeff and Alice to their Madison home for dinner. Jeff had tried for weeks to persuade Alice to go to the Avery house to sort through the Averys' belongings for anything that might be useful in the wilderness. When the dinner invitation came Jeff accepted over Alice's opposition. When Jeff and Alice came back to the farm from Madison they were pleased to report that the Averys had a microwave, a refrigerator, a washer and dryer and some Corelleware that the group, purged of evil, would be able to use.

The pit was completed by Friday, April 14. It was on this day that Richard first saw the grave. He did not know what the pit was for or why it was there. He does not recall why he was in the barn. He does remember trying very hard at that time *not* to speculate on the reason for the pit.

On Sunday Sharon noticed that for some reason Richard had not taken the trash out, so, hoping to prevent any criticism of him, she took the bags to the barn. She was unable to open the barn doors, they seemed to be nailed shut. As she was standing outside the doors wondering what to do, she heard a sound that seemed to be metal striking dirt. Damon called down to her to leave the bags where they were, that someone else would take care of them.

On Saturday morning Dennis Patrick had arrived at the farm hoping to be able to appease Jeff by offering to help in any way he could. Jeff sent him out to the barn, telling him to do whatever he could to help Ron and Keith with their project. Ron told Dennis that they were digging a baptismal font and since they were nearly finished they did not need his help.

On Saturday Richard was playing a game of basketball with some of the other men, including Damon. Jeff joined the game and at one point stopped it by holding the ball. He looked directly at Richard and said, "Tomorrow is the day." Richard took that comment to mean that the Averys would be killed on Sunday.

On Sunday Greg was instructed to make a reservation for the Averys at the Red Roof Inn, but the reservation had to be cancelled since Dennis and Cheryl were not yet ready to move out of their house. Also, Jeff and Dennis had to take their shopping trip. Little was accomplished on Sunday.

The next day was Monday, April 17, 1989.

12

THE SECOND SEAL

At sunrise on Monday, April 17, 1989, Dennis Avery, his wife Cheryl and their three daughters, fifteen-year-old Trina, thirteen-year-old Becky and six-year-old Karen, slept in sleeping bags in the tiny frame home they had rented in Madison, Ohio, for more than a year. But by sunset, the five Averys had finished their last dinner, just a few minutes from the time of their execution and a few feet from their burial in a common grave.

It was a typical spring day in northeastern Ohio. The sun rose at twenty minutes before seven through a sky dotted with Lake Erie's heavy, rain-foretelling clouds. The afternoon temperature reached a high of seventy degrees. Sunset came at eight-fifteen that night, though it was invisible through a bone-chilling, impenetrable fog. That evening, the thermometer dipped to near forty. Anticipated showers never developed.

The emotional climate among the Lundgren group living in the old farmhouse at 8671 Chardon Road paralleled the weather on that early spring day. At dawn, the twenty-eight adults and children who followed the self-proclaimed prophet Jeffrey Lundgren felt that the arrival of God and the ability of the group members to see Him in the flesh was a clear probability marred only by the lack of repentance and occasional sinfulness of group members. At dusk, the future and intent of the group and its leader were as cold and opaque as the fog surrounding the farmhouse.

For Debbie the day began as had every other day in the eight months since she had injured her back, except that she woke up next to Greg, her husband of less than two weeks.

A prerequisite to the group's departure into the wilderness was the killing of the Averys, but few in the group knew that the executions were to be that night. Debbie did not learn that that day was different from any other until afternoon. That morning, as Debbie was dressing, Alice came into the bedroom. Draping herself casually across the bed, head propped on her hand, Alice instructed Debbie that she would need to alter the menus she had prepared for the wilderness trip. She said that the two of them would have to purchase additional food and supplies because five people had been saved, and those five now would be part of the wilderness experience. Alice matter-of-factly reported that the five had been saved by the women's submission, which Debbie understood to mean that Richard, Sharon and Tonya, Molly, and Dennis Patrick would not be killed at the same time as the Avery family. Despite her mixed relief and confusion, Debbie revised her menus and planned for the purchase of extra supplies without question, as she had been taught.

For all the others, this day was different from any other in recent memory. Debbie, Jeff, and Alice were the only adult group members living in the communal house not employed outside the home. All the others had been instructed to take vacation time from their jobs or to quit, beginning that day. Everyone knew that these changes in the routine were made because the group would be leaving soon, and were busy packing and preparing camping equipment. Only Jeff and Alice knew when they were leaving or where in the wilderness the group was headed.

At 9:13 in the morning a one-minute telephone call was made from the Lundgren phone to the Avery home, presumably to tell the Averys when they could expect the men to arrive to move the last of their belongings. At 9:48 A.M. a reservation was made for the Averys by Greg Winship at Jeff's instruction at the Red Roof Inn, a motel located at the corner of State Route 306 and Interstate 90 in Willoughby, Ohio. (Jeff later would tell the group that the reservations were necessary so that there would be no connection between the Averys and Jeff's farm on that day.)

Sometime during the morning Greg was sent to take his Honda to the dealership to have the transmission repaired. Ron Luff picked up Greg at the dealership and took him into Cleveland, where Greg had been instructed by Jeff to locate and purchase a stun gun. After some searching Greg found a Power Shield stun gun at Galco Army Supply Company on East Seventy-first Street. He bought the stun gun and some rapelling rope, Ron picked him up and the two men returned to the farm.

Richard remembers being present in the living room when the stun gun arrived. Jeff was delighted with it. He strutted about the living room snapping the switch and listening to the crack and sizzle of the current surge. As he watched, Richard felt the usual stress increase almost to the breaking point. Abruptly, Richard found himself offering to let Jeff test the stun gun on him if Jeff felt it needed to be tested. Damon looked at Richard in amazement. "Why would you want to do that?" Richard wanted to know what the effect would be if the stun gun were used on him. He did not answer Damon.

While Ron and Greg were in Cleveland, Alice and Jeff called on Tonya Patrick at the Patricks' apartment and informed Tonya that, because of her submission to Alice, Tonya had saved herself, her husband Dennis, and their nine-year-old daughter Molly from destruction. Tonya asked no questions. She was not shocked since, according to her own account, she did not really believe that Jeff would carry out the death threats he had so often made against members of the group. In fact, according to both Dennis and Tonya, Tonya was so unimpressed by the news that she did not even bother to mention it to Dennis.

At eleven-thirty, after the men had moved the last load of furniture and belongings from the Avery house to the Lundgren barn, the Averys were brought to the farm from their house in Madison. Debbie served a lunch of sandwiches and leftovers. The entire group was present. Jeff let it be known that he did not want the Averys at the farm that day, and they were taken to the Red Roof Inn. Red Roof Inn records show that Dennis Avery checked in two adults and three children at 1:00 P.M. Dennis paid cash for the room, and with the advance cash payment it was not necessary for the family to check out formally the next morning. Leaving the keys in the room would be all that was required.

Shortly after lunch Alice took Sharon with her to the bank. Several deposits were made that day, from paychecks various group members had received over the previous few days. During the drive, Sharon remembers, Alice turned to her and said, "The Averys are going to die tonight, and I've known for a long time that you and Richard were going to be in the pit with them." Alice went on to say that she was very proud of Sharon, and that her obedience to Alice had saved both herself and her husband Richard. Sharon barely heard that last part of

Alice's comments. Unlike Tonya Patrick, Sharon was struck dumb with shock and could only think, What have I done?—but she asked no questions. Alice has denied that this conversation ever took place.

Sharon also remembers that shortly after she and Alice returned to the farm, they met Jeff in the living room and Alice told Jeff that she was so excited that she hadn't been able to wait and had told Sharon that she and Richard were to be spared. According to Sharon, Jeff was not pleased but indulged Alice's excitement and called Richard downstairs to share the good news with her. Richard does not remember such a meeting; he simply remembers being told almost casually by Alice that he would be spared. Alice has also denied that that conversation took place.

Later that afternoon Debbie and Alice drove to the Giant Eagle supermarket in Chardon, about ten miles east of Kirtland on Route 6. They were to shop for additional supplies for the wilderness and food for that evening's dinner—prescribed by Jeff to be roast beef, mashed potatoes, gravy, and corn.

During the drive, Alice now told Debbie that the Averys would be killed that night but that the Patricks and Richard and Sharon would be spared because of Sharon's and Tonya's obedience. According to Debbie, she was too terrified to say anything, realizing that her words might well be misinterpreted when repeated to Jeff by Alice, as she knew they would be. Her thoughts were in a jumble. She thought that it must be God's will for this to happen, even though the thought of it was too horrible to face up to. Alice, she has said, was completely calm as she discussed the coming murders while she steered the Toyota pickup along the winding country road. Alice also denies that this conversation with Debbie ever took place.

At some point during the afternoon Greg returned to the rental agency the U-Haul truck that the group had rented to move the Averys out of their home. All of the Averys' belongings, except for one suitcase per Avery, were now at the farm. The suitcases went with them to the Red Roof Inn. No doubt the family had been eagerly anticipating the wilderness trip; their lives in Madison had been drab and difficult and a short stay in a motel would have seemed to be an indication that their fortunes were changing. They were soon to see God, and their worldly trials would no longer be significant.

*　　*　　*

Still afternoon: Richard and Sharon were in their bedroom packing and talking when Jeff came up the stairs. Jeff called Richard out of the bedroom into the hall, where he told him that he would be helping him in the barn that night. Richard said nothing, simply returned to the bedroom. Richard and Sharon knew what Jeff had meant but did not discuss it. Sharon said nothing because she didn't know what Richard would want to hear from her; Richard was silent because he was afraid Sharon would repeat his comments to Jeff. A Gestapo mentality had taken hold.

Late in the afternoon: Alice drove Greg back to the Honda dealership to pick up his car. On the way, according to Greg, Alice said, "How do you feel about people having to die for your sins?" Greg replied that he would that all men would repent and come unto God. Alice has denied that this conversation ever took place.

Sharon remembers that at the end of the afternoon, before the Averys arrived for dinner, Jeff called a meeting of the adult members of the group. He then proceeded to tell those present that the Averys were to be killed that evening, gave a general outline of how the murders were to be carried out, and asked if they were in or out. All said they were in. No one else has admitted being at this meeting or that it ever took place.

Between five and six that evening, Richard drove to the Red Roof Inn in Jeff's pickup truck. As instructed, he drove between the north and south buildings of the motel and parked on the north side of the south building. From this location the truck could not be seen from the street. Again as instructed, Richard went up to the second floor of the south building where the Averys' room was located. Richard greeted Dennis and Cheryl, who were waiting on the balcony with their daughters. The family was dressed for a camping trip, with Dennis and the girls in jeans and jackets and Cheryl wearing her usual gray hooded sweatshirt and sweatpants with the hood tied tight around her face. Trina's thick dark brown hair was drawn in a long braid that hung down her back. The girls were rambunctious, as children thinking they were about to go on vacation would be. All six now filed down to the truck, where they crowded in for the ride to the farm.

Still acting, as he has said, in strict accordance with his instructions,

Richard drove south on Route 306 past the Kirtland police station to the farm. He couldn't say a word to Dennis or Cheryl, knowing that they were soon to die and that he would help with their executions.

Immediately after their arrival, Jeff questioned Cheryl about a letter he had told her several weeks before to write to her mother, a letter to explain that the family had suddenly decided to move to Wyoming and that they would contact relatives later to let them know more about the change. Jeff told Cheryl that the letter was necessary so that no one would know that the group had gone into the wilderness. When Jeff discovered that Cheryl had not written it, he ordered her to sit down immediately and write the letter. She did, addressed the envelope, and handed both to either Alice or Jeff.

Debbie served dinner at precisely six-thirty, as she had been instructed, which was shortly after Richard and Dennis, Cheryl, Trina, Becky, and Karen arrived at the farm. Keith and Kathy Johnson and the Patricks were not invited to dinner by Jeff. Even so, there was not enough room around the dining room table, which comfortably seated twelve. The Averys, the Lundgrens, and one or two others sat around the table. The rest of the group filled their plates and sat wherever they could find room. The air in the house seemed almost too thick to breathe, crammed with a mix of terror and despair. The Averys were the only ones oblivious to the atmosphere. The others endlessly repeated to themselves that the coming deaths were God's will, or, unable to anesthetize their consciences, simply did not think at all. Jeff had repeatedly told them, as with a litany, that sinners had to die and that the Averys were ripened in iniquity and would never repent. But the self-control of those at dinner that night was strained right up to the breaking point. Killing Karen, the youngest child, would be particularly difficult. Very little was eaten by anyone.

After she laid out supper Debbie went upstairs—she couldn't bear to be near the Averys. Upstairs, she found that she couldn't stay still and paced about her bedroom. She did not come downstairs again until the house was quiet. Only the Averys, Sharon, and Susie and her children remained inside.

When the men had finished eating, Jeff called them into the downstairs bedroom shared by Damon and Danny. Richard, Greg, Danny, Damon, Ron, and Jeff all crowded into the room. Dressed in his camouflage combat fatigues, Jeff withdrew the .45 Colt Combat Elite from the holster at his hip. He repeated his question to each man in the room: "Are you in or are you out?" Each one responded that he was in. Jeff then sent them out to the barn.

As the men walked through the kitchen to the back door, Richard noticed Dennis Avery still seated at the table finishing his dinner. Cheryl was standing at the kitchen sink, helping Sharon with the dishes. Sharon was not able to speak or even think, but she did hear Alice say, "Come on, kids, we're leaving," to Jason, Kristen, and Caleb. According to Sharon, Alice was tight-lipped and intent on escaping the situation as soon as possible. As Richard was on his way to the barn he saw Alice walking rapidly toward the pickup truck with the three younger Lundgren children. Jeff stopped at the truck to talk with her just before she drove away. He then went to the barn.

In the barn, Jeff and Ron instructed the men on what was to be done, although they did not assign particular duties to anyone. In contrast to the plan which Jeff had discussed in class in which Dennis Avery was to be required to watch as his wife and daughters were executed, the men were told that the Averys would be brought out to the barn one by one from oldest to youngest, that the stun gun would be used to immobilize them, that some of the men would be needed to tape their wrists and their ankles with silver duct tape, that all five should have their mouths taped but that only Cheryl and the girls should have their eyes taped. Jeff wanted Dennis to look him in the eye and to know with whom he was dealing when he died. His early resentment of Dennis had never changed.

The Averys were to be taped in the small, concrete-floored room located on the east end, lower level of the barn. They were then to be carried down a corridor to the large, dirt-floored room that comprised the entire west end of the lower level of the barn. This was the room in which the group had been storing its trash for the past several months. The area was now piled with trash of all sorts to a depth of three to four feet, except in the northeast corner of the room, where Keith and Ron had dug a pit approximately six and one-half feet by seven and one-half feet by three to four feet deep. A path had been cleared through the trash from the corridor door directly west for ten to twelve feet, then north to the heaps of dirt surrounding the pit. Damon had rigged a light in the room by fastening a light bulb surrounded by a reflector to one of the supporting pillars. Except for the light from that lone bulb, the room was completely dark, dank, and cold. There were about two inches of mud in the bottom of the pit.

The men were told that the Averys would be carried one by one after the taping to the pit room, lowered into the pit, and shot. Jeff would do the actual killing. The other men would do the rest. Someone would also be required to run a chainsaw during the executions to cover the sound of the gunshots.

Jeff asked if there were any questions. There were none. Jeff and Ron walked around the driveway and barn area, apparently to see if any unexpected visitors had arrived and to check on whether or not the group's activities had been observed. Jeff glanced at Ron and said, "Let's do it." Jeff went into the pit room; Ron walked the one hundred yards to the back door and entered the house. It was dusk, almost nightfall.

Ron entered the house and found Dennis Avery in the kitchen. He told Dennis that the other men needed Dennis's help in the barn sorting through the camping equipment. Dennis and Cheryl briefly discussed whether or not he should wear his glasses outside; it was misting and Dennis, ever meticulous, disliked getting water spots on his glasses. In the end, Dennis laid his glasses on the counter and went with Ron through the fog to the barn.

At about this time, perhaps shortly before, Alice arrived at the Patricks' apartment. According to Keith Johnson, Alice was upset when she entered and said only, "The fog is blood red at the farm tonight." Alice left her children Kristen and Caleb with the Johnsons and the Patricks and with Jason went on to Makro, a discount store, where a receipt shows that she bought two picnic tables and some candy at approximately nine o'clock.

While Alice was talking with the Patricks and the Johnsons, Ron was attempting to immobilize Dennis Avery with the stun gun. However, as neither Ron nor Jeff knew how to use the gun properly, and as the gun was of rather weak voltage, instead of stunning Dennis, the shock was simply very painful, making him cry out. When Ron, Richard, Danny, Damon, and Greg realized that Dennis was not going to become unconscious, the five men jumped him and wrestled him to the floor. Dennis struggled, but not a strong man, he was no match for the others.

"No!" he shouted. "No, no! This isn't necessary! Please! This isn't necessary! Goddammit, goddammit, goddammit!" Finally the taping was completed and he could no longer protest. Richard and Danny picked Dennis up and carried him into the next room, where they found Jeff waiting for them, lying on one of the mounds of earth surrounding the pit, one arm crooked and the palm of the hand supporting his head, while the .45 dangled in the other hand.

Richard and Danny struggled across the mounds of trash with Dennis, lowered him into the pit onto his feet, but because his ankles were bound he lost his balance and fell to his knees and then forward onto his face. Dennis struggled to his knees. Richard and Danny broke free from the horrified fascination with which they had been watching the bound man and ran for the door into the room where Ron and Damon waited.

Just as Richard reached the door, he heard the first shot and the door was slammed in his face. He turned back to the pit in time to see Jeff fire a second shot into the hole, standing and shooting from an angle directly behind Dennis Avery as Richard had last seen him in the pit.

During the shooting Greg Winship was outside the barn, immediately beside the driveway ramp, which led to the second floor, running a chainsaw to sound as if he were cutting wood. Several of the neighbors heard the chainsaw but none suspected anything sinister on the part of the strange group down the road.

The women in the house also heard the chainsaw, and Debbie and Sharon both noticed that Cheryl frequently gazed with a worried frown out the dining room windows toward the barn.

In the barn, Damon broke down. "I can't believe he's dead; I can't believe he's really dead . . ."

Jeff came out of the pit room and called out to the others, "I guess you'd better see what this looks like."

The men filed obediently into the room and took up positions surrounding the pit. Richard heard a noise that sounded like a last breath escaping from Dennis's body. Blood stained the bottom of the pit. No one moved while Jeff scanned their faces.

After a few moments Jeff ordered Damon to jump into the pit to retrieve the motel keys from the corpse. Damon ran out of the room. Ron looked at each of the other men in turn, then sighed and said something to the effect that if no one else was going to do it he would. He jumped into the pit and reached into Dennis's shirt pocket, which, as he said later, was extremely bloody, but found nothing. He then reached into the jeans pockets, where he found a wallet that he removed, but he did not find the motel key.

The men moved from the pit room to the taping room, where Damon was sobbing. Jeff put his arm around his son and told him that he had to grow up very fast but that he was proud of him. He then reassigned Damon from taping to lookout. Damon was to sit at the top of a short flight of stairs leading from the taping room to the second level of the barn, where there was a small window that overlooked the barnyard and the back door of the house. He was to watch for intruders and to warn the other men when Ron approached with another of the Averys.

Jeff then glanced at Ron. "We have to have those keys." Either Ron, or Ron and Jeff, went into the house and asked Cheryl for the motel keys. Cheryl turned them over.

The keys were placed on a shelf next to Dennis's wallet and other papers. Jeff then went back into the pit room, Damon went up the stairs and Ron went back into the house, where he told Cheryl that Dennis needed her help in the barn. Cheryl left with Ron.

In the barn, Damon peered out his window. "Here they come," he said.

The other women sat in the living room or paced from the living room to the dining room. The Luff children and Becky and Karen Avery played video games. Trina was reading a magazine, sitting in one of the living-room chairs. After their mother left, Becky and Trina went to the refrigerator and stood there looking in at what might be to their liking. Debbie asked them what they were doing, and the girls replied that they were hungry. Debbie told them to find something to eat and close the refrigerator.

*   *   *

In the barn Ron tried once again to use the stun gun, this time on Cheryl. Again, the gun did not work. Ron put his hand on Cheryl's shoulder and told her, "Just give it up, it'll be easier this way. Just let go, let go." Cheryl did not struggle, she sank down to the floor. The men taped her ankles and wrists, and taped her head so that her mouth, eyes, and ears were covered. Richard and Ron carried her into the pit, Richard having complained that Danny was not strong enough to help with the weight. Cheryl was lowered into the pit as Dennis had been, and came to rest sitting in the southwest corner. Richard, who could see only the top of Cheryl's head, watched as Jeff fired into Cheryl's body. Richard has said that the first shot was to the back of the head or the top of the back, clearly remembering how Cheryl pitched forward and then back with the first shot.

Greg Winship was running the chainsaw.

In the house Debbie, Susie, and Sharon heard the chainsaw. At first Sharon thought the sound was just a motor running and wondered why someone would be running a motor after dark. But then she decided it was the chainsaw. Debbie was pacing in the dining room when Susie walked up. "Do you think it's happening?" Debbie said. "I hear the chainsaw. I think so."

After killing Cheryl, Jeff and Ron walked around the barn to check for any indication that the shots had been heard or that the group's activities were now being observed. They then returned to the barn, where Ron or Jeff told the others that they were to pretend to play games with the girls since the stun gun was not working. They would play hide-and-go-seek or hear-no-evil-see-no-evil. The girls would believe that the group were just playing since several months earlier at Halloween the barn had been used for just that sort of activity.

Ron then went into the house and told Trina that her mother wanted her in the barn. Trina sighed, put down the magazine she was reading, got up, and left with Ron.

Damon called out, "Here they come."

Becky and Karen continued to play video games while they waited for their parents.

*   *   *

In the barn the men played word games with Trina while taping her ankles, wrists, and head. She stood quietly during the taping. Richard and Ron carried the girl into the pit room, but at one point during their passage down the cleared pathway, either Richard or Trina bumped the cord connected to the light and the light fell, breaking the bulb. The room was suddenly dark. Jeff told Richard to get another bulb, then shouted for another bulb. Richard put Trina down and went to the door to get the new bulb. Originally Richard told prosecutors that Damon had handed him the bulb, but he later testified that he could not remember who had done it.

When the light was repaired, Richard and Ron carried Trina to the pit. She was lowered in, as her parents had been, and sat against the west wall. The first bullet grazed her head, ruffling the hair on the left crown. Richard believes that he heard Trina say "ouch!" even though her mouth was covered with tape. The next bullet did not miss. It entered Trina's skull at the crown on the left side and exited below her right ear, killing her instantly.

After Trina's death, Damon, the lookout, was very upset and began crying again. Not for Trina, but for having hung the light improperly and thereby jeopardizing the night's operation.

Once again Jeff comforted his son, and once more he and Ron reconnoitered the premises. After they reentered the barn someone said that the ruse of playing a game had worked well and suggested that it be used for the other two girls. All agreed.

Ron went into the house to get Becky.

Once in the house, Ron asked the two little Avery girls if they would like to see the horses. Both jumped up eagerly and headed for the back door. Ron told them to slow down, he would have to take them out one at a time or they would frighten the animals. He told Karen to sit back down and that he would come back for her after Becky had seen the horses. Karen obediently sat down in front of the television.

Damon called out, "Here they come."

At one point Karen became impatient and jumped up from the television, saying, "I want my Mommy," and headed for the back door. According to Sharon, Debbie stepped into the child's path and directed her back to the floor. Debbie has said she doesn't remember that.

*   *   *

In the barn the men taped Becky as they had taped Trina, without taking her to the floor. Richard and Ron then lifted the child and carried her into the pit, placing her almost on her dead mother's legs. Jeff fired at least twice, shooting the child in the chest and possibly in the shoulder, although the bullet was discovered in Becky's left thigh. Again Greg ran the chainsaw.

After Becky was shot, Greg remembers standing next to the grave. He cannot remember when or why he entered the room, nor can he recall leaving. What he does recall is that the child was still breathing, making rasping, gurgling sounds. She was unconscious.

After Ron and Jeff did their walk into the barn, the stage was set for Karen. Ron went into the house, told Karen it was her turn to see the horses and bent down for her to climb on his shoulders for a piggy-back ride to the barn.

Damon called out, "Here they come."

Karen was taped like Trina and Becky, then Ron flung her over his shoulder and carried her into the pit. She was placed in the pit next to Becky. Like Trina, Karen was shot in the head and died within moments.

After Karen's execution Jeff came out of the pit room, saw Richard, and sent him in to help Ron. When Richard arrived at the pit he saw that Ron was spreading lime over the Averys' bodies. Richard began to help with the lime, and Jeff instructed Greg and Danny to assist with the burial. After the bodies were covered with lime the men added on rocks brought into the barn from the pond two days earlier. They completed filling the hole with dirt and, finally, covered the dirt mound with several feet of trash. Richard estimates that they worked from an hour and a half to two hours.

Some five minutes after Ron had left the house with Karen the phone rang. Debbie answered, not knowing whether she would be punished for her boldness but afraid not to do so. Alice was calling from the Patricks' apartment. Alice said, "Is the company gone? Can I come home now?" Debbie, not knowing how to say what was happening over a telephone she had been told was probably bugged, said, "You'd better wait for about fifteen minutes." Alice said she would wait, then hung up.

Fifteen minutes later Jeff came into the house, and immediately went to take a bath. Sharon remembers asking him a question at this point, although she can't remember what it was. She does, though, recall his response—"I can't think about that now. I just killed five people."

Damon came into the house five minutes later, and his mother and brothers and sister arrived a few minutes after that. Jason wanted to know what the men were doing out in the barn, but Alice sent him up to bed with Kristen and Caleb.

Sharon recalls that a few minutes later Jason came back downstairs, saying he was going to go out back to find out what was going on. He headed out the back door. Sharon ran to Jeff's and Alice's bedroom, knocked on the door and told Alice what Jason had done. Alice screamed at her, "Stupid, you stupid, how could you let him do that!" and ran from the room to the back door, where she shrieked to Jason to come back into the house.

Alice denies that this ever happened. According to Alice, when she got home she could tell by the behavior of the people there that something terrible had happened and guessed that the Averys were dead. Then, she testified, Jeff pulled her out onto the front porch, stuck the .45 in her face and said, "Alice, now I don't want any of your bullshit!"

Shortly after Alice returned home Jeff called the Patricks, telling them that they and the Johnsons should come to the house for a class. Then Alice, Jeff, and Damon left and drove to the Red Roof Inn, where they stuffed all the Averys' belongings into trash bags and removed them from the room. Apparently, they also left the room keys in the room so there would be no questions from motel staff in the morning.

When the Lundgrens returned to the house the Johnsons and the Patricks had arrived and the men had come in from the barn. When the adults assembled in the living room for the class there was a somber dead silence. Some appeared to be in shock. Alice told Dennis Patrick and Richard Brand that they should be very proud of their wives, since the women's obedience had "pulled their cookies out of the sand." Jeff praised them for helping him in his hour of need, then he asked each around the circle for his or her feelings about what had happened. No one can remember the response of any individual except Richard, who was upset enough to say, "No one should have to die that way. . . ."

No one remembers much of anything about that class, but all agree that details of the murders were not discussed at that time. Afterward the Johnsons and the Patricks went back to the Patricks' apartment. The others went to bed.

Sharon says she and Richard talked about nothing after they went to bed.

Richard says he told her the whole story of what happened in the barn.

Alice says that Jeff said to her, "It had to be done. It was God's will."

13

BY HASTE
AND BY FLIGHT

Tuesday, April 18, dawned clear and bright. The group was subtly different, but no one could, or perhaps would, determine in what way. Most had not slept well.

Everyone was up early. Debbie and Ron were sent to the store to buy more supplies for the wilderness trip. Jeff and the other men went to the barn to work on arranging equipment for the trip and to sift through the Averys' belongings for anything useful the group might take with them. Alice was going through the Averys' effects in the house. While Alice was examining things packed in a cardboard box, Kristen spotted a doll that had belonged to one of the girls. The child demanded the doll, and it was turned over to her without a word.

Everything of the Averys from the motel room that was not to be used was packed into plastic trash bags. Greg was assigned to deposit the bags in various dumpsters around the area. At least some of the dumpsters were in Cleveland. It was probably at this time that Cheryl Avery's last letter to her mother was mailed, carrying a Cleveland postmark.

Meanwhile Ron and Richard were assigned to take any of the Avery children's books and notebooks that identified them, to tear the identifying information from the books, then to hide the books inside the wall beneath the window over the mass grave.

As these members busied themselves with their assigned tasks, another group was assembling what would have a profound effect on the family's immediate future.

Jeff had never realized that the group was actually under surveillance by the FBI. Debbie had once spotted the surveillance van and warned him, but Jeff had decided she didn't know what she was talking about. Even though the group had not realized the extent of the FBI interest in them, they had still concealed their activities and intentions to the extent that there was not enough information to justify continued federal involvement. Neither the FBI nor the Kirtland police had ever been able to accumulate enough information to establish probable cause for a search warrant.

Any FBI investigation that does not bear fruit in six months is usually either abandoned or the agent in charge receives special permission to continue the investigation. In this case the agents involved were certain that permission would not be given to spend further time investigating the activities of an apparently obscure religious nut. The story was too farfetched, in spite of Chief Yarborough's insistence that the group was a very real threat. During the months between Kevin Currie's revelations and April of 1989 Yarborough became increasingly convinced that Jeff Lundgren was actually going to do something terrible. He began to make random middle-of-the-night foot patrols of Kirtland, concentrating on the Temple area, and at one time carried up to four hundred pounds of ammunition in his car. FBI Agent Alvord believed that the group was dangerous but did not share the intensity of Yarborough's concern.

This shared worry did have its impact when Jeff was making his final preparations for mass murder and the Kirtland police convinced the FBI to plan to come with some twenty agents and police officers at least to interview the group members. The idea was to separate members and interview them individually about the alleged plot to assault the Temple, as well as to give each group member a chance while protected by the officers and agents to leave the group if he or she chose to.

Robert Alvord, an urbane man in his mid-forties, an agent in charge of the Painesville office, was coordinator of the FBI corps. He hoped that in the course of the interviews someone would give up information which would provide probable cause for a search, or some agent or officer would see something that would provide probable cause. The interviews would be voluntary, since neither the police nor the FBI could compel cooperation. Alvord set the date of the interviews for

April 18—one day too late—which was just before the six-month period expired. Since April 18 was a Tuesday, it would provide time for
final coordination on Monday. Of course, there was no opportunity
for the FBI or the Kirtland police to be aware of the plan for the
slaughter of the Averys, but Agent Alvord has lived with the pricking
thought that *if* the interviews had been scheduled just one week, or
even one day, earlier, the Averys might still be alive.

The agents and police officers did arrive at the farm at 10:00 A.M. on
Tuesday, April 18. Yarborough and Bob Alvord got there first and
proceeded to the front door of the house. Alice answered the door.
Yarborough greeted her, then asked if he could speak with Jeff. Alice
told him that Jeff was in the barn, closed the door, and walked
through the house to the back door to call her husband. Yarborough
and Alvord left the front door and walked quickly across the barnyard
toward the main door of the barn. Both were aware of the excellent
targets they provided as they crossed the seventy-five to one hundred
yards between the house and the barn.

By the time Alice had reached the back door Yarborough and Alvord
were inside the main front door of the barn. Yarborough called up,
"Jeff, come on out. I'd like to talk with you." When Jeff appeared
Yarborough introduced Alvord and explained that the police and the
FBI wanted to interview him and the others. Jeff turned and called the
other men from the upstairs of the barn. Richard would later say that
he knew something was wrong just by the tone of Jeff's voice.

Yarborough and Alvord were beginning to feel extremely uncomfortable as the men streamed down from the upper parts of the barn.
The fact that these men, whom they knew by report to be armed, were
concealed above their heads, was enough to make them aware of their
vulnerability to sudden attack. They were relieved somewhat when
the other agents and officers arrived and the barnyard was suddenly
crowded with unmarked cars and Kirtland police cruisers.

Sharon and Susie, upstairs watching the children, were unaware
that anything was happening until Alice called up the stairs at an
agent's instruction to bring the other women down. Although their
initial impulse was to hide, the two women came down the stairs and
Alvord and Yarborough took Jeff into the living room. As they entered
the room Alice darted past them into her bedroom and tried to slide
the connecting door closed. The men gently but firmly prevented her
from closing the door and requested that she make herself available
for an interview. Later Alice would say that she had attempted to

enter her bedroom to make the bed because she was embarrassed about her home being seen in disarray. She was, after all, a tidy lady.

The prophet's spouse was escorted to the back seat of Yarborough's station wagon so she would have a place to sit during her interview. She would later claim that she had been imprisoned in the car and harassed during her interview. According to Ron Andolsek, who conducted the first interview of Alice, and according to the FBI agent who also interviewed her, there was no pressure and no harassment. The door of the car was open at all times and she was free to end the interview and leave whenever she wanted to. In fact, Alice's later statements to Jeff about her mistreatment by Andolsek were so harrowing that Jeff added Andolsek to the list of people he would surely kill when the mountain was made. Both officers found Alice's attitude and demeanor during her interviews to be arrogant and condescending.

Alice denied knowing anything about a plot to take over the Temple, denied any knowledge of a cache of weapons other than a black-powder rifle which Jeff kept as a collector's item, and claimed she had never heard that some people referred to Jeff as a prophet. Ron Andolsek thought that Alice seemed amused that he and the other officers would even think that their efforts had any chance of success. Alice later claimed that she answered as she did because she was afraid for her life and the lives of her children. She would swear during her trial that she thought that Jeff would kill her or Damon, Jason, Kristen, or Caleb if she said anything to the agents about the Avery murders.

Yarborough and Alvord got nothing from Jeff except his consent to a search of the secret closet upstairs in the younger Lundgren boys' closet, where they found an unusual if not especially alarming number of legal weapons.

Alvord and Yarborough had been hoping that access to the inside of the house would reveal something that would provide clear evidence of criminal conduct. There had been speculation that one or more of the semi-automatic rifles might have been illegally altered to fire automatically. But there was nothing that would provide probable cause to search further into areas where the family could legitimately demand that its privacy be respected.

The other group members interviewed on the front porch or in agents' cars answered questions just as Jeff had instructed them to do if they were ever questioned by law officers. All denied any knowledge of a plan to assault the Temple, all denied that any military training ever took place, all rejected the opportunity to leave. The agents found the people they interviewed to be mostly polite and intelligent, if a touch arrogant, with an apparent conviction of superiority and a barely concealed attempt to hide their amusement at the questioning. Later, like Alice, all questioned would state that they said nothing about the Averys out of fear of Jeff and his terrible swift retribution.

After some two hours Yarborough and Alvord gave up. They were sure they had been lied to, but nothing that had been done or said or that the agents had seen had given them any legal basis for probing further. They left the farm, the FBI agents to write up and file reports of the interviews, the Kirtland police officers to continue to watch and worry.

The group was in an uproar. Jeff was convinced that one purpose of the encounter had been to get inside the house to plant listening devices. He told everyone to keep their voices down to a whisper at all times in the house. He demanded and received complete reports of each person's interview, both questions and answers. After he had been assured that no one had said anything that could threaten the group or, more importantly, him, he said that it was a good thing he had shot the Averys the night before, because they would have been too weak to hold out and would have revealed the group's plans.

Jeff told all to burn notes from class, including military notes. Only Greg Winship's notebook was spared, whether by accident or by design, Greg doesn't recall. Jeff suddenly seemed to come apart; he was shaking, disoriented, a prophet with no idea what to do next.

Alice and Greg took over. No one really believed that it was coincidental that the FBI and the police had come to the farm the morning after the killings. They were afraid someone had heard something, or that somehow someone in authority at least suspected what had happened. They figured that no one was *certain* that the Averys had been killed because if there had been sure knowledge they felt they all would have been arrested without the preliminary interviews. But they also believed that if there were suspicions that *something* illegal had happened the evening before, Yarborough and Andolsek wouldn't stop until they had learned more—maybe all. Clearly they had to vacate the area as soon as possible and find a hiding place where fourteen adults and ten children would not be conspicuous. They would have to avoid the places previously scouted in case they had been followed on any of their reconnaissance trips.

Alice remembered that in the Book of Mormon, Moroni had at one time been told to flee south-southeast, so she and Greg decided that that was the direction God would want them to travel. Head immediately east into Pennsylvania, then south toward West Virginia until they found a spot that Jeff, when he was in control, would designate as the proper place.

The decision made, the group prepared in frantic haste. All had been living out of their suitcases for some two weeks, so clothing was mostly packed. Even so, essential supplies had to be purchased and most importantly an additional truck had to be rented and loaded along with the pickups. Everyone except for Jeff and Alice labored for hours. Shortly after dark Jeff and Alice left in their truck, taking Susie and her children with them. The others left after midnight. They would meet for breakfast at a restaurant in Pennsylvania.

The Averys and their belongings were left rotting in the barn, not to be discovered for more than eight months.

Early the next day Ron Andolsek drove casually past the farm, as he had done now for almost a year. This time the farm looked different, and he realized with a chill that it appeared to be abandoned. Andolsek was apprehensive, and so was Yarborough. Neither knew why Jeff —they assumed it was his decision—had picked that day for the group to leave, but they were sure that the sudden departure must have been linked to their visit the day before. So what was it that Jeff thought they knew? What would be such an immediate threat that the group would suddenly leave en masse and this abruptly?

Later that day Andolsek went back to the farm with landlord Stan Skrbis. The two wandered around the barnyard and through the orchard, snapping photographs. Andolsek wasn't sure why he wanted the pictures, he just felt a record was a good idea. They tried to look in windows of the house and the barn but could see little. The house did seem to be empty. The group had certainly left, abandoning their property in the house and the barn with apparently no intention to return.

Andolsek reported to Yarborough. And the chief had a dilemma. Families of the young people in the group, particularly the Brands and the Krafts, had kept up sporadic contact with the chief as they tried to find various ways to pry their children loose from the Lundgrens' orbit. Wilbur Brand, in fact, had just a few months earlier, in January, 1989, contacted the Internal Revenue Service with information about Jeff's finances, hoping to trigger an income-tax-fraud investigation and prosecution that would finally free Richard from Jeff's grasp. Yarborough and Alvord, however, had been afraid that such an investigation would not discourage the group members' faith in Jeff and would make it impossible for the police to monitor the group at all since Jeff would become much more secretive. So they asked the IRS to delay.

Now those families would want to know where their children had gone.

Yarborough felt a good deal of sympathy for the solid, middle-class families whose children were trapped by the Lundgrens, but because the group members were adults he could no more intervene than could their families. But he had no idea of Jeff's destination, and without some concrete evidence of criminal activity in his jurisdiction he really had no legal reason to press his investigation.

There were, though, the nagging doubts. In spite of the discouragement from the failed FBI investigation and that he hadn't been able to turn up evidence to support the allegations made by C.I.'s I (Kevin) and II (Shar), Yarborough felt in his gut that Jeff and his group were dangerous and he had a dark suspicion that he had not seen the last of them. His only real choice was to try to track the group down and keep an eye on them. Wherever Jeff might come to roost, Yarborough could make the local authorities aware that a dangerous and possibly unbalanced man was among them.

While Yarborough and Andolsek tried to make sense of the situation at 8671 Chardon Road, Jeff and the group were making their way south-southeast. At the end of the second day they came on a second-rate motel outside of Davis, West Virginia, The Highlander. They thought that the motel name was an omen of significance. Part of the group was lodged at The Highlander and part at another motel down the road.

The next day Jeff, having recovered from his earlier disorientation, began checking out the surrounding countryside, searching for a campsite relatively inaccessible but close enough to town to make access to food stores and other amenities reasonably easy. He also wanted a campsite that was either free for the taking or available for a minimal fee. Three days later Jeff decided on land that belonged to a local power company available to the public for free camping. The initial campsite was one-tenth of a mile off the end of the access road some fifteen miles from town. A few days later Jeff decided that the group should move to a more out-of-the-way place, and a second campsite was chosen, nearly a quarter mile from the end of the access road.

The Kirtland police had tracked the rental truck to a small town in Virginia, then notified ranger stations and local sheriff's departments throughout a wide adjacent area to be on the lookout for Jeff and his group. Within a few weeks the group's campsite was located by Tucker County, West Virginia, Sheriff Hank Thompson. When Thompson reported in, Yarborough told him that he was dealing with armed and potentially dangerous individuals.

He still had no idea how right he was.

14

THE WILDERNESS

Davis, West Virginia, is a town of a thousand citizens located in the Canaan Valley about sixty miles southwest of Wheeling. It is surrounded by the Appalachian Mountains and sits some thirty-two hundred feet above sea level. Davis, established in 1885, was one of the first lumber towns in the state and now is part of a recreational area featuring ski resorts.

The camp area the Lundgren family settled in was strip-mined for coal at one time and later reclaimed by the mining company. While the camping area is covered with pine forests and crisp mountain streams which are as beautiful as any in the state, the topsoil is only a few inches thick and rests on solid rock. Any amount of rain turns the ground to slippery, sticky mud. The spring and summer that found the group in the wilderness were unusually wet and cold in Davis, and they suffered accordingly. Debbie Olivarez remembers that there were only two days all summer when she wore shorts, and, worse, only one evening warm enough to wear shorts until bedtime.

However, on the cold, rainy April 23rd when the group first established camp their physical unhappiness was still in the future. All they knew was that Jeff had said that this was the site where they would continue to purify themselves until they were ready to see God. The execution of the Averys had not, apparently, done the job. Jeff knew that this was the proper place, he said, because he had gone to the mountain to meditate, and God had told him that the group would stay here. Jeff made much of the fact that Davis was located in the Canaan Valley, the promised land of the Bible.

Two weeks after the group left Ohio Jeff sent Richard and Greg back

127

to the Kirtland area to pick up the paychecks waiting for them and to see if there was any suspicious activity at the farm. The two men were able to pick up their checks, cash them, check out the farm and return to the wilderness—their faith unshaken by murder.

Still, not even the beauty of the surrounding countryside and the elation of believing they were all much nearer to their goal of seeing God would blot out thoughts of the Averys. No one dared speak his or her thoughts aloud, but neither could anyone forget what had happened back there in the Kirtland barn. There was no laughter, little conversation. Tones were hushed, individuals tended to break into tears at unexpected moments.

Jeff went into action. A little more than two weeks after the murders he convened a class about the Averys' deaths. He castigated the group for seeming to mourn the dead, reminding them that the Averys had been ripened in iniquity and already dead unto God. He said he didn't want anyone to mention the Averys' names again after this class, forbade any further expressions of grief and called on the men who had been present in the barn that night each to give a detailed description of his role in the killings; Jeff's description of his own conduct was less detailed, but he left no doubt that the Averys were dead, and that he was their executioner.

No one, it seems, can remember this class in detail, although the women believe that this was the first time that they learned exactly what had happened to Dennis and Cheryl and their three children. Even so, both Debbie and Sharon have separately said that they sometimes believed, because they did not see the executions, that maybe the Averys actually did go to Wyoming and that maybe the murders were just another of Jeff's lies.

The class was mostly intended to be a threat. And now that the Averys were gone, Dennis Patrick—ever a perceived problem—was the focus of Jeff's intimidation. Dennis was reminded at this class that what had happened to the Averys could also happen to him and his family. Dennis and Tonya were terrified; they were isolated in the wilderness with a man who had killed before and would likely kill again.

From the time of the group's arrival Jeff was, as always, security-conscious. The group was organized into various segments, each commanded by one of the men who was designated "sheriff" of a particular task or responsibility: the "horse sheriff" in charge of caring for the horses, the "trash sheriff" of garbage disposal and so forth. Jeff was in charge of camp security. A guard was posted at all times, and all the men except Dennis Patrick were assigned guard duty on a rotating basis. It was impossible for Dennis to stand guard duty since Jeff had taken away his weapons, saying he was too unreliable.

By mid-May Jeff's anxiety about camp security made him decide the group would have to move the camp several miles farther into the woods to a spot less accessible from the road. The move was no simple matter. There were three days of preparation, packing and sorting for the most efficient transportation, then three days of moving the three refrigerators, the two stoves, the two freezers, and the generators by hand or on the ATVs. Alice, of course, was responsible only for seeing that her own things and Jeff's were packed. The other women were assigned to tend to the Lundgren children's belongings.

Meanwhile, Jeff seemed to be growing increasingly displeased with the group's spiritual progress. Instead of coming nearer to the day when they would see God, their goal was becoming more and more difficult to reach. And Jeff's threats were becoming more violent, overt. Each individual realized that there, in the wilderness, it would be simple for Jeff to kill them and to dispose of the bodies where they would never be found. Terror was a daily companion.

Indeed, a few days after the move Jeff approached Debbie while she was cooking the evening meal and told her in detail how he had killed the Averys, saying that he had shot Dennis in the heart, and Cheryl and the girls in the head. He said he had not been able to break Dennis's heart on the Word, so he had had to break it with a bullet. "You know, death stinks," he said. "But I guess I'm just going to have to get used to it." He went on to say that according to Scripture he would personally kill ten thousand people. "Now," he said, "I just have nine thousand nine hundred ninety-five to go."

In late May Jeff decided that he now wanted Tonya Patrick, a hankering that had begun when he'd first met the Patricks and undoubtedly had to do with his animosity toward her husband Dennis. He told the others that Dennis continued to be a sinner and that he was endangering his own life *and* the lives of his wife and child. Jeff said that Tonya's obedience was no longer sufficient to atone for her husband's iniquity. The only way, he said, that Tonya and Molly could be saved would be for Tonya to be taken into his tent. He pointed his .45 in Dennis's face. "And if there are any problems with that from this quarter, we can just take care of them right now." Dennis said nothing.

Tonya and her daughter Molly moved into the Lundgren tent. Alice, of course, was not happy with the situation but apparently comforted herself with the belief that Tonya and Jeff were not sharing the same bed. Alice was wrong. After the group broke up, Tonya would tell the others that Jeff had begun coming into her bed almost as soon as she moved into his tent but that he had concealed his activities from Alice. She also said she didn't find Jeff's attentions satisfying, which infuriated him.

Tonya has also said she accepted the arrangement out of fear for the lives of her daughter and her husband. Dennis has said he didn't protest for the exact same reason. But many of the group members have said that at the time Tonya did seem at least to enjoy the elevated status of living in the prophet's tent.

In any case, Jeff decided to take Tonya as his second wife, increasing her status even further. He justified this by teaching that the Bible didn't actually mean that each man should have one wife. As Jeff put it at his trial, the Hebrew word for one also means several or many; therefore, an English translation does not accurately reflect God's intent. Any man can be allowed more than one wife, and Jeff said he believed Tonya was *his* true wife rather than Dennis's.

According to Alice, Jeff announced his intention to take Tonya as his wife by telling Alice that it was her responsibility to choose Tonya's fate and that Tonya's state of sin was such that she must be pierced in order to be saved. It was up to Alice, said Jeff, whether Tonya would be pierced with the sword and killed, or pierced with his penis and survive. Alice said that she was forced to choose and that when she chose that Tonya not die she was forced to make the bed for them with fresh sheets and then to leave the tent.

Whatever the truth and whatever Jeff hoped to accomplish by making his relationship with Tonya public, the change apparently did not change Tonya's lack of enthusiasm for his attentions, which, according to Tonya, Jeff continued to find puzzling and frustrating.

Jeff's military training and planning reached a new level of intensity in the wilderness. In mid-June he assigned command ranks to some of the men. Jeff was a five-star general. Ron was appointed a major general, designated by three stars—not the proper two; Damon was a lieutenant general, designated by two stars, instead of the proper three; and Danny was a brigadier general, with one star—he got that one right. No four-star general was appointed, presumably so the rank would be available for Damon when he became second in command. In the absence of Jeff, the general of the army of Israel, the next senior officer was to take command. The women were assigned to make battle flags for the generals. The one Alice made for Jeff was a purple banner sporting an embroidered spread-winged eagle and a seven-pointed star.

Jeff took the group to Gettysburg to study the battlefield and told the group that a great battle would be fought in the meadow near the camp. Later in the summer, he said they would be attacked across "the battlefield" by police and SWAT teams but the group would be victorious and God would come down to the top of the hill in the meadow after the battle was won.

Sometime in June Jeff began to teach either that he had progressed beyond the point where his status was analogous to that of a prophet such as Moses or Moroni or even Jesus, or that he had *always* been of a more exalted status and the group had not been able until this time to appreciate his true role. Group members have said they weren't clear which interpretation was being taught, maybe both. In any event, whether Jeff had just realized it himself or the group was just now being blessed with the news, Jeff announced one day that he was not simply a prophet but that he was the god of the earth. He was, therefore, all-powerful, and as such it was no longer necessary for him to explain why he wanted what he wanted or to persuade them that it was right to follow his will. As god he could not be questioned or even doubted.

Still, some of the group members were finding Jeff's teachings difficult to believe. Richard, Greg, Debbie, Dennis and Tonya in particular have said they were having problems. All, however, badly *wanted* to continue to believe. They all had invested, literally and spiritually, so much in what Jeff had taught them. They were afraid *not* to believe. Sharon, for instance, was so intent on not doubting that it apparently never crossed her mind not to believe until much later. But first cracks were appearing.

One reason was the increasing extremeness of Jeff's teachings, but just as important was the unrelenting physical misery the group lived in. They were constantly wet, muddy and cold. Their tents were never completely warm and the weather was so humid that clothing and equipment were always damp. Money began to run out. Jeff did not bring back as much food from his frequent trips to town. Later Hank Thompson would remember seeing Jeff's car parked at a popular local restaurant when Jeff was in town.

The unequal treatment of the naturals over the other children in the group began increasingly to rankle the parents. The naturals got candy and treats from McDonald's while the other children were hungry. The naturals had warm clothing and a warm tent while the other children had no boots in the snow. Jason Lundgren was even given his own handgun. The fifteen-year-old was so careless with the weapon that one day while he was playing with it in the tent the gun fired by accident and nearly shot his sister Kristen. When Jeff and Alice returned to camp after that incident Greg was reprimanded for having told Jason it was a stupid thing to do.

One day toward the end of July Jeff and Alice planned a little party for the family to take their minds off the difficulty of their lives in the wilderness. There was dancing, and Debbie was asked to dance for Jeff, who remembered her high school reputation for dancing. Debbie, claiming to be embarrassed and self-conscious about performing in front of the group, clearly displeased Jeff.

Debbie would later blame her failure for causing "The Intercession" that followed.

15

INTERCESSION

During July of 1989 Alice was particularly vocal during and outside class in her support of Jeff and his teachings. She shrilly reminded the group of the sacrifices made by the Lundgren family for their benefit. After all, she pointed out, Jeff was perfect, the god of this earth, and there was no doubt that he was ready at any time to see God. But Jeff's reward was being frustrated by their obtuse insistence on sin and refusal to change. Not only that, Jeff was caused severe physical pain by their iniquity. The pain was so cruel she could not bear the discomfort of removing it from his body through massage as she had taught the women to do for their husbands. Her hands, she said, hurt so from absorbing the torment from Jeff's body that she would be forced to stop.

And, Alice emphasized, the naturals suffered because of the presence of the rest of the group. After all, the naturals were the Lundgrens' own children, who had been required to sacrifice the closeness they should have had from their mother and father because of the time Jeff and Alice were forced to spend with the group preparing its members to see God. "If Jeff tells you that there is rebellion in the group, and the thought comes, 'There is no rebellion,' *that* is rebellion!" she told them. "It seems to me that the only time you get into trouble is when you try to think for yourselves. Always ask, 'What would Dad do? What has Dad said to do?' Every situation we're in is an open-book test and you keep forgetting to use the book."

Actually, Alice was probably becoming more aggressive because she felt her own control of or influence on Jeff seeping away. She continued to be indulged over everyone else in camp, but Jeff's marriage to

Tonya must have made it clear to Alice that her position was being undermined and at any moment might even end.

Alice has said that during this period Jeff would take her into the wilderness on the ATV and threaten her life, telling her that he could kill her then and there and no one would ever know. She has also said that these sessions would sometimes begin or end with Jeff's bizarre sexual demands. Group members confirm that on one occasion when Alice was having a temper tantrum Jeff set her down on one of the picnic table benches, sat on her legs and threatened her life. No other such instances of physical intimidation by Jeff toward Alice are recalled by anyone in the group. And that incident happened after Jeff had publicly taken another wife. Alice must, indeed, have been panicked, and if the relationship with Tonya had been more gratifying for Jeff, her worst fears might well have been realized. Jeff likely took satisfaction from Alice's discomfort, and it's certain that Alice was increasingly willing to go along with anything to maintain some control over her relationship with Jeff.

Which explains her going along with Intercession, conceived by Jeff to help him exercise complete power and abase everyone, including Alice, who was getting bothersome. On August 8 Jeff began to teach Intercession. . . .

In ancient times, he said, a wife had been permitted to intercede with her husband's lords for mercy when the husband was so sinful that his life was to be forfeit to the lord. Jeff had taught for years that sin and error were rampant in the group. Since the trip to the wilderness he had been even more insistent that the sole reason that the group had not long before succeeded in its goal of seeing God was that each group member was so prideful that he or she was unable to humble himself or herself to Jeff and give up individual thoughts and become perfect like Jeff.

Therefore, said Jeff, it was essential that the group strip itself of pride. Furthermore, since the men had been unable to teach themselves and their families to become without sin, God was losing his patience with the group and was unwilling to wait any longer for matters to proceed in the normal course. So Jeff, speaking for God, said it had become necessary that the women intercede for their families. The price of resistance: physical and spiritual death.

The women chosen for the intercession ritual were Kathy Johnson, who would intercede for herself, Keith, and their sons; Susan Luff, who would intercede for herself, Ron, and their two children; Debbie

Olivarez, who would intercede for herself, Greg, her children and their future children; and Sharon, who would intercede for herself, Richard, and their future children. Tonya Patrick, of course, had already atoned for her and Molly's sins by becoming Jeff's second wife, and as Jeff's wife was no longer capable of interceding for Dennis. Also, since Alice was Jeff's wife there was no one she needed to intercede for.

It was essential, Jeff said, that the women should be stripped of their pride for the intercession to be successful. To assure that they were symbolically stripped they should literally strip themselves naked. They then would be required to perform some act to please their God. If their sacrifice was acceptable, their Lord would shed his blood for them and their families, completing the act of atonement for their sins and the sins of their families.

For several days classes dealt only with Intercession. Through consultation with the Scriptures, Jeff revealed, he had designed a ritual that would satisfy the conditions for a successful intercession. Each woman would be required to dance for him. In preparation for her dance the woman would make herself as attractive as possible. Her husband would put on his full battle gear. The wife would then walk alone to Jeff's tent. Everyone else in the group was required to avoid the area of Jeff's tent while Intercession was in progress, and the husband of the woman dancing was to remain in his tent—studying Scripture.

The woman would enter Jeff's tent, perform her dance, and after she had been informed whether or not her offering had been acceptable, would leave. She would return to her own tent, where she would read a prepared statement to her husband. The husband would then walk to Jeff's tent, where he would swear an oath of personal loyalty to Jeff. The details of the dance ritual were meant to be humiliating. As described by Sharon and Debbie, Alice was present as a cheerleader, for "emotional support" for the dancing woman, and to assist Jeff.

On her entrance, the woman handed her underpants, which she was carrying, to Alice. Jeff was seated on his cot, nude at least from the waist up. The women weren't able to see below the waist, where he was covered by a sheet. Alice in a loose housecoat then sat on the cot next to Jeff, also covered by the sheet.

The woman brought with her a previously prepared tape of music Jeff particularly liked. The tape was one hour long. When Jeff indicated that he was ready, the woman turned on the tape and began to dance. During the first song she stripped, then danced for the rest of the hour as erotically as she was able.

The dancing was exhausting, the women were humiliated and afraid; no one refused. Sharon remembers being in considerable pain from the combination of physical strain and her pregnancy, although at the time she didn't realize she was pregnant. Even so, she was too afraid for herself and for Richard to dare to complain or to stop dancing.

During the dance Jeff masturbated into the woman's underpants. He explained that the shedding of his semen was analogous to Christ's shedding of his blood for the redemption of sin. Alice provided whatever assistance he needed. Sharon remembers noticing at one point during her dance that Alice was completely under the sheet covering Jeff's lower body.

At the end of the dance the woman lay down flat on her face and did not get up until given permission to do so. Only then was she permitted to dress. When she left the tent, if her dance had been satisfactory, her underpants were returned to her by Alice with Jeff's semen staining them. She was obliged to put on the underpants and wear them for the rest of the day.

Alice, the lord's helpmate, tutored the women in the procedure and gave suggestions about what would please Jeff, including appropriate music. Sharon says that she danced to selections from the music of *Beverly Hills Cop.*

Alice was also assigned the job of persuading the women to go through with the ritual in the first place. Debbie and Sharon say they remember Alice screaming at some woman, "You will do this thing or I will beat you myself!" No one was permitted to express reluctance, much less rebellion.

Ron and Keith were extremely upset, but each had invested too much and was too afraid for himself and his family to refuse to go along with his wife's dancing naked for Jeff. Richard and Greg found it distressing but didn't have the same emotional attachment to their wives as Ron and Keith.

On August 14 Susie and Kathy danced. The next day it was Sharon and Debbie. All the dances were found acceptable. Kathy Johnson's must have been particularly so.

A few days after the dances Jeff was spending some of his free time, of which he had a great deal, with Debbie and Kathy, both of whom he found very attractive, frequently calling Debbie "a vision of loveliness," and talking about Kathy's attractive mouth. Talk turned to Dennis Patrick and his precarious situation, with no wife to intercede for him.

Dennis, in fact, lived in constant terror. He had not been allowed to carry a weapon since even before his wife Tonya was taken to Jeff's tent. Dennis had long been aware that Jeff not only heartily disliked him, but that Jeff could easily believe that his continued presence was a threat to Jeff's domestic harmony and the compliance of the entire group. Dennis never forgot, nor did anyone else, that Jeff had recently slaughtered five people, and that the group had helped him do it. Many nights Dennis would lie awake, terrified by every sound, worried that any snapping twig might mean that Jeff was on his way to execute him in his bed. Dennis not only had no weapon—he had no rank, no authority, no option except to try to find an opportunity to sneak away into the woods and make his way to Davis alone. But he couldn't do that, couldn't leave Molly and Tonya at Jeff's mercy. So he stayed, hoping to survive long enough to help his wife and child.

Other members were at least uncomfortable about Dennis's plight— in spite of Jeff's dislike of the man, Dennis was generally well liked. So when the discussion between Jeff and the two women turned to Dennis, Debbie and Kathy were pleased to hear from Jeff that it might be possible for Keith to intervene on Dennis's behalf; Keith was assigned to be in charge of Dennis and so was, to an extent, responsible for Dennis's survival. Jeff did counsel Kathy, however, that she should not tell either her husband Keith or Dennis that he had made the suggestion. Keith's intervention should be voluntary to be effective.

Kathy passed on the suggestion to Keith, making it sound as if it were her own idea. Keith was happy to help Dennis and reduce the stress in the camp and soon approached Jeff with the proposal that he somehow might intercede for Dennis.

Jeff instantly went into a rage, attacked Keith for overstepping and implying that Jeff's judgment of Dennis was incorrect, improper. Jeff said that the punishment for such an offense was death and that Keith had just signed his own death warrant and his family's. Keith should be aware by now that the sins of the husband and father were visited on his family.

After a few minutes, though, Jeff seemed to subside and relent. Oh, he still insisted that the proper punishment was death, but he also reminded Keith that death meant to be pierced by a sword and said that Kathy had successfully interceded for herself and her family. Jeff added that while a man could only be pierced by a literal sword, a woman could be pierced by a different sword. So it followed that Keith could save himself and his family by giving Kathy to Jeff to be appropriately pierced. And since the initial sin was a sin committed through Keith's mouth, Kathy's mouth would be pierced as well.

Keith was devastated.

Keith was afraid of what Jeff would do if his edict was disputed.

Keith could hardly stand to think about giving in to what Jeff had demanded.

Keith gave in.

Kathy was pierced by Jeff's sword on August 25.

Alice was not pleased. Jeff tried to appease her by returning Tonya to Dennis, telling the group that it seemed Tonya had not actually been his true spiritual wife. Jeff told Alice that Tonya never had been able to satisfy him as she did, that he did not find Tonya attractive because she was too fat. According to Tonya, the truth was the reverse. Alice was not appeased. In fact, she became so out of control that two days later Jeff was obliged to tell the group that Alice was not to function independently and that no one was to speak to her without his permission.

Stress was beginning to fracture the group. Keith was becoming more and more upset over the relationship developing between his wife and Jeff but could see no way to stop it. Debbie was doubting more and more but believed she had no life outside the group. Richard and Greg both had thoughts about leaving the group, which they began to talk about with each other in a sort of joking way, trying to guard against the possibility that the other would report to Jeff. Ron was dedicated to remaining with Jeff and to seeing God in the flesh but was finding it necessary, almost forcibly, to restrain his doubts about multiple wives and other questionable doctrines. Danny stayed convinced that Jeff was the prophet. Susie was loyal to Ron. Sharon was dedicated to Jeff. Jeff was convinced that he could persuade the group to do anything and was increasingly entranced with the power he held over their lives. Alice was angry and bitter, feeling unneeded and unwanted and that all her efforts on Jeff's behalf were not appreciated. The group was reaching a crisis point.

On the morning of September 15 the crisis arrived. Jeff managed to leave for town with Kathy on the ATV before Alice was up and dressed. Some time later a helicopter arrived and hovered over the camp. At various times during the summer copters, usually flown by game wardens making sure that the group was properly caring for the area, had flown over the camp. Sheriff Thompson occasionally visited the campsite on foot or by copter to check on the group's activities. The sheriff visited, often concealed himself in the woods and silently watched. This time the sheriff's copter hovered over the camp low enough to blow wash from the line.

As the copter left, Jeff and Kathy appeared on one side of the clearing while Alice emerged from her tent on the other side. Alice, it seemed, snapped. She marched across the clearing and began screaming at Jeff. Then she stalked back toward the tent, yelling at the group, "So *that's* your God!" In the tent she began throwing clothing into a suitcase.

When Jeff approached the tent to talk to Alice she came outside and began hitting him on the head and shoulders with her purse. Jeff put up his arm and tried to talk to her but she only shouted obscenities at him. Finally the two went into their tent, and the group heard Alice rant on and on.

No one knew what to do, except, as always, wait. Eventually Jeff emerged from the tent with the news that the arrival of the helicopter indicated that things were becoming too dangerous and that he was sending Alice, Jason, Kristen and Caleb, and Susie, Matthew and Amy Luff to Mack's Creek to stay with Alice's parents. The two women and the children left that same evening.

Alice, to Jeff's relief, was at least off the premises.

16

BATHSHEBA

Jeff had promised Alice when she left that he would not spend time with Kathy, but the day after Alice left Jeff gathered the other men and explained to them that he was taking Kathy as his second wife—Kathy was his Bathsheba.

Jeff had convinced Kathy that he, not Keith, was her true husband, and Kathy, unhappy with Keith for some time, had little difficulty accepting the idea. Keith did not share these sentiments. He also did not dare challenge Jeff, but he did think about killing him. Eventually, though, he accepted or rationalized the situation . . . as time passed Kathy would come to her senses . . . Jeff would get tired of her, the way he had of Tonya Patrick . . .

When that same day the sheriff's helicopters came again Jeff decided that the camp would have to be split. He said, though, that he'd need to keep his three witnesses with him, the three being analogous to the three witnesses who had testified by affidavit for Joseph Smith, Jr., that they had actually seen the plates from which the Book of Mormon was translated. According to Jeff, since he was soon to enter the treasury where the plates and the Sword of Laban were stored, he would need three witnesses just as Joseph Smith, Jr., had had. The witnesses were to be Damon, Greg and Ron.

Jeff, Damon, Debbie, Greg and Ron moved to a new campsite, and Jeff manipulated the arrangement so that it would appear to Alice, if she were to learn of the move, that he and Kathy were in different camps while they were actually living openly as a married couple at the original camp.

Kathy almost immediately became pregnant.

*   *   *

In September Damon, favorite son and group armorer, was assigned to alter the murder weapon, to switch the barrel of the gun Jeff had used to kill the Averys with that of another Colt .45, apparently hoping that if the gun were ever found the alteration would foul up any positive identification as the killing weapon. Damon couldn't manage it.

The group was beginning to be a real burden to Jeff. They had little food, no money, winter was coming and the weather was sliding from chilly to cold. He was forced to make trips back and forth between the two camps to be sure both groups were functioning. He also had to visit Mack's Creek to see that Alice didn't feel too neglected. Alice had a tongue. Being a prophet and god of the earth had become a lot of work.

Richard remembers that during this period he was told to dig fox-holes. Jeff had apparently decided that his new status as god of the earth changed the proper protocol for the appearance of god to the group. Because the Bible taught that God required man have no other god before Him, Jeff said that he would have to stand behind the other men when God appeared, so that the group would have no other god before them. He instructed the men to dig foxholes at the base of the hill, in the battlefield, for the coming conflict, and when they were done he told them they would now practice the proper ritual for the coming of God—stand behind their foxholes while Jeff, armed with his .45, stood behind them. Richard not unreasonably was afraid that Jeff would start shooting them one at a time, that the foxholes were intended to be their graves. Jeff, he thought, had decided to rid him-self of the group that had become too much of a burden. As it turned out, it was another of Jeff's sadistic control games.

It was also during this time that Debbie and Damon were alone at their campsite when police officers approached. Debbie remembers that Damon shoved his semi-automatic rifle into her hands, quickly tried to show her how to fire it, told her to hide and that if he wasn't able to talk the officers into leaving the area without entering the camp she was to shoot to kill. Damon, already a practiced con man, managed to persuade the officers to leave.

And a few days before this, Sharon, in the fifth month of pregnancy, finally realized her condition. The other group members, and particularly Alice, had assured her for months that she wasn't pregnant and she had doggedly ignored all the usual telltale signals her body was sending her. When her condition could no longer possibly be ignored Sharon was delighted; Richard, though, felt further trapped and suspected that the baby might be Jeff's. A couple of weeks earlier Jeff had told him he foresaw that Richard would soon be a father. Richard took this prediction as another proof of Jeff's ability to prophesy, which doubtless was Jeff's intention—another control tactic. Of course, having observed the pregnant woman, such prescience required little divine insight.

On October 12 Jeff made a last trip to a pawnshop in Elkins, West Virginia, where he had been a regular customer, and sold two Colt .45 pistols. They would not be discovered, in spite of an intensive search by law-enforcement officials, for nine months.

On October 13, fed up with West Virginia, Jeff left for Missouri with Dennis, Tonya and Molly Patrick. Ron and Damon had individually left for Missouri some days before. Jeff had made no arrangements for the rest of the group, which had no money, no truck, and were so estranged from their families that they felt they couldn't call on them to help. Kathy came to the rescue when she called friends in Missouri who had a large truck and begged them to haul the group back to Missouri. They rode to Missouri jammed in the truck like illegal aliens desperately seeking the land of milk and honey north of the Rio Grande.

In Missouri the group camped in a barn owned by an old friend of Kathy's, just outside Chilhowee, a small rural community southeast of Independence. Jeff, Kathy and Damon spent time in a rented trailer with the family living there and relaxing in ways they couldn't when they were with the group. Mostly they listened to heavy metal rock music, drank beer and watched pornographic videos.

Jeff now traveled back and forth from Chilhowee to Mack's Creek to see Alice, apparently trying to save—or control, or both—his marriage while holding on to Kathy. A week after the move to Chilhowee he took Kathy with him to Mack's Creek, a strange way to win back a wife. Alice later would say that Jeff came to her bed right after having had intercourse with Kathy, and that she became so upset that she had a "nervous breakdown" and tried suicide with an overdose of Excedrin washed down with beer.

Jeff, she said, walked her around all night, forced her to drink coffee, then when he was convinced she wouldn't die, took her into the bathroom, had a bowel movement, forced her to rub the feces on his genitals and to have oral sex with him, swallowing some of the feces in the process. She tried to resist, she said, and next remembers waking up on the bathroom floor, the side of her face sore and blood flowing from an ear.

Later that day Jeff and Kathy took Alice back with them to the barn in Chilhowee, where, according to Alice, Jeff told her that she would have to tolerate that he was also married to Kathy. Jeff was also teaching their children to call her "one of daddy's wives."

Debbie says that when Jeff and Kathy appeared with Alice and reported that Alice had had a nervous breakdown, they couldn't detect any evidence of it. She was too alert. As Debbie said, "Dennis and I agreed that those eyes were just too bright."

The next day Alice returned to Mack's Creek, and Jeff would tell the group that if Alice tried to kill herself again, well, he thought he might just let her die.

The group had arrived at Chilhowee on October 21. Jeff now told the men that his plan for the winter was that the group should scatter, each man to find a job to provide for his family while accumulating some extra money so Jeff could take his family for a vacation in the spring before the group once again left to attempt some sort of wilderness experience.

For Richard and Greg this was the proverbial last straw. Greg had—and it wasn't easy—concluded that he no longer could believe that Jeff was what he said he was. Jeff had told him too many lies. Richard still couldn't decide whether or not he believed that Jeff was a prophet. What he did know was that life with Jeff and Sharon had become a torture for him. He would rather live in hell for eternity than with Jeff and Sharon for another day. He also believed that his days were numbered whether or not he stayed with Jeff. He was sure that if the group reassembled in the spring according to Jeff's plan, he would be killed by Jeff after he turned over his accumulated earnings.

So for different reasons both Richard and Greg were looking for a way out. On October 29 Greg's dad located the group and tried to talk Greg into leaving. Greg did not tell his father at that time how near he was to leaving because he was very afraid that Jeff would try to prevent it.

Two days later Greg and Richard each packed a suitcase, took them outside the barn and hid them. Neither said a word to anyone about their plans, especially not to their wives—both Debbie and Sharon were, to all appearances, still disciples of Jeff and likely would tell him about the escape plan.

But before the men could leave, Debbie noticed that Greg's suitcase was missing from their tent, confronted and challenged him about his intentions. When Greg admitted that he'd intended to leave without saying goodbye and without letting her know where to contact him, Debbie lost control and smacked him in the face.

She then walked off toward where Jeff was about to have breakfast. Passing Sharon on the way, she told her that Richard was leaving. Sharon, confused, ran to Jeff. After the women had told Jeff that Richard and Greg were leaving, the husbands decided that now that Jeff knew, the best strategy was to try to deflect at least some of his anger by talking directly with him. Wrong.

When Richard told Jeff that he and Greg had decided they needed some time away from the group to get their thoughts in order and decide what they wanted to do, Jeff picked him up by his shirt front and shoved him against one of the barn support pillars and told him that the two of them would never survive on their own and if either of them ever told what he knew, Jeff would kill him. A few minutes earlier Jeff had told Kathy he would slit the men's throats if they ever told.

But Greg and Richard were able to walk away from the group. They stayed with Greg's brother for a few weeks, not telling friends where they were out of fear that word would get back to Jeff. Both knew that they were out for good. Neither had any intention of returning. The crack was widening.

With Greg and Richard gone, those left behind had to sort out their reactions. Sharon continued to be convinced Jeff was all he said he was. Danny, too, held tight to his faith in the prophet. Kathy was, in a fashion, falling in love with Jeff. Keith hated Jeff for taking his wife but wasn't sure that Jeff wasn't a prophet as claimed. Debbie had questions but . . . what if Jeff *was* what he said? The Patricks were plain afraid for their lives, and Ron and Susie had too much invested in their relationship with Jeff to allow their struggles with the teachings to undermine their faith. Still, things were rapidly changing for all of them. In five weeks it would be a drastic change.

After Greg left, the equation was changed for Debbie. She no longer, she realized, had to be afraid that anything she did might negatively affect Greg. Now she only had to fear for herself. She waited two more weeks, then just walked away from camp one day when Jeff was not at the barn. She had decided that she was going to see her children, even if she had to die for it.

She walked into town, where she called a friend who came to pick her up. She arranged to see her children one at a time while she stayed with her friend, but all the time was very much afraid for herself and her friend. Jeff, she still believed, could read her thoughts and know where she was. He would come to her friend's home and kill both of them. Finally she could no longer stand the fear, and ten days after she had left she called Jeff and asked his permission to return. It was the day before Thanksgiving.

While Debbie was gone the group had moved to property owned by Ron's brother Rick Luff in Warrensburg, Missouri, another small town near Chilhowee, Mack's Creek and Independence. The Luffs had a loft in their house where the children would be able to sleep instead of being outside in the tents with winter setting in. Jeff and Kathy were living in a trailer that belonged to Ron's and Rick's parents. Rick had also attended a few classes and seemed to be interested in Jeff's teachings about the chiasmic pattern.

However, on the Wednesday after Thanksgiving, Rick suddenly announced to Jeff that he could not tolerate plurality of wives and that Jeff and Kathy would have to be off the property by that night if they continued to live together. Rick then called the others into his house and told them that they would have to leave by that weekend if they intended to continue to follow Jeff, but if they wanted to leave the group they were welcome to stay as long as they wanted.

The group scattered. Jeff, Damon and Danny went to Mack's Creek, where they reunited with Alice. Kathy went to stay with friends. Keith went to his father's farm. Debbie and Sharon went to stay with Debbie's friend. Ron and Susie stayed at Rick's. The Patricks went to her parents' home.

Debbie was glad of the chance to escape again because she had known almost immediately on returning that she had made a mistake and wanted out. Sharon, finally, was able to understand after long conversations with Debbie that almost everything Jeff had said was a lie, but was unable to bring herself to make a final emotional break with the group. In fact, she called Jeff, telling him that she needed to talk to him, that she was confused, and arranged to meet him a few days later. It was not until the next day when Ron called to tell Sharon and Debbie that he was out of the group that Sharon finally felt that she, too, could leave. She called Jeff and left a message saying that she no longer wanted to meet with him. She never heard from him again.

The crack was becoming a chasm.

17

EXODUS

Kathy Johnson was frightened. Keith was still her legal husband but she couldn't trust him with her life—or the life of her unborn child, child of the prophet. After she left Jeff, Keith called and tried to talk her into coming back to him. When she refused, he began to threaten, implied that as her husband he could have her committed to a mental hospital and that he could force her to abort Jeff's child.

Kathy grieved for her sons because she didn't believe Keith was a fit person to care for them alone, but she could not provide for them by herself. She knew that at least some of Keith's threats were probably serious; he had always been a jealous husband and her relationship with Jeff had driven him beyond his emotional endurance. She also knew that Jeff intended to go back to Alice and wouldn't keep her as a second wife. Even so, in Kathy's mind the child she was carrying was the prophet's son, the son of the god of this earth. Jeff had told the entire group that both Kathy and Sharon were carrying sons. So the survival of the baby was even more important. Finally in December, to get away from Keith, Kathy went to stay with friends in Kansas to try to figure out what in the world to do for herself and the prophet's baby.

In Mack's Creek Jeff, Alice, Damon and Danny were trying to evaluate and plan what to do next. Once Jeff and Alice knew the others were abandoning the group, they also figured it was only a matter of time until the Averys' execution would become known to the police.

Alice claims she was oblivious to any of Jeff's planning and simply happy to have him back, apparently without Kathy. She also claims not to have known what he was thinking and to have operated only at his instruction. Given the way the group in Kirtland had always functioned, that seemed highly unlikely. More plausibly, Alice and Jeff together planned to return to San Diego, an area familiar from Jeff's Navy days.

In any event, in mid-December the Lundgrens and Danny Kraft headed cross-country from Missouri to southern California. In California Jeff and Alice established themselves in a residential motel in a San Diego suburb, stored many weapons and supplies in a rented storage locker and waited to see what would happen.

Back in Missouri Debbie decided that they ought to get together to talk about their experiences with Jeff and in particular what to do about the Avery murders. The meeting was in her friend's apartment, where she and Sharon were staying, and everyone invited came, except for Danny and Kathy.

In some ways—terrible as they were—they were closer than most families. In some ways they were also strangers to each other. It was only at this meeting that each began to learn the full extent of Jeff's deception. No one had been told precisely the same things as any of the others. Jeff talked behind backs, separating them from each other, building suspicion and distrust. But none could compete with Jeff's knowledge of the Scriptures, no one could *prove* Jeff wrong through the holy books. Together now, they could agree that Jeff was not a prophet, but they weren't *too* confident about that. They had been able to base their belief in Jeff as a prophet on the Scriptures, but their rejection of him had no such authoritative foundation. Against the written word of God, seeming to support Jeff's claim, was conscience and reason that said he could not be what he professed. God-fearing people, long conditioned and vulnerable, it was no easy position for them. Finally, it was less faith or lack of it, or reason or even conscience that was decisive in their rejection of Jeff's claimed exalted status. Every one of them had been so *miserable* for the months and years they'd spent with Jeff and Alice, *and* they just no longer could tolerate the misery, the terrible fear.

Much of the meeting was about what they should do about the deaths of the Averys. Keith began by telling them he had written a letter detailing the murders and had sent it to his lawyer, directing that it be sent on to the Kirtland police chief if he were to die suddenly under suspicious circumstances. Keith was afraid that Jeff would try to kill him because of Kathy, and equally afraid, he said, that Jeff would kill Kathy to get her out of the way. The rest of the group sympathized but insisted that he destroy the letter immediately after the meeting because it put them all in danger.

No one, it turned out, felt in any way responsible for what had happened to the Averys. All agreed that the whole plan had been Jeff's and that if they hadn't all been so deathly afraid of Jeff and Alice, no one would have stayed at the farm while the killings took place. The same rationale applied to any participation in the plan—their fear for their lives and their families' lives.

They also agreed, though, that even though the killings had been done by Jeff and wouldn't have happened if Jeff hadn't directed them, they were probably all in trouble with the law because of what Jeff had done. No one knew how much trouble legally, but all thought that there was a possibility they might be treated lightly because none of them was the actual killer.

There was brief talk about denying that they knew anything about the murders. Ron suggested that he and Keith might say that they had actually believed, as originally told, that they were digging a baptismal font when they dug the grave. That was quickly rejected, however, and the group solemnly agreed that all would have to face up to whatever their responsibility was under the law. The men reassured the women that they probably had nothing to worry about since they weren't in the barn during the killings. The Patricks also felt that they would escape legal blame because they weren't even at the farm when the Averys were shot.

They finally decided they would more likely receive favorable treatment if they went to attorneys and told their story to the law together. But not just yet. Debbie pleaded for time to spend a few months with her children and her family, and then she would be ready to face whatever had to be faced. The group agreed to give her a few months.

A few days later Greg flew back to Cleveland, where he visited friends he had made before he moved to the farm. He also drove by the farm, looking to see if anyone was living there, mostly concerned that anyone might soon locate the bodies in the barn. The group also wondered what had happened to their belongings. All Greg could report was that no one was living at the farm. He hadn't wanted to be seen or contact anyone to ask questions that might later seem suspicious.

* * *

When Sharon went back to her parents' home in Beaverton, Michigan, the family didn't quite know how to handle the fact that she had come back after more than four-and-a-half years of estrangement, unmarried and pregnant with the child of a man she had been living with; but at least she was home again and they welcomed her and said they would help in any way they were needed. In less than a month that commitment would come to demand more than they could ever have imagined.

Beginning with the evening of December 22, 1989, when Sharon gave birth to a daughter, Dawn Heather Bluntschly, Richard, not surprisingly, considering the paternity, was not exactly entranced.

Debbie moved in with her sister and brother-in-law in mid-December, and one day went to her parents' home unannounced and told her mother that she would either have to be accepted as she was or she would never again see her parents. The family did begin to work out a new, more honest relationship, which was more than she had realistically hoped for.

A few days after Greg's return from Kirtland with the news that all seemed quiet at the farm, several group members met at a local Pizza Hut restaurant. Keith Johnson said he had contacted an old friend who was an agent for the Federal Bureau of Alcohol, Tobacco and Firearms who could help them get a deal from law-enforcement agencies if they would trust him to set up contacts and interviews. The group, though, was still not ready to turn themselves in, most saying wait at least until after the holidays.

Keith pressed hard to convince the others it was necessary to contact officials to assure that Kathy would be safe. He said again he was worried that Jeff would follow through with a plan he'd mentioned before to enlarge his group by recruiting members of motorcycle gangs, that Kathy would be in danger from such people or that Jeff would kill her if he got tired of her. The others were not overly impressed. Actually, they felt that Kathy was safer with Jeff than anyone else would be. They also believed that Keith, considering his well-known jealousy, was more concerned with having law-enforcement agencies search for Kathy to return her to him than he was for her safety. Keith also seemed to think he was not in danger of going to prison because he wasn't at the farm the night the Averys died, but to make sure he wanted to arrange for special treatment through his friend. The others said no, not yet, and he agreed to wait.

The day after Christmas Kathy left her friends in Kansas by bus and apparently headed for Texas. Actually the ticket to Texas was intended to misdirect anyone who might be looking for her. She was really headed for San Diego, to be with Jeff, having decided she would be safe from Keith only if she were with Jeff. She also still had the old faith in Jeff's professed special powers and divine status, which meant that no one else could protect her from harm as Jeff could. She had earlier contacted Jeff by telephone and he had told her how and where to come to him.

The situation was awkward for Jeff, knowing as he did he wouldn't be able to tell Alice that Kathy was coming to California. Alice believed Jeff had abandoned Kathy; she had no idea that they had been in contact with each other.

When Kathy did arrive Jeff instructed Danny to rent a room in a motel in a nearby suburb where Danny and Kathy would be safe and inconspicuous. The pair had along with them a significant portion of the group's remaining arsenal, including the .50–caliber rifle. Jeff would make at least daily calls to Kathy and Danny from neighborhood phone booths.

Kathy at the time believed Jeff intended that he and she and Alice would have a conventional plural marriage—they would establish a household together in which the two women would share the housekeeping and child-rearing *and* their husband. Of course, Kathy was well aware that Alice was hostile to any such arrangement but convinced herself that Alice's hostility was based on a mistaken idea that she, Kathy, wanted to replace her altogether in Jeff's life. Kathy, for her part, believed that she and Alice each had a unique role in Jeff's affections, that Jeff needed Alice, and she wanted Alice to be her friend again. She just wanted Alice to accept the situation and move aside a little bit to allow her to have some space next to Jeff too. Kathy even labored over a letter to Alice begging her to be a part of Jeff's proposed plural family; the letter was never sent.

Whatever Jeff had told Kathy about his plans, he never could bring himself to let Alice know that Kathy was living nearby. He seemed to have the same problem explaining plural marriage to his wife that Joseph Smith, Jr., had had, and with much the same result. Whatever else Alice had been able to accept from Jeff in their years together, plural marriage was definitely not to be tolerated. No one knows what if anything Jeff intended as a solution to his problem, but Alice's attorneys say they believe Jeff planned to kill her somewhere in California.

It was New Year's Eve and Keith Johnson had reached the limits of his ability to tolerate the suspense, the jealousy and the fear. He contacted his friend, who was actually an informant working with ATF agents from the Kansas City post, and asked him to arrange a meeting for him with his ATF contact. The informant contacted Larry Scott, a short, compact man who had been a special agent for the Bureau of Alcohol, Tobacco and Firearms since 1976. Scott called his group supervisor, Richard Van Haelst, also a fourteen-year veteran. Even though it was Sunday afternoon and New Year's Eve, the two special agents agreed to meet Keith and his contact on a street corner where Scott and the informant had met in the past.

At the meeting place Scott and Van Healst excused the informant, then the special agents and Keith Johnson went to ATF offices, where Keith proceeded to tell the agents the whole bizarre tale of Jeff Lundgren. Strange and terrible as the story was, both agents knew from their years in the Missouri area that the RLDS church did spin off splinter groups and that many of these groups were small personal cults. True, it was unusual for an RLDS sect to preach, let alone practice, the violence Johnson was laying out, but both agents also knew that violence as a religious practice wasn't rare within certain Mormon sects, especially in Utah. The agents did not have enough to evaluate fully Johnson's information, but they did believe there was at least some chance that Keith was telling the truth. Scott had Johnson draw a diagram of the lower levels of the barn to indicate its rooms and the location of the alleged grave. The agents then contacted their office in Cleveland.

But the agent taking the call in Cleveland felt the tip was simply another report from another nut, dutifully passed on by the Kansas City office. So the Cleveland agent took no action, except to give the Kansas City agents the name and telephone number of the Kirtland chief of police, in case Kansas City wanted to waste Yarborough's time on New Year's Eve.

Van Haelst and Scott got the message but persisted in the feeling that there was something about Johnson's story that couldn't be shrugged off. Maybe it was that there was just too much detail for the story to be entirely fabricated. Whatever, at least some checking was in order. And they wanted it done as soon as possible, since Johnson apparently believed that Lundgren was still dangerous and might even be headed out of the country.

They contacted Yarborough, who was more responsive than the Cleveland agent. As an RLDS member himself, he knew better than Van Haelst or Scott that some doctrines from the early days of the Mormon church, before the death of Joseph Smith, Jr., could be bloody enough to justify even a mass execution. Blood atonement, a doctrine personally espoused by early church leaders, could be a credible motivation for the Averys' deaths.

Blood atonement was, and still is among some Mormons, thought to be necessary to cleanse a soul of egregious sin. The sinner dies by his own hand or by execution in such a way that his blood is spilled on the ground. The steam from the fresh blood rises to Heaven like incense in atonement for the sinner's terrible sin. Blood atonement, though, is appropriate only for a sin so severe that the sacrifice of Christ on the cross is not sufficient expiation. Such a sin might, for example, be murder, or perhaps a lack of belief in Joseph Smith, Jr., as the prophet of God. In any event Yarborough believed that Jeff Lundgren would have known about blood atonement and could have made it a part of his teachings to encourage his followers to take over the Temple and kill those in the surrounding area. But he found it difficult to believe that Jeff actually would have killed his own followers. More, like members of the group but for different reasons, Yarborough did not trust Keith Johnson. Was Johnson acting at Jeff's instruction to buy some future leniency for fessing up? Did Keith have his own plan for revenge that had little to do with reality? In spite of such doubts, Yarborough, who had long been uneasy about Jeff, decided that such harrowing information had to be investigated, and that evening assigned Ron Andolsek, his deputy, to begin checking on the whereabouts of the Avery family.

18

THE PARTING OF THE RED SEA

Ron Andolsek tried to contact neighbors and relatives of the Averys, but neighbors had not seen or heard from the family since the previous spring, and the telephone numbers of family members were no longer current.

He did find a friend of Debbie's in Missouri who told him that she had recently been contacted by Debbie, who was currently living with her sister. The friend told Andolsek that Debbie had contacted her in November of 1989 at Jeff's direction to learn whether or not the friend knew anything about an on-going police investigation of the group. The friend said that Debbie had told her that the group at that time was living in a barn in Chilhowee, Missouri. Andolsek sent a teletype to the Chilhowee police department asking them to find out whether or not the Avery family was now or had previously been in the area. He made no further progress that evening.

The next day, January 1, 1990, Andolsek picked up the investigation when he came on duty in mid-afternoon. He spoke with the Averys' Madison landlord, who said he had received a letter in the spring of 1989 from Dennis Avery that said he was taking a job in Arizona. The Averys had not paid their last month's rent and had disappeared sometime in the second week of April, leaving nothing behind.

Andolsek again tried reaching relatives of Dennis and Cheryl but again with no success. Next he called Gerald Winship, Greg's father, who told Andolsek how he had gone to the barn where the group was living on October 29, 1989, to try to persuade Greg to leave the group. Mr. Winship said that on October 31 Greg and Richard had left, and that Sharon, Debbie, Keith and possibly the Luffs had also left. Greg, he added, had never mentioned the name Avery to him and he didn't believe that the Avery family was with the group in West Virginia. He said he would ask his son that day and would call the Kirtland police to let them know whatever he found out.

Andolsek tried to call the Brands—no answer. He called Sharon Bluntschly, who told him that she was done with the group. She also said, following Jeff's instructions to the end, that the last she had heard, the Averys were on their way west to Montana or Wyoming, and that they did not go to West Virginia with the group. When Andolsek asked her when she had last seen the Averys, Sharon said, "I just got over a big mess and I don't want to talk about it." Andolsek then asked whether the Averys were at the farm when the FBI agents and the police interviewed the group. Sharon answered, "Ron, I just got through telling you that I do not want to talk about it." And that was it.

Later that evening Andolsek contacted Stan Skrbis to let him know that some of the group members were missing and that the police wanted to search the barn at 8671 Kirtland–Chardon Road. Skrbis told Andolsek that the rent at the farm had been paid through February or March of 1989, that the Lundgrens had abandoned the property and that the property had since been put on the market. He gave Andolsek written permission to search the property at 8671 Chardon Road.

That same evening Andolsek was contacted by Donna Bailey of Centralia, Washington, who identified herself as Cheryl Avery's mother. She gave Andolsek some background information on Cheryl and told him that she had information from Ron Luff that the Averys had left the group shortly after they moved from Kirtland to Madison. Mrs. Bailey went on to say that she had had no contact with Cheryl since she had received a letter from her in April of 1989 that said the family was moving to Wyoming. She had then contacted the Salvation Army Missing Persons Bureau.

Andolsek next contacted Jim Fincham, Jeff's former friend from the Temple, who said he did not know the Averys but he had gotten the impression that Jeff did not want the Averys in the group.

Andolsek also talked with Shar, who told him that Alice was living in Mack's Creek and that Jeff, Kathy and Danny were together but she didn't know where. Shar said she'd heard that Jeff was thinking about recruiting from motorcycle gangs. As for the Averys, she said they didn't go along with the group to West Virginia and that Jeff had always said that the Averys were expendable and would end up dead. All, of course, true, so far as it went.

At about 9:30 that evening Andolsek and Yarborough examined the barn at 8671 Chardon Road. Following the information from Kansas City as they understood it, they checked the floor in the northeast corner of the ground floor of the barn. To their relief, the floor was a concrete slab that showed no sign of having been disturbed. The only portion of the barn the officers could find with a dirt floor was the western one, but that room was filled with junk, looking like a giant Goodwill box, as Andolsek would later describe it.

Yarborough and Andolsek examined some of the personal property left in the barn and discovered numerous items that apparently had belonged to the Averys, including children's school notebooks, personal papers and family photographs. But they found nothing to indicate that a grave had been dug in the barn.

Later that evening Andolsek contacted Dennis Avery's sister in California, who said that the last time she had spoken with her brother was in April, 1989. She was told that he and his family had intended to go to West Virginia but had changed their minds and were going to Wyoming.

On January 2, ATF Agent Larry Scott called Yarborough to find out what progress was being made in locating the area of the barn described by Keith Johnson. Scott was told that Yarborough and Andolsek had searched the barn the night before but could only find a concrete-slab floor, although they understood Keith to have said there should be a dirt floor and a grave.

Scott said that he thought the officers were looking in the wrong area of the barn and offered to fax to Yarborough a copy of the diagram drawn by Keith on December 31. They agreed that the diagram would be useful, and Scott transmitted it to the Cleveland ATF office, where Group Supervisor Patti Galupo arranged for it to be sent on to Kirtland. The fax arrived at Kirtland City Hall at about 2:30 that afternoon.

Dennis Patrick had arrived at the Kirtland police station and had spoken briefly with Chief Yarborough. Yarborough arranged for Patrick to return later that afternoon, when he would be able to speak further with him. Meanwhile, Yarborough contacted FBI Agent Bob Alvord, who arranged to be on hand during the interview. The two hoped that Dennis, who was possibly one of the weakest members of the group, might confirm what Keith Johnson had said and maybe give even more information.

When Dennis returned at about 3:00, Tonya, Debbie and Shar were with him; they waited outside in the car.

Dennis told Yarborough and Alvord that he and his wife had left Jeff Lundgren's group on or about December 8, 1989, along with most of the other members. He said that Danny Kraft had stayed with Jeff, as had Kathy Johnson, who was pregnant with Jeff's child. He had no idea where Jeff was.

Dennis also said that on April 17, 1989, the day before the Kirtland police and the FBI had come to the farm, he had been with Keith Johnson the whole day. Johnson's Chevy was being repaired and so the Johnsons and the Patricks had stayed at the apartment the entire day. He said that on the day and the evening of the seventeenth neither he nor Keith Johnson was at the farm.

He had last seen the Averys, he said, at the farm about two weeks before April eighteenth. He said he understood that the Averys had left for Wyoming and he hadn't seen or heard from them since they'd left Ohio. He said that he had never been part of a meeting in West Virginia in which the killing of the Averys was discussed and that he had never heard anyone in the group talk about killing the Averys.

Dennis, who showed a building uneasiness as the interview went on, said that he and his wife Tonya were very angry with Jeff and that they as well as other members of the group had decided that they'd been badly taken advantage of. He said he and Tonya and Debbie had come back to Kirtland to retrieve some personal items left when they had gone into the wilderness thinking that they would have no further need of worldly goods—after all, they were going to see God.

At the end of the interview Dennis told Yarborough and Alvord that he thought it was too late that afternoon to try to go to the farm for any of their household goods and made an appointment to meet Alvord and Yarborough at the Kirtland police department the next morning at 10:00 to arrange to go to the farm.

*   *   *

After they left the police department Dennis, Tonya and Debbie dropped Shar off at her apartment, then they went to see a local attorney they had known from their contacts in Kirtland. They told him the whole story, including the fact that someone apparently had been talking to the police and that Yarborough seemed to know a great deal about the murders. The attorney told them all to return to Missouri immediately and to talk with attorneys there as soon as they arrived. They did exactly as they were told.

Andolsek now contacted Stan Skrbis for another consent to search. This time, the consent covered the time period of January 2, 1990, through January 17, 1990. He also continued to contact anyone and everyone he could in the Lake County area who might have information about the Averys. It was slim pickings; the Averys appeared to have been socially isolated, loners by choice, who left barely a ripple behind them as evidence that they had ever lived in Lake County.

After driving all night Debbie and the Patricks reached the Independence area the following morning, where they immediately contacted attorneys and the other group members. Keith Johnson admitted that he had gone to the ATF and encouraged the others to go in too, saying that the agents had agreed that anyone who came in voluntarily would receive immunity from prosecution. In fact, no such offer had ever been made. Keith had learned a thing or two about manipulation himself.

Ron, not surprisingly, resisted the idea of turning himself in. He said that he would go to the authorities only if the bodies were actually found. They all decided to sit tight.

Debbie, however, went to the attorney who had handled her divorce. When she told him the story he said, in a masterpiece of understatement, "Debbie, you have serious problems." She promptly went home to her sister's house to wait.

On January 3 Andolsek contacted Skrbis to ask about the type of flooring in the lower level of the west side of the barn. Skrbis told him that the floor was dirt with the exception of a concrete pad that reached approximately two feet in from the walls. He also said that the trash in the room had accumulated during the last six months that the Lundgrens had occupied the farm.

At mid-afternoon a local attorney arrived at the police station to report that he had information that five bodies were buried in the barn at 8671 Chardon Road. The location that the attorney described was consistent with what was indicated in the drawing that had been faxed from Kansas City.

Between three and four o'clock that afternoon Yarborough and Andolsek went back to the barn. This time Andolsek climbed over the trash to the northeast corner of the westernmost lower-level room. He discovered clumps of dried clay on top of some miscellaneous objects on the floor. It definitely appeared that someone had been digging in the room. The men both felt their hearts sink and had to swallow several times at the thought that Johnson's story appeared to be true— that an entire family was buried somewhere below their feet.

Andolsek also noticed that the trash was stacked higher in the northeast corner, and that with the exception of that corner the floor appeared to be hard-packed. There was also a north-facing window immediately above the northeast corner, which corresponded with the window Johnson claimed had been used to throw rocks into the barn to cover the bodies.

Chief Yarborough, feeling poorly, asked for assistance from the Kirtland Fire Department in excavating the barn.

At about seven o'clock in the evening Yarborough and Andolsek went to the Kirtland Fire Department to brief the firefighters on the investigation. Andolsek assigned two photographers, Volunteer Firefighter John Florentine with a 35–millimeter camera and Fire Chief Richard Martincic with a videotape camera.

The officers and the firefighters arrived at the barn at about twenty minutes after seven. It was completely dark with a penetrating, damp chill in the air. Freezing rain had been falling earlier in the day, but with darkness the precipitation had turned to soggy snow. The grim-faced men set to work as soon as they arrived.

The trash-filled westernmost room of the barn was photographed as it was, filled with the furniture, keepsakes and necessities accumulated by a middle-class family over several years. The stacks of household trash accumulated by the Lundgrens were heaped side-by-side with school pictures, baby books, bills and receipts, college and high-school diplomas and knickknacks, all once part of five human lives trashed by Jeffrey Lundgren. The piles of trash and household goods, including some items of furniture, were three- to four-feet high throughout the room.

The safety forces cut a door in the north wall of the room to allow easy access for the workers without requiring that entrance and exit be made by crawling over the heaps of debris. The men then began clearing the northeast corner of trash, stacking it toward the south side of the room and tossing some of it out the window in the north wall. Andolsek cut the power to the room because of unsafe wiring and installed floodlights for the work crew.

When the northeast portion of the room was finally cleared the area was photographed and examined. The dirt in the eight-foot-square area roughly surrounded by the support posts seemed to be spongy. Taking the condition of the floor as a guide, the men began to dig.

When the ground was disturbed, an almost overpoweringly foul odor began to fill the room. The men gagged, and a few had to leave quickly to be sick outside, or at least to inhale a few gasps of fresh air before they ventured back into the barn. As the firefighters continued to dig, the smell became stronger, and red water began to fill the hole they were creating. Bits of flesh and corn and unidentifiable matter floated in the water.

At approximately 9:07 P.M. a clothed human body was discovered approximately thirty inches below the surface of the concrete pad. The body appeared to be that of a male, lying on his side, with his head toward the north. Only his buttocks, lower back, and upper thighs were excavated, but his large, thick belt, his pants and shirt were clearly visible.

Chief Yarborough immediately notified Dr. William Downing, the Lake County coroner; the Kirtland safety director and mayor; the Federal Bureau of Investigation; Rick Kent, laboratory supervisor for the Lake County Regional Forensic Laboratory; and Charles Coulson, the Kirtland prosecutor. Kent called his boss, the Lake County prosecutor, Steven C. LaTourette.

Dr. Downing arrived at the barn at about ten o'clock. He had met Yarborough at the police station and had been briefed as to what to expect. Dr. Downing was given high boots to wear because of the mud, then Yarborough escorted him to the barn. After they arrived, the two entered through the large double doors, which had been pried open, and laboriously climbed over the heaps of trash to the gravesite,

Dennis and Cheryl Avery and their children, (from left)
Rebecca, Trina and Karen, are shown in a spring 1988
photograph by a family friend. *(AP/Wide World Photo)*

Alice, Damon, and Jeff Lundgren after their arrest in
San Diego. *(Union-Tribune Publishing Co.)*

Defense attorneys, R. Paul LaPlante *(left)* and Charles R. Grieshammer *(right)*, pass through metal detectors set up in the Lake County Courthouse. *(Photo credit: John Kuntz)*

Lake County Prosecutor Steven LaTourette. *(Photo credit: John Kuntz)*

Cult members Richard Brand *(left)* and Gregory Winship *(right)* being led into the courtroom for their arraignments in February, 1990. *(Photo credit: John Kuntz)*

Jeffrey Lundgren's defense
attorney, R. Paul LaPlante.
(Photo credit: John Kuntz)

Cleveland criminal attorney
Gerald Gold, who defended cult
member Gregory Winship.
(Photo credit: John Kuntz)

The Kirtland, Ohio farmhouse where Jeffred Lundgren and
his followers lived when the murders of the Avery family
were committed. *(Photo credit: John Kuntz)*

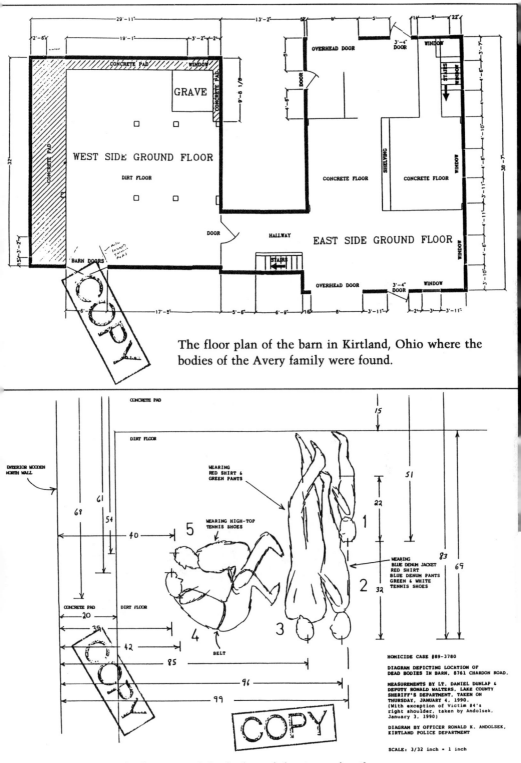

The floor plan of the barn in Kirtland, Ohio where the bodies of the Avery family were found.

A diagram depicting the location of the bodies of the Avery family.
(Diagram by Officer Ron Andolsek of the Kirtland Police Department)

The historic Kirtland Temple at which Jeffrey Lundgren once worked as a tour guide, and which he was plotting to destroy. *(Photo credit: John Kuntz)*

Jeffrey Don Lundgren delivers his five-hour sermon in the Lake County Courthouse during his murder trial. *(Photo credit: John Kuntz)*

Jeffrey Lundgren's 19-year-old son Damon leaves the courthouse to await the jury's recommendations of life or death. *(Photo credit: John Kuntz)*

The Kirtland, Ohio barn where the bodies of Dennis
and Cheryl Avery and their three young daughters were
discovered in January, 1990. *(Photo credit: John Kuntz)*

Jeffrey Don Lundgren is escorted from the Lake County Courthouse by two uniformed officers after hearing the jury's recommendations of the death sentence for the murders of the five Avery family members. *(Photo credit: John Kuntz)*

During testimony at her trial, Alice Lundgren uses her finger to describe how husband Jeff had pointed a gun at her head, threatening to shoot her. *(Photo credit: Willoughby News Herald/Duncan Scott)*

Alice Lundgren being led from the courtroom following the jury's guilty verdict in her murder trial. *(Photo credit: Willoughby News Herald/Duncan Scott)*

Cult member Ron Luff stares at the arriving jury members prior to the start of his trial in the deaths of the Avery family. *(Photo credit: Cleveland Plain Dealer/Curt Chandler)*

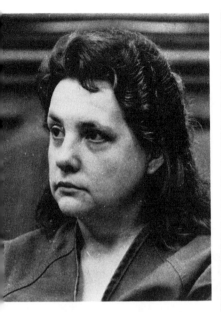

Deborah Olivarez, cult
member and cousin of Jeff
Lundgren, during her
arraignment in the Lake
County Courthouse.
*(Photo credit: Cleveland Plain
Dealer)*

Dennis Patrick enters the
courtroom for his arraignment in the deaths of
Dennis and Cheryl Avery
and their three daughters.
*(Photo credit: Cleveland Plain
Dealer)*

Sharon Bluntschly during her Lake County arraignment in the killings of the five Averys. *(Photo credit: Cleveland Plain Dealer/Curt Chandler)*

Kathryn Johnson, who bore a daughter for cult leader Jeff Lundgren. *(Photo credit: Cleveland Plain Dealer/ Curt Chandler)*

Cult member Richard Brand enters the courtroom for
plea bargaining in the deaths of the Averys. *(Photo credit:
Cleveland Plain Dealer/Curt Chandler)*

Danny Kraft pleading guilty to aggravated murder charges in the deaths of the Dennis Avery family. *(Photo credit: Cleveland Plain Dealer/Curt Chandler)*

where Yarborough bent over to point out the officers' grisly discovery. Dr. Downing remembers that Yarborough suddenly became sick there at the side of the pit. Yarborough remembers the incident differently. He believes that he lost his dinner later, outside by a squad car. In any event, the aroma of death attacked everyone. No man present was untouched by the horror of the scene they were uncovering.

Dr. Downing was closely followed by the other officials, including Rick Kent. It was agreed that because of the cold and the lateness of the hour no further digging would be done that night. The barn was sealed off with police barricades and "police line" yellow tape.

A press release was issued that same evening at about ten o'clock. The shocking news of the discovery of a human body buried in a Kirtland barn found its way to the local television late news. For the next year the lives of the Kirtland police and the staff of the Lake County prosecutor's office would be engulfed by the volume of the data, research and investigation necessary to resolve the baroque tale of religious and sexual perversion that would soon be revealed.

At 8:00 the following morning, two meetings directly involved with the future handling of the investigation were conducted. At the Kirtland Police Department, Yarborough and Andolsek met with Deputy Ronald Walters of the Lake County sheriff's department. The chief had requested assistance from the sheriff because of the nature of the apparent crime and the necessity to commit more man hours to the exhumation than were available from the tiny Kirtland police and fire departments. Deputy Walters was briefed by Yarborough and Andolsek about the details of the murders that had been provided by Keith Johnson and was asked to arrange for help in processing the crime scene. After his briefing Deputy Walters contacted the sheriff's department with a summary of the situation and the sheriff's department assigned Lieutenant Daniel Dunlap, a fourteen-year veteran of the department and a recent graduate of the FBI Academy in Quantico, Virginia, to assist the Kirtland police in processing the crime scene.

At this same time Rick Kent was meeting with the prosecutor to inform LaTourette of the steps taken by the KPD up to that time and to discuss procedures to follow in the investigation. Kent and LaTourette agreed that the prosecutor would go to the scene with his chief assistants later in the morning after he had appeared at hearings scheduled that morning in court on another case.

Rick Kent and David Green, another forensic specialist from the crime lab, arrived at the barn at about 8:30. Walters and Dr. Downing arrived at about 9:00, and seven firefighters arrived between 9:00 and 9:15. Andolsek also had a local towing service install a portable jack to support the ceiling because the existing beams were cracked and not providing proper support. Everyone set to work taking out debris and trash from the barn to a driveway that skirted the west side of the barn.

The prosecutor, Dale Kondas, the chief assistant, Karen Kowall, the chief criminal assistant, and Ron Graham, another assistant prosecutor, arrived at about 10:00. Lieutenant Dunlap got to the scene at about 10:15 and began to recommend procedures to be used in handling the evidence and in establishing security. Dunlap recommended and Andolsek established an inner perimeter with access restricted to those who would be directly involved in gathering evidence and in removing the bodies from the grave. Andolsek also arranged for an area in which the soil excavated from the pit would be isolated on top of a blue tarpaulin until it could be sifted, so that any evidence hidden in the lumps of thick clay would be exposed. An evidence-processing table and an evidence-holding area were constructed at the south side of the room.

A simple preliminary inspection of the trash in the barn revealed an empty box for a Colt pistol, complete with model and serial numbers. The box was turned over to Patti Galupo, who had arrived at the barn with one of her agents at Rick Van Haelst's request to help in any way she could.

The stage was set for the serious work to begin.

19

SIGN OF THE FALSE PROPHET

The prosecutors at the barn met with Yarborough, Andolsek, Dunlap, Kent and Green. Prosecutor Steven LaTourette was very concerned that everything done at the crime scene be precisely legal so there would be no question later about the admissibility of any crucial evidence.

LaTourette was certain there would be several trials; after all, if the information he'd received from Kansas City ATF was accurate there might be more than a dozen defendants in this remarkable case. Only thirty-six at the time, LaTourette had been elected Lake County prosecutor fourteen months before. He had hardly anticipated a case like this one—who could?—but LaTourette was and is the sort that thrives on the unexpected.

A northern Ohio native, he attended Michigan State University. After graduation LaTourette returned to the Cleveland area, where he attended law school at Cleveland Marshall College of Law, affiliated with Cleveland State University.

At law school LaTourette was perceived by other students as an individual intensely committed to his vision of things, which was a tilt left of center.

After law school he was hired by a downtown Cleveland law firm that paid him well and, typically of such firms, believed that the good salary bought the body and mind for eighty to one hundred hours every week and paid for the soul forever. LaTourette couldn't live with that and left for a job as an assistant with the Lake County public defender, R. Paul LaPlante. Public defenders are paid worse than assistant prosecutors, whose low salaries are notorious, but LaTourette loved the work and the people-contact, believing there are many more important things in life than money.

After some years with the public defender, establishing a reputation as one of the best trial lawyers in the area, LaTourette left to go into private practice. Then in 1982 he ran for Lake County prosecutor against the incumbent, John Shoop. Shoop was a popular prosecutor and a Democrat in a county that had a virtually unblemished record for electing Democrats to every public office for almost twenty years, but LaTourette thought that Shoop's office was poorly run and that the county needed a prosecutor who could run the office and prosecute criminals more efficiently and effectively. So he ran as a Republican with a campaign staff consisting of himself, his wife Sue and his secretary. The race was not even close. LaTourette went back to private practice and worked on generating support to run for prosecutor in 1988 with backing from the county Republican Party. In the five years between campaigns both the Democratic Party in Lake County and John Shoop fell on hard times. Shoop's office was responsible for several well-publicized fiascos and the citizens of Lake County apparently finally got fed up with the petty feuding between many of the elected officials. In 1986 a Republican was elected to the three-member Board of Commissioners, which had not held a Republican since the early 1970s. In 1988 Shoop was defeated in the primary election in May, and in November LaTourette was handily elected prosecutor.

From the start, LaTourette was disgusted and enraged as a man and father that a group of people could have callously executed three children and their parents. He strongly believed that all responsible should be executed, and publicly—and perhaps universally—said so a few hours later at a press conference. He and his staff then returned to their office to discuss the situation and contact the Kansas City ATF office for more direct information about Keith Johnson and the allegations he was making about the murders and the story surrounding them.

At the barn the police officers, firefighters and deputies continued to prepare for the excavation. They discovered in the pit a white powdery substance that both Dunlap, who had some construction experience, and Kent believed to be lime. The presence of lime was, of course, consistent with the scenario Keith Johnson had told Van Haelst and Scott to expect and tended further to confirm his story. The initial diggers had also found large field stones, some weighing between twenty and forty pounds, when they began the excavation. This, too, was as Johnson had told them it would be. Eventually the men would find between seventy and eighty of the field stones and other stones resembling cement blocks or large bricks in the grave.

Just a few minutes before noon Andolsek was asked to contact LaTourette as soon as possible. When he did he was told that the prosecutors had decided that it would be advisable to get a search warrant before any further investigation was done in the barn. Andolsek ordered all work stopped immediately and went to the Lake County Courthouse in Painesville to testify in front of Judge James Jackson for a search warrant.

The decision to seek a search warrant had been made by LaTourette after consultation with his young assistants, none older than the late thirties, who had gone with him to the scene. Dale Kondas, LaTourette's chief assistant, had been his good friend for many years and had been an assistant prosecutor under Shoop's administration. Karen Kowall, an assistant prosecutor since 1985, had only recently been promoted to chief criminal assistant. Ron Graham, also an assistant prosecutor since 1985 and a Painesville city councilman, was frequently called "Rambo" by the other assistants, a moniker based on his all-or-nothing courtroom style.

They worried that if the search were not conducted properly, any evidence collected at the barn, including evidence regarding the corpses, would not be admissible at trial. The prosecutors agreed that the initial search probably had been done properly, since the police had gotten a consent to search from the property owner before they had even entered the barn. Still, there was some question in the prosecutors' minds about the status of Jeffrey Lundgren with regard to legal title of the property at 8671 Kirtland–Chardon Road. They couldn't determine on what basis the property had been rented since the agreement between Lundgren and Skrbis appeared to have been amorphous and might be open to several interpretations, and it also wasn't clear whether Lundgren had abandoned the property or whether there might be some valid argument that Lundgren could still be said to have some claim to the property, or at least some ownership-type expectation of privacy in the barn and/or the house. So Kowell, Kondas and LaTourette in particular agreed that it would be best to foreclose any possible question about the legality of the search by stopping operations until they could obtain a search warrant. After all, a search warrant granted by a judge would be much more difficult to contest than a consent to search from a man whose authority to consent might be challenged.

Before the excavation had been stopped the men had been hampered by water running into the depression from under the concrete slab at the eastern end of the barn. No one could figure out whether the source of the water was run-off trapped beneath the barn or whether the concrete slab had been poured on top of a spring that had been freed by digging the original pit. In either case the free-flowing water threatened to make any orderly exhumation and gathering of evidence all but impossible. So while Andolsek was gone, Kent and Dunlap drove boards down into the soil as near to the east wall as possible. These boards cut down the flow of water but the men weren't able to stop it completely. After the water was blocked the workmen spent the rest of the time bailing out water that had already flooded the hole.

After the search warrant was issued and served on Skrbis by LaTourette and Andolsek, the digging began again. Dunlap and Kent did most of the exhumation by themselves, carefully and slowly using small digging tools such as hand trowels to avoid damaging the bodies.

Once again the entire barn was filled with the smell the workmen had found overpowering the evening before. Dunlap would pause as long as possible before drawing each breath. The barn was also bitterly cold, the temperature outside in the twenties with a whistling wind and a dusting of powdery, blowing snow. Inside, the diggers were protected from the wind but not from the snow, and the dampness that was an integral part of the barn seemed to leach away whatever warmth their bodies generated.

As the two men dug carefully around the first body discovered, a male body curled in a near-fetal position with knees drawn up toward the chest, they located another body, apparently an adult female, lying east to west and south of the feet of the first body. Dunlap and Kent decided that it would be difficult to remove the first body without removing the female body before it, so they began carefully to excavate the second body.

The soil that was being carefully scraped trowel-by-trowel from the bodies was extremely thick clay heavy with water. It was so thick that Dunlap and Kent would often be forced to help each other move his feet. Neither had the strength in his legs to pull his feet from the mud and so they had to help each other by grabbing the other man's boot or leg and then pulling his feet free one at a time. The mud also coated the corpses to such a degree that it was impossible to determine much about the bodies except for their relative sizes and, with the adults, their probable sex.

As Dunlap and Kent carefully unearthed the second body, they discovered a third smaller body on top of the second. It was at this point that Dr. Downing left the barn to go to his office to contact Dr. Elizabeth Balraj, the Cuyahoga County coroner in Cleveland. It had become apparent to Dr. Downing that the most difficult portion of the autopsies he would shortly be called on to perform would be their positive identification. In Lake County, where aggravated murder was rarer by far than snow in late April, the coroner's office did not have the sophisticated equipment that made for identification under difficult circumstances such as the advanced decomposition and partial reduction to a skeleton that was the case with these bodies. Cuyahoga County, on the other hand, did have such facilities, and the staff of the Cuyahoga County coroner's office was trained and competent in performing challenging forensic analysis. Dr. Balraj assured Dr. Downing that her office would be glad to assist.

At the barn Kent and Dunlap continued to unearth the pit's grisly contents. In uncovering the third body they discovered a fourth, smaller yet, with the head positioned almost on the hips of the third body. Slowly, carefully, they uncovered the small child, but as they tried to lift her the water and the clay created a powerful suction, as if reluctant to let her body leave its grave. The men were afraid that the stress would actually pull the body apart, because the joints and hands and fingers were particularly decomposed and partially skeletonized. During the process of removal the left foot did fall off and was never recovered. Dunlap remembers thinking that it was helpful that this little girl had been wearing tough denimlike clothing, which helped support the body during removal from the pit. This body, although the fourth discovered, was tagged Number 1 because it was the first removed from the grave. On its removal at about 4:45 P.M., like all the others to follow, it was wrapped in plastic to preserve any evidence that might have been clinging to the body or clothing and was then placed in a body bag that was carried out of the barn and placed on the ground along the north side of the building.

It had become obvious that all of the bodies were taped with silver duct tape just as Keith Johnson had said they were. On some of the bodies the tape had decomposed to an extent so that only traces remained about the wrists or ankles, but all the faces were taped, with tapes also arranged around the head. The second corpse disinterred, also clearly a child's body, was labeled Number 2.

Kent and Dunlap, their cold-numbed fingers protected with plastic gloves, finished their work with the second body and proceeded to the third. This time they were very concerned that because of the body's position, semi-immersed in the muck of the depths of the pit, the suction of the moisture would be so great that they would be unable to remove the corpse intact. Dunlap suggested that they use the clean sheets that were part of the standard equipment carried in the ambulance waiting to transport the bodies to the morgue. The sheets were passed under the body, the upper trunk and under the legs, and the body was carefully pulled free from the mud at about 5:20 P.M. The head of this female body was almost completely covered by the tape and by the hood of the sweatshirt, which was pulled tight around the face under the tape. The body was wrapped in the plastic sheets, placed in a body bag and labeled Number 3.

Dunlap was exhausted from the cold and physical labor in excavating the bodies from the omnipresent muck. After the removal of the third body, he asked that Walters take his place in the pit. Walters and Kent finished exhuming the first body discovered, and lifted it out, using fresh sheets, at about 6:05 P.M. This body, the male corpse, was labeled Number 4.

As they finished exposing the male corpse Walters and Kent had discovered a fifth body, another female, lying on her side, curled in a fetal position like the male, face-to-face with the male body. This body was carefully revealed using hand trowels, just as the other four had been, and then removed with sheets. Walters still too vividly remembers that as he reached under the body to lift the head, the entire scalp, complete with long, braided ponytail, came off in his hand. This final corpse was tagged Number 5.

The bodies were loaded into the ambulance, which Kirtland Police Officer Steve Sutch followed to the Cuyahoga County morgue in his patrol car, where he relinquished their custody to a representative of the Cuyahoga County coroner. The bodies were removed from the ambulance and received into the morgue in the same order in which they had been removed from the grave, to make record-keeping easier and more efficient.

At the barn the men checked the remaining unexcavated area of what had apparently been the original pit to make sure that there were no more bodies unreported by Keith Johnson. To their relief, they found that nothing more appeared as the soil was turned.

Autopsies were performed the following day at the Cuyahoga County coroner's office. Dr. Downing was present and observed. Dr. Balraj supervised each autopsy.

The autopsy of Body Number 1, later identified through x-rays of the sinus cavities as that of Karen Diane Avery, was begun at 11:00 A.M. by Dr. Jiraki. He determined that Karen Avery's body was forty-two inches in height and weighed thirty-six pounds. The face was decomposed. The body was clothed in a blue jacket with beige, green and red patches on the sleeves. Underneath the jacket was a long-sleeved white shirt with a purple collar and a picture on the front of a rainbow with red, purple and green horses on the rainbow and colored hearts over the main body of the shirt. The pants were light green jeans. The right foot was detached and was dressed with a white sock with blue-and-red stripes at the top. The shoe was a white tennis shoe with three colored designs. The panties were white with purple flowers. The eyes, ears, nose and mouth were covered with silver gray duct tape that ran all the way around the head. The wrists and ankles were bound with silver gray duct tape holding the arms and the legs together. Two gunshot wounds were discovered, one a wound to the head, the other a gunshot wound of the chest.

The autopsy of the second body, later identified through dental x-rays as that of Rebecca Lynn Avery, was begun at 12:10 P.M. by Dr. Carlos Santoscoy. Rebecca Avery's body was found to be sixty and one-half inches in height and to weigh seventy pounds. The body was clothed in a blue denim jacket, red sweatshirt, blue denim pants, white tennis shoes, white sweat socks, a brassiere and panties. Yellow metallic earrings were present in the ear lobes. The arms were bound at the wrists with duct tape, the left over the right. The legs were bound together at the ankles with duct tape. The head was wrapped with duct tape, completely covering the eyes, ears, nose and mouth. Two gunshot wounds were discovered, one of the posterior trunk, one of the left thigh.

The autopsy of Body Number 3, later identified from dental x-rays as that of Cheryl Lynn Avery, was begun at 11:15 A.M. by Dr. Murthy. The body was sixty-three and one-half inches tall and weighed one hundred thirteen pounds. The body was clothed in a hooded, zippered sweatshirt, a blouse with a white-and-green design, a white brassiere, a pair of sweatpants with a string-tie waistband, a pair of white panties and a pair of socks and tennis shoes. The eyes, ears, nose and mouth were covered with silver gray duct tape that passed completely around the head. The hood of the jacket was pulled over the hair, and the duct tape passed over the hood of the jacket. Both wrists were bound using silver gray duct tape. A watch was around the left wrist. A yellow metal ring was found in the clothing overlying the abdominal region. Three gunshot wounds were discovered, two to the right breast, and one to the abdomen.

The autopsy of Body Number 4, later positively identified from dental x-rays as that of Dennis Leroy Avery, was begun at 2:00 P.M. by Dr. Stanley F. Seligman. The body was found to weigh one hundred twenty-four pounds and to be sixty-seven and one-half inches in length. The body was dressed in a black belt, blue jeans, briefs, a black athletic shoe on the right foot and no shoe on the left foot, a white sock on each foot, a camouflage green tee-shirt, a short-sleeved shirt and a long-sleeved flannel shirt. The ankles were bound with gray duct tape. The hands were wrapped in gray duct tape but were free, apparently because of decomposition of the tape. The mouth was covered by gray duct tape wound around the head with the ears exposed. There were two gunshot wounds to the trunk.

The autopsy of Body Number 5, later positively identified from dental x-rays as that of Trina Denise Avery, was begun by Dr. Stanley F. Seligman at 4:00 P.M. The body weighed one hundred forty-five pounds and was sixty-three inches tall. The body was dressed in white athletic shoes, white socks, blue jeans, blue panties, a denim long-sleeved jacket, a white brassiere and a purple, blue and red blouse. There were gold earrings in the ear lobes. The hands were taped with gray duct tape but were not bound together. There was a watch on the right wrist. There was gray duct tape on the mouth and around the head with the ears exposed. There were three gunshot wounds to the body, one to the head and two to the trunk.

On January 6, 1990, Dr. Downing prepared the death certificates reflecting the results of the autopsies.

20

AN EYE
FOR AN EYE

The news of the bodies discovered buried in the dirt floor of a barn in a tiny suburb of Cleveland hit the national television networks and the wire services on the morning of January 4. That morning Ron and Susie Luff came into the ATF office in Kansas City with their children to talk with Larry Scott. Keith Johnson and the television news had convinced Ron that it was time to free himself of the guilt he had carried since he had become certain that the killings he had had such a significant part in had been cold-blooded murder, not a sacrifice ordered by God. The Luffs had contacted an attorney who had advised against going directly to law-enforcement authorities, but Ron believed it was right, or better for him, to tell the truth now.

He told Van Haelst and Scott that Keith Johnson had convinced him to come in to tell the truth. Later Ron would claim that Keith had promised him that if he voluntarily cooperated with the authorities he would be given leniency. Both Scott and Van Haelst, as mentioned, deny that any such promise was made, specifically or by implication. If Keith Johnson did tell Ron Luff he would be treated leniently, it was apparently only Keith's assumption, or perhaps his hope, that such treatment would be given.

Van Haelst and Scott told Ron that anything he would say could be used against him in a court of law and that he did not have to talk to them. Luff said that he understood, that he was "man enough" to take his punishment and that he still wanted to talk with the agents. He signed an ATF Waiver-of-Rights form, indicating that he understood his Constitutional rights to refuse to make statements that could incriminate him and that he wanted to forego those rights.

He then gave a complete statement to the agents about his participation in Jeff Lundgren's group, the deaths of the Averys, and the group's stay in the wilderness and later breakup. Van Haelst asked Luff if he would be willing to repeat his statement on videotape. Luff agreed. He gave his entire statement again in front of the camera, omitting only some detail about his religious beliefs and his life before and after joining the group.

The statement took more than two hours to complete. On the tape Ron Luff appeared detached and remote, speaking with no apparent emotion about the murders of Dennis, Cheryl, Trina, Becky and Karen. His voice was cold, almost a monotone, and his phraseology was artificial; he described himself as "disappointed" when the stun gun failed to work. As he chain-smoked his slightly high-pitched voice with its Missouri twang related an incredible story of deception and death without pause or hesitation.

Susie Luff also provided a statement for the ATF agents. Susie also did not appear to be nervous or particularly worried about the circumstances of her conversation with Scott and Van Haelst. She was told that her remarks could be used against her in court and that she did not have to talk to the agents, or that she could choose to have an attorney with her while she did talk with them. Like Ron, she chose to tell her story to the ATF agents.

In Susie's videotaped statement she rattled on, much the way she usually spoke, as she told of her involvement with the Lundgrens. She admitted having been present in the farmhouse on the evening of April 17, 1989, but denied having had any part in the preparation for the Averys' deaths. She claimed she had not believed that this prophecy would be any different than many of Jeff's other prophecies that hadn't come true. She said she believed that the entire plan was an elaborate test of faith and that the lives of the Averys would be spared at the last moment, just as Sharon's, Richard's and the Patricks' lives had been spared. She maintained that she did not know that the executions were to take place on the seventeenth, that, in fact, she did not even know that they were actually occurring until after either Becky or Karen, she was not sure which, had been taken to the barn. It was Debbie Olivarez, she said, who told her at that point that the murders were happening.

Susie went on to tell about the class held after the killings and to talk about the visit by the FBI and the Kirtland police to the farm the following day. She said that she had lied at that time as she had been programmed to do by Jeff, and that she had not been able to tell the police and the agents about the bodies in the barn because she was afraid for her life and the lives of her children. Susie also talked about the group's stay in West Virginia, described her stay in Mack's Creek with Alice and the breakup of the group. She said that she and Ron had talked about going to the authorities earlier but that they had been afraid to do so because they were afraid of Jeff and didn't know where he was.

While not as cold as Ron, Susie did not appear to be overly moved by the facts of the murders; instead she appeared to be more involved in denying any responsibility on her or Ron's part for what had happened. Clearly she felt that Jeff was altogether responsible for the killing, and denied that she personally had had any knowledge of what was to happen.

When Agent Van Haelst contacted Lake County Prosecutor LaTourette after the interviews with the Luffs, LaTourette told him that arrest warrants were being prepared for all who were implicated by Keith Johnson in the deaths of the Averys. Warrants for aggravated murder were prepared for Jeff Lundgren, Damon Lundgren, Ron Luff, Richard Brand, Greg Winship and Danny Kraft; Alice Lundgren, Deborah Olivarez, Sharon Bluntschly, Susan Luff, Tonya Patrick, Kathryn Johnson and Dennis Patrick were to be arrested on charges of complicity to commit aggravated murder. The warrants were faxed to the Kansas City ATF office, and Ron and Susie Luff were placed under arrest and taken to the Jackson County jail.

That afternoon the Patricks were arrested at Tonya's parents' house. After their arrival at the ATF office Dennis told Larry Scott that he and Tonya had contacted an attorney and that they wanted to talk with his attorney before making a statement.

Debbie Olivarez was arrested at her sister's house that evening. Armed officers came to make the arrest, having been told she was an armed and dangerous fugitive. She told Larry Scott that she would be retaining an attorney and did not want to make a statement.

*   *   *

On January 5 the news media in Missouri and across the country were filled with more sensational news about the bodies of the family that had been found buried in a barn in Kirtland, Ohio, adding that a strange religious cult had murdered the family in a horrible religious ritual.

Sharon Bluntschly now turned herself in to the police in Bay City, Michigan.

In Kansas City Richard Brand and Greg Winship surrendered to the ATF, accompanied by their respective attorneys. They did not make any statements at that time. Later that morning Dennis and Tonya Patrick were returned to the ATF office from the jail where they each waived their right to remain silent and provided videotaped statements.

The Patricks' statements were very similar to those of the Luffs, except that neither Tonya nor Dennis was present during the murders. Dennis and Tonya also both described the nude dances in the wilderness that Jeff had justified through his teachings on Intercession. Tonya also talked about her life as Jeff's second wife and said that she had lived with Jeff to save her own life and those of Dennis and Molly. She said that she had been forced to have sex with Jeff.

In the early morning of this same January 5 Donna Keehler, Alice Lundgren's mother, contacted the Kansas City ATF office and offered to make herself available for an interview later that day about her daughter and Jeff. That evening an agent spoke with Mrs. Keehler and her husband at the home of her sister and brother-in-law. Mrs. Keehler said later that she was willing to speak with the agents because she was afraid that Alice was dead. She said she had recently had a conversation with Damon, and that when she had asked about Alice she had been told, "She's being taken care of." Given what she had learned over the last several hours about the activities of her son-in-law, Mrs. Keehler's worry about that statement was understandable. She had little of importance to offer.

But just after midnight Mrs. Keehler contacted one of the agents who had interviewed her earlier in the evening, and sounding very shaken she said she had just spoken with Jeff, who had told her that he wanted her to come west to pick up the younger children and that after she had the children he and Alice would turn themselves in to the police. The agent told Mrs. Keehler that he and other agents would talk to her first thing in the morning.

At 8:30 the next morning the agents again arrived at Mrs. Keehler's sister's home. Mrs. Keehler said that Jeff had told her to begin driving west toward San Diego. He had called twice, giving her two telephone numbers in California. During the first call he told her to begin driving west on January sixth and that she should call the number he had given her at about nine o'clock in the evening, when she would be given further instructions. A short time later he called back and gave her the second phone number, saying that he had discovered that the first telephone couldn't receive incoming calls.

Mrs. Keehler said that she wanted to cooperate with the authorities but that she was very concerned for the safety of her grandchildren. When the agents assured her that the safety of the children would be their main concern Mrs. Keehler provided the agents with the two telephone numbers, which were immediately relayed to the ATF office in San Diego, where agents located the telephones assigned with the numbers Mrs. Keehler had relayed. Both telephones were pay phones located in National City, California, a suburb of San Diego, just six miles north of the Mexican border. The first was outside a 7–11 store; the second, outside a restaurant.

Just after noon Mrs. Keehler and her sister and brother-in-law began driving west in a 1985 Ford LTD station wagon. Four ATF agents in two cars followed. At about 9:00 P.M., as she had been instructed, the group stopped at a restaurant in Oklahoma City and placed a call to the second pay phone. Damon answered. He told his grandmother that everything was all right and that she should continue to drive west and call again at noon the following day Kansas City time.

While Mrs. Keehler was talking with Damon one of the agents traveling with her used another public telephone next to the phone she was using to relay the information from Mrs. Keehler's conversation to the special agent in charge of the Kansas City ATF office, who in turn relayed the information by telephone to the special agent in charge of the San Diego office. The San Diego office also relayed information from agents in the field who were watching Damon to a second agent on the telephone on the other side of Mrs. Keehler. Damon was under surveillance during the entire conversation by agents from the San Diego ATF office. After the conversation he was followed to the Santa Fe Motel, located near the pay phone.

On Sunday, January 7, at about noon Donna Keehler again did as she was instructed and called from a ranger station in the Petrified Forest National Park near Holbrook, Arizona. Again Damon answered the phone and told his grandmother that everything was fine. He told her to keep driving west and to call the same number at midnight after she got to San Diego. He said that the younger children would be sent to her in a cab. The information from the calls was relayed in the same way as it had been before. Mrs. Keehler and her escort proceeded on west.

Rick Van Haelst had flown to San Diego to supervise the arrest of the Lundgrens and, he hoped, of Kathy Johnson and Danny Kraft. No one at the time knew where Kathy and Danny were. Van Haelst hoped that the remaining members of the group would all to be together. He was reasonably certain that Jeff and Damon and the three younger children were together from the comments Damon had made to his grandmother, but he had no idea whether Alice, Kathy and Danny were with Jeff or not. Van Haelst worried, like Alice's mother, that Alice might even be dead. Van Haelst also did not know whether Jeff, whom he knew to have had numerous guns and hundreds of rounds of ammunition, had prepared armed resistance to any attempt to arrest him. All he could do was hope to locate the Lundgrens within the next few hours before the Keehlers arrived, and to take them quickly before anyone was hurt.

Van Haelst was waiting in one of the surveillance vehicles parked outside the Santa Fe Motel, where the agents believed the Lundgren family was staying, as Damon made his noon telephone contact with his grandmother. Unfortunately, because of the floor plan of the motel, the agents had not been able to follow Damon to his room the day before without danger of being seen, so they didn't know just where the family was located. No Lundgrens were registered at the motel, and the agents could not afford to be spotted questioning the motel staff about the guests. This time the agents, including a young female masquerading as a jogger running through the motel complex, had the entire motel property covered.

She spotted Damon as he entered Room 29 on the second floor of the motel, then made her way quickly but casually to a telephone booth on the sidewalk just outside the motel complex to report the number of the room Damon had entered. As she was standing in the phone booth Jeff walked out of Room 29 and stepped into the adjoining booth. The agent reported Jeff's presence as calmly as possible, trying not to let him know that he was being observed. Van Haelst instructed her to check to see if Jeff was carrying a gun. When she said that he was not, five agents converged on the phone booth, pulled Jeff out, put him on the ground on his stomach and handcuffed his hands behind him in spite of Jeff's vigorous protests. After Jeff was cuffed Van Haelst put his service pistol to Jeff's ear. "Jeffrey Don Lundgren, you are under arrest for murder."

As Van Haelst and the others were taking Jeff down, other ATF agents ran to the motel room Jeff had left just a few moments before, announced themselves and demanded that the door be opened. When there was no immediate response the agents burst through the door, where they found Alice, Damon, Jason, Kristen and Caleb watching television. Alice and Damon were immediately arrested. Damon was handcuffed outside the room, and as the young agent placed the cuffs on Damon's wrists, Damon turned toward him and said, "I didn't do the actual shooting."

Alice, Damon and Jeff were taken to the jail and the younger children were taken to the ATF offices to wait for their grandmother. Rick Van Haelst spent the next several hours on the telephone with a local district attorney obtaining a search warrant for Room 29. After the search warrant had been issued the local agents searched the motel room while Van Haelst talked with the suspects at the ATF offices.

Jeff and Damon refused to make any statements. Alice agreed to talk with Van Haelst after she had signed a grant relinquishing custody of her three children to her mother. Alice's statement was videotaped, as the other suspects' statements had been. In her statement Alice claimed that she had not believed that Jeff would actually kill the Averys but that she had supposed the entire plan was similar to God's test of Abraham's faith recorded in the Bible, in which Abraham was required to go to the brink of killing his son Isaac. She had thought that at the last moment Jeff would tell the Averys and the others that the Averys did not need to be killed, that Jeff had been testing the group's faith in him.

Even so, Alice said, "You would have had to be stupid not to know what was going on," with reference to the planned murders. She also said that she knew that God would never require the deaths of innocent people and that she had stopped believing that Jeff was a prophet at about the time that the group moved out to the farm. She did not go to the police the night of the murders because she had no idea that anything out of the ordinary was to occur that night. She had simply followed Jeff's instructions when she left the house to go shopping and was very afraid of Jeff and feared for her own life and her children's. So that was why she could not say anything about her knowledge of the murders to anyone.

Alice stated that her marriage to Jeff had been difficult, that he had been financially irresponsible for years and that she'd had to put up with his sexual infidelity many times. In spite of her unhappiness with her marriage, she said, she hadn't been able to leave Jeff because he always saw to it that she didn't have all the resources that she needed to leave at one time. She also said that Jeff always kept at least one of the children with him whenever she went anywhere to make sure she'd come back. She talked about Jeff's taking two other wives while the group was in the wilderness, which she hated.

At the time of her arrest Alice weighed some 240 pounds. On the videotape the viewer saw a sad, pathetic woman, her voice soft and hesitant, with open sores covering her face, sores she picked at while she spoke. It hardly seemed possible that this could have been the unchallenged matriarch of a group that had executed five people.

Alice, like Jeff, was very good at manipulating any situation.

Alice's mother, Donna Keehler, arrived at the San Diego ATF office at approximately 11:00 P.M. that evening, and Jason, Kristen and Caleb were immediately released to her. The ATF agents were relieved when the Lundgren children left. They had barely spoken while they were in the office. Whenever a question or comment was directed to either Kristen or Caleb, the child would glance at Jason as if for permission to speak. Jason kept sullenly silent.

During the search of Room 29 the agents found an AR–15 semi-automatic rifle, two .44 magnum revolvers, a .45–caliber pistol, hundreds of rounds of ammunition, knives, gas masks, books about the M–60 machine gun, camouflage outfits, maps, a Bible and a "three-in-one" that contained in one volume the Book of Mormon, the Doctrine and Covenants and the Bible. The agents also found a business card and a receipt indicating that Jeff had rented a storage locker in Chula Vista,

California, another San Diego suburb. Later that afternoon the agents obtained another telephonic search warrant for that storage locker and found photographs and papers, two trunks, one of which was filled with gunpowder, ammunition reloading dies, hundreds of rounds of ammunition, three long guns, including one paramilitary semi-automatic rifle and one 9–mm semi-automatic handgun.

On January 8, 1990, at 10:00 A.M. Alice, Jeff and Damon appeared in San Diego Felony Arraignment Court before Judge Timothy Tower. Judge Tower denied a request by their court-appointed attorneys for an identity hearing, required when a suspect arrested on a warrant claims that he or she is not the individual named in the warrant. In this case the judge found that there was ample evidence discovered in the motel room to demonstrate that the individuals before him were the same Jeffrey Don Lundgren, Alice Elizabeth Lundgren and Damon Paul Lundgren named in the warrants from Ohio.

When the three refused to waive extradition from California to Ohio, the court ordered they be held without bail and scheduled a review hearing for February 8.

Kathy and Danny were still at large, and there had been no clue in the Santa Fe room about where they might be. All local, state and federal authorities in southern California were alerted, as well as law-enforcement officials in Baja California, Mexico. Their photos were shown that evening on all local television stations and were provided to local newspapers.

On January 9, just after twelve noon, the maid at the Moana Motel in Chula Vista entered Room 7 to clean it. She found two weapons, including a .50–caliber rifle, a large quantity of ammunition and documents and letters. The maid notified the manager, who contacted ATF. The documents identified the occupants of Room 7 as Kathy Johnson and Danny Kraft, and the manager identified the two from photos.

According to the manager, Kathy and Danny had paid for the room through January 7. Danny was seen by the maid at about 7:00 A.M. on January 8 leaving the room in a hurry. Agents removed the guns from the room and began a twenty-four-hour surveillance on the motel and the room. An all-points bulletin on the two was again requested, and neighboring states were also warned to be on the lookout for them.

On January 10, just after two in the afternoon, Danny and Kathy were spotted by a lieutenant from the San Diego County sheriff's department travelling westbound on State Route 78 in a remote part of eastern San Diego County. The lieutenant recognized their Nissan pickup truck from the APB broadcast and requested backup. A California highway patrol unit responded and assisted with the stop.

Kathy and Danny gave false identification but were recognized by the officers, arrested and taken to the Julian Sheriff sub-station. Both refused to make any statements, but Danny did consent to a search of the truck, which had been partially repainted. There were no guns in the truck. The campsite where Danny and Kathy had stayed the previous night was also searched but no weapons were found there either.

They were then taken to San Diego, and on January 11 appeared before Judge Tower. They too refused to waive extradition and were held without bail, a review hearing scheduled for February 8.

Lake County residents felt better. The cult murderers were captured. Now the populace could settle down to watch the spectacle of the trials.

Yarborough was very pleased. For the first time in two years he could sleep knowing that Jeff Lundgren was not a threat to his community. He knew that some of the most difficult work still lay ahead, that the trials would demand hundreds of hours from himself and from Andolsek. This was work he would gladly do.

LaTourette was at once relieved and apprehensive. He knew that the spotlight would now be focused almost exclusively on himself and his office.

21

THE WAGES OF SIN

On January 5, 1990, the case against all of the members of the group, including those not yet arrested, was presented to the Lake County grand jury for indictment. If the grand jury found probable cause to believe that a crime had been committed, and that a particular person had committed that crime, it would vote for an indictment.

The grand jurors indicted Jeffrey Don Lundgren, Daniel David Kraft, Jr., Richard Brand, Ronald Luff, and Damon Paul Lundgren, each for five counts of aggravated murder with death-penalty specifications, and each for five counts of kidnapping. Each count of the indictment charged a separate crime; each count charged aggravated murder related to a different victim, as did each count charging kidnapping. Deborah Olivarez, Sharon Bluntschly, Alice Elizabeth Lundgren, Gregory Winship and Susan Luff were each charged with five counts of conspiracy to commit aggravated murder, five counts of complicity to commit aggravated murder and five counts of kidnapping. Dennis Patrick, Tonya Patrick and Kathryn Johnson were charged with five counts of conspiracy to commit aggravated murder.

Aggravated murder is the name in Ohio for the crime that charges the deliberate, premeditated killing of another human being, or the killing of another human being in the process of committing several specified crimes, one of which is kidnapping. Conviction of aggravated murder, however, doesn't automatically cause a defendant to be eligible for the death penalty. Other facts surrounding the murder must be charged and proved to invoke the death penalty. These facts, aggravating circumstances, are specifically enumerated by statute. Among the aggravating circumstances that can be charged are commission of the murder during a kidnapping, and commission of the murder as a part of a course of conduct that involves the killing or attempted killing of two or more people. All the men charged with aggravated murder were also charged with both applicable aggravating circumstances. All five could be sentenced to death if convicted as charged. At a press conference LaTourette said: "As surely as I am the prosecutor, the people responsible for this will fry."

On this same January 5 Richard Brand and Greg Winship were surrendered in Kansas City by their attorneys, with orders not to make a statement. On the other hand, signals were given by the attorneys that their clients would be willing to cooperate with information in exchange for lesser charges than they might otherwise expect. Also, whatever they said would not be used against them in court. In short, a deal.

LaTourette and his associates had a conundrum they didn't like but which they had to face. Early on, along with his associates Kondas and Kowall, LaTourette had decided that all the information collected by the Kirtland police and ATF agents made it clear that Jeffrey Lundgren was primarily responsible for the murders. He pulled the trigger each time; he alone contrived the purpose and plan for the killings. The prosecutions would be successful, LaTourette believed, only if Jeffrey Lundgren were sentenced to die. The others were guilty of participation in the crime, no question—Lundgren couldn't have done what he did without their cooperation, passive and active. But none, with the possible exception of Lundgren's chief assistant in the killings, Ron Luff, was as completely guilty as Lundgren or, in LaTourette's mind, as completely evil.

Without the corroborating testimony of at least one person who had been at the barn that night, it was going to be difficult if not impossible to place the murder weapon in Jeff Lundgren's hand as each of the Avery family was killed, and it would be equally difficult to prove Lundgren's unique role in the group. Keith Johnson couldn't testify from personal knowledge about the events of April 17, 1989, or about the history of the group. He also had other liabilities as a witness. Because of Jeff's relationship with his wife Kathy, he had an obvious motive to lie about Jeff and paint him as worse than he was—or so a jury might find. And during interviews LaTourette had found Keith less than candid, mercurial, perhaps emotionally unstable. He was hardly the sort of witness upon whom to build a capital case or any other case.

Which left the need for honest, credible testimony from either Richard or Greg to convict Jeff. Like it or not, LaTourette felt he had little choice other than to take the deal offered by Richard's and Greg's attorneys. Once he did, Richard provided a videotaped statement to the ATF agents on January 21. Richard, it became clear, was an eyewitness to four of the five murders. Greg, who had seen none of the deaths, could and would confirm Richard's observations of events as he knew them on the evening of April 17. At one time Greg's diary, which LaTourette and Kowall had learned about, was considered important prosecution evidence, but in fact turned out to be not much more than religious notes.

LaTourette still would have to evaluate the relative strengths and weaknesses of the cases against the various defendants, not only as individual cases but in terms of how each case would impact on the others. And, in the more mundane but nonetheless crucial area, he had to figure out whether his small office had the capacity to prosecute all these defendants, and if not, how to supplement the staff.

But he was on his way.

At the same time LaTourette was putting together a prosecution strategy, defense attorneys were assessing their clients' positions and trying to devise an approach to minimize the penalty each would face. Extradition proceedings were the first item on the agenda.

In California, all five defendants had at first resisted extradition, apparently at Jeff's direction. California and Ohio have very similar extradition statutes.

At the February 8 review hearing the California court ordered that Jeff, Damon, Alice, Danny and Kathy be held in the San Diego County Jail pending further proceedings. After the arrest it was necessary for the initiating jurisdiction (Ohio) to submit a Governor's Warrant from the governor of that state to the governor of the state holding the prisoner, notifying the holding state of the charges pending against the defendant and requesting that the holding state surrender the defendant to the initiating state. Such request is routinely granted, but in this case the defendants, represented by court-appointed California attorneys, all challenged the Governor's Warrant. The defendants' challenges were made and strategies were plotted with the help in some cases of defense attorneys from Lake County.

Courts generally appoint the local public defender to represent an indigent defendant unless the public defender's office finds that for some reason a conflict of interest exists. Generally a conflict exists when the public defender already represents a co-defendant of the individual the defender is currently asked to represent. Representation of co-defendants by one attorney or by one firm of attorneys is almost always considered to be a conflict because the best defense for each defendant may arise through that defendant's willingness to cooperate with the authorities to the detriment of his confederate. One attorney would not conscientiously be able to advise his clients to betray each other, so a claimed conflict is almost always enough reason for a court to excuse an attorney from representation of a co-defendant.

Appointment of counsel for the group members was complicated because so many of them were subject to the death penalty, but there were built-in protections for the defense in a capital case. An attorney appointed to represent a capital defendant must meet certain criteria of experience and training. A defendant may choose for himself and hire any properly licensed attorney; even an attorney who has no criminal experience may represent a capital defendant if that defendant hires him to do so. But the court may only appoint to a capital case an attorney who has had previous experience in several murder cases and who has attended a seminar in death-penalty litigation presented by the Public Defender Commission.

As part of its statutory function the Public Defender Commission is required to provide assistance to court-appointed counsel with advice and investigation resources, and provide a staff of investigators who usually investigate not the circumstances of the crime but the background of the defendant, hoping to find information that can be used to persuade the jury that the defendant does not deserve the ultimate punishment. The commission also provides the services of a social worker who assists in preparation of death-penalty defenses and maintains a significant number of attorneys for the sole purpose of pursuing death-penalty appeals and researching legal questions relating to capital cases.

With such resources to draw on, the Lake County public defender, R. Paul LaPlante, decided to reserve the resources of *his* office for the leader of the group, the one defendant whose life was most in jeopardy —Jeff Lundgren. In fact, shortly after Jeff was arrested, LaPlante and his most senior assistant, Charles Grieshammer, flew to San Diego to confer with their most famous client. At the time rumor had it that LaPlante advised Jeff to shave before all court appearances, to lose weight and to cut his hair. The same rumors had it that Jeff said that shaving and losing weight would be no problem but that he would not be able to cut his hair because Jesus had had long hair.

Alice maintained the same position she had taken during her video-taped statement—that she had not believed that Jeff would actually kill the Averys, that she had not known that the killings would take place when they did and that she had been a battered wife and had not reported the murders out of fear for herself and her children. Her attorney in California consulted with Albert Purola, a well-known Lake County defense attorney, about Alice's best course of action.

Ultimately Alice decided to waive extradition and to return volun-tarily to Lake County to face the charges against her. Her California attorney expressed confidence that once her position was presented to a jury, Alice would be acquitted of all wrongdoing.

That the public defender was able to represent only one of the thir-teen defendants was a problem for Judge James Jackson, the presiding judge, a veteran of more than ten years on the bench. When Judge Jackson heard about the cases he knew that selection and appointment of defense counsel would be a significant, difficult job. He was deter-mined to appoint attorneys who had demonstrated themselves compe-tent defense counsel and who did not appear interested in handling the cases simply for their publicity value (as several did who wrote him offering their services, all of which he rejected). Richard and Greg retained their own private counsel, James Krivok and Gerald Gold, the public defender would, as we know, represent Jeff. Judge Jackson chose John Hurley to represent Deborah Olivarez, Robert LaForce to represent Sharon Bluntschly, Louis Turi to represent Susan Luff, Mark Ziccarelli to represent Alice Lundgren, James Koerner to represent Dennis Patrick, Clifton "Pat" Jones to represent Tonya Patrick, and J. Ross Haffey to represent Ron Luff.

On March 7, 1990, Richard Brand pled guilty to five counts of mur-der at his arraignment in front of Judge Jackson. The five counts of kidnapping were to be held in abeyance and would be dismissed at the time of his sentencing provided that he cooperated as promised with the prosecution and gave truthful testimony about the deaths of the

Averys. Richard's hand shook when he signed the guilty pleas, his voice barely audible in the small courtroom. Immediately after the hearing he signed affidavits saying that Damon had been in Kirtland between April 16 and April 18, 1989. The affidavits were necessary to dispute the claim recently raised in documents filed in California claiming that Damon had not been present at the location of the crime on the dates charged.

Richard and his memory were now completely available to the state. All other defendants had pled not guilty.

22

YE LIARS AND HYPOCRITES, YE LAWYERS

The first moves would be made by the prosecutor.

In a county with a population of approximately 250,000 people the Lake County prosecutor employed eleven assistant prosecutors in January of 1990. Some assistants were employed on a part-time basis, specializing in functions from commissioners' counsel to prosecution of sexual assault and abuse. As LaTourette marshalled his resources for the so-called cult prosecutions, it was clear to him that reassignments would have to be made and that the office would need outside help to prosecute effectively the large number of defendants charged in connection with this terrible crime.

His planning was complicated by the fact that his office was currently prosecuting two other capital cases scheduled to go on trial in March and May. But LaTourette was determined that his office would successfully prosecute all of the seven death-penalty defendants charged in Lake County, and he personally would try Jeff and Ron. So appropriate assignment of his assistants to the remainder of the trials and recruitment of special assistants were his first priority.

Two of his part-time assistants were Karen Lawson and Sandra Dray, assigned to prosecute sexual assaults of adults and children. Lawson, a delicate-featured blonde in her early thirties, had been with the public defender's office first as a law clerk, then as an attorney when LaTourette had been a public defender. Lawson had always admired LaTourette as a person and as an attorney and had served as his campaign manager when he was elected prosecutor. She was an experienced, respected trial lawyer who had been in private practice for several years. Her agreement to join the prosecutor's staff part-time to handle some of the high-visibility cases was made at some personal sacrifice because of the demands her private practice placed on her time and energy. Dray, blonde and in her mid-forties, is a partner of Lawson in private practice. Dray attended college and law school as a housewife and mother, graduating in 1981. Her ambition had been to be a prosecutor, and she had worked as a law clerk and assistant prosecutor for the previous prosecutor, John Shoop. Dray, also an experienced and respected trial attorney, had agreed to return as a part-time assistant to her first love, prosecution, when LaTourette was elected.

When the group members were first arrested and information about them was first becoming public, Lawson told LaTourette that she would like to prosecute Alice along with Sandra Dray. Lawson would later say that her interest in trying Alice Lundgren was based on her judgment that Alice, as the leader's wife, would certainly have been one of the most powerful members of the group. Lawson knew that she would not have the opportunity to try Jeff, so she wanted to try someone she felt might well have been second in importance.

LaTourette did assign Lawson and Dray to try Alice. He also decided that his assistants couldn't reasonably be asked to do both their regular jobs and the prosecutions of the cult defendants. LaTourette began to recruit attorneys from outside his office whom he was confident could serve as special prosecutors.

He first approached Joseph M. Gurley, a private attorney in Painesville, former Painesville city councilman and at the time Painesville law director. A man in his early forties of medium height, Gurley bears an uncanny resemblance to the actor Harrison Ford. He had graduated from law school at Louisiana State University in New Orleans fifteen years earlier and had served as an assistant prosecutor with John Shoop, rising to chief criminal assistant before he left the office. Gurley had tried several murder cases during his time with Shoop's office, earning himself the nickname "Mr. Murder," but he had never tried a capital case. Never personally close to LaTourette,

Gurley was surprised and flattered by the invitation and was pleased to accept.

David Joyce, recently elected prosecutor in Geauga County, the largely rural and upper-income suburban county directly south of Lake County, offered his assistance. LaTourette and Joyce had had an informal mutual assistance agreement for some months, each office offering to assist the other when appointment of a special prosecutor was necessary. A handsome, square-jawed blonde young man, Joyce was not as experienced or confident in trial as some of the others, but LaTourette nonetheless believed that he would be a valuable asset.

LaTourette also hired Thomas Lobe and Joseph Delguyd, partners in private practice and young men in their early thirties, whom he had come to know in law school. Both had been successful assistant prosecutors in neighboring Cuyahoga County, and LaTourette had the highest respect for their experience and ability. The two young men, Lobe blonde and Delguyd with dark hair and dark complexion, make a striking pair. Both were enthused about being asked to take part in the cult prosecutions.

One more problem remained to be handled. Death-penalty cases generate an astounding amount of paperwork, mostly in the form of pretrial motions. More than a hundred motions are not unusual in a single capital case. LaTourette's office was faced with seven death-penalty cases. The Ohio Public Defender Commission, as a part of its death-penalty seminar, presents each participant with a three-ring binder containing prewritten form motions regarding every issue on every phase of the trial the commission believes significant regarding a possible steering of the jury toward a less-death-penalty-prone result or toward later appellate reversal of a death penalty, perhaps even by the U.S. Supreme Court. Since death-penalty motions are likely to be similar it made little sense for each prosecutor to reinvent the wheel. Each could be given access to form responses recommended by the Ohio Prosecuting Attorneys Association to the form motions generated by the Ohio Public Defender Commission. But there was still no guarantee that each motion would be filed according to the recommended form, and there was certainly no guarantee that the various defense attorneys would not devise unique motions. And either approach would necessitate further legal research and writing.

So LaTourette decided that it would be most practical to assign one assistant full-time to respond to motions in the capital cases and apparently he felt he had the right person already on staff. Cynthia Sassé (co-author of this book) had been an assistant prosecutor since the previous November when she had been sworn in as an attorney, and had also been a law clerk with the office since shortly after LaTourette was sworn in. In her early forties, she had been a social worker at one time, had begun law school in her early thirties and had finally graduated after some eight years, with time out to have her third child. At the time she was assigned to the IV-D unit, which, under a contract with the local Department of Human Services, was responsible for collection of delinquent child support. She had made it plain to La-Tourette that she was unhappy with her position and that she was eager to become a part of the criminal-trial rotation. LaTourette believed that, although responding to death-penalty motions was not actually a part of the trial rotation, Sassé would be willing to accept the reassignment. He was right. She was scheduled to move to her new responsibilities on Monday, February 5.

LaTourette also decided to use his old friend and former employer Richard Collins as a part of the cult prosecutions. Collins, a tall gray-haired man in his late thirties, has a quiet charming manner and is well-liked and well-respected by fellow attorneys. Collins is a fine legal tactician with excellent reasoning skills. He was a part-time assistant prosecutor, serving as commissioners' counsel. LaTourette felt that Collins's insight and skill would prove valuable to the prosecutions.

Now that his staff was on board, LaTourette needed to decide which prosecutors would be assigned to which defendants and to brief us fully on the case. (Please forgive the first-person switch at this point, but it seemed to me, Cynthia Sassé, more natural and less pretentious, perhaps, than referring to myself in the third person.)

This was my first contact with the Kirtland police and my first view of the interior of the Kirtland police station, where we gathered early that morning. I was sleepy-eyed like the other prosecutors as we milled about the small cramped offices waiting for Steve LaTourette. Yarborough, his characteristic pinch of chewing tobacco in place, and Andolsek, chain-smoking as usual, seemed particularly on edge as they paced from one group to another.

When Steve did arrive he brought along copies of the police report in thick black three-ring binders that he distributed to the special prosecutors. Then we piled into our cars and followed the police to the farm.

On earlier trips to the area on my own I hadn't known which house

was the notorious one, and when we pulled into the driveway I con-
fess I was surprised. I'd expected the farm to be solitary, isolated.
Instead, it was surrounded by other homes and small businesses. Several others made the same observation.

Inside, the house seemed comfortable and well-kept. In my mind,
the image of a communal religious cult that engaged in alleged ritual-
istic acts of murder had carried with it the impression of a dark, dirty,
weirdly decorated flophouse reminiscent of the drug-culture com-
munes of the late 1960s. Instead the house, painted pale blue with
white trim, seemed almost cheerful and airy, like the comfortable old
farmhouse which it was. The master bedroom, which had been occupied by Jeff and Alice, might originally not have been intended to be a
bedroom at all. Two of the walls were filled with windows, and the
third outside wall, on the southwest side, was covered with built-in
brickwork shelves and a mantel above built-in cupboards. According
to Yarborough, Alice had reputedly kept her Miller Lite in the cupboard on the extreme southwest corner, where it was kept chilled by
the cool brick, thereby saving herself trips to the refrigerator. A photograph was found, apparently depicting the shelves after Alice had finished decorating the bedroom. The wall and the mantel contained
several black-powder guns and a powder horn. Sliding oak doors separated the bedroom from the living room.

The group had apparently kept the house in good repair, although
the roof seemed to have been leaking into at least one of the upstairs
bedrooms they'd left. The floors were well-maintained hardwood
floors. Even though the house had been unoccupied for months it
appeared to be relatively clean, with the exception of the footprints of
a raccoon that appeared to have discovered the downstairs commode.
A few board games had been left in a stack in the back room when the
group moved, and there were curtains hanging in the windows as well
as other odds and ends in the house, including clothing hanging in
one of the upstairs closets. It *could* have been a house that your average middle-class family might have just moved out of a day or so
before.

The barn was huge and quiet and cold. Yarborough and Andolsek
led us first into the small room where the taping had taken place. The
concrete-floored room was cramped and dirty, lined along the walls
with an unused workbench and free-standing storage shelves down
the center of the room, beginning about a dozen feet from the door. A
small tractor was stored in the room, as were some children's bicycles.

I noticed that a girl's bicycle leaning along the east wall was identical to the bicycle we had bought the spring before for our ten-year-old daughter Meggan.

A few at a time, we walked down the hallway between the taping and burial rooms, oppressed by its dark, dank chill. Most of the men moved down into the burial room, the almost two-foot drop broken by a small wooden stool that had been found in the room near the door. Others, particularly the women, went back through the taping room.

We also went up the uncovered wooden steps leading to the barn's second level from the taping room and peered out the window where Damon had sat on lookout. Upstairs, the barn was filled with an astonishing number of household goods in conditions ranging from new to unusable. There was also an antique car sitting in the second level of the barn.

Downstairs, the lowest level, westernmost, dirt-floored room had been cleared of trash. The pit gaped in the corner, huge and empty. Andolsek pointed out where he had discovered the children's books under the window through which the rocks had been thrown into the barn. Yarborough indicated the height of the trash, and traced the path left in the trash from the corridor to the pit.

We walked around the farm, exploring the pond behind the barn from which the stones had been taken, and the small apple orchard beside the barn. Some of the group returned to the house to examine whatever else they found of interest. Then we drove back to the Kirtland police station, where we parked to walk to the Temple Visitors' Center.

At the Visitors' Center we were met by Dale Luffman and were given a complete tour, including an explanatory film strip by Eleanor Lord, wife of Bill Lord, the site director. Eleanor Lord's tour included many of the explanations and interpretations of Temple decoration first incorporated in a tour by Jeff Lundgren, but Mrs. Lord said that this was her standard tour. The whole experience was fascinating. I had never been inside the Temple and was impressed with its simple beauty, but the religious symbolism that decorated the building and pervaded Mrs. Lord's talk was so alien to me that I felt oddly out of synch.

Yarborough then led us across the street and around the RLDS church to the embankment behind the church. He pointed out the spot where Jeff had planned to lead the group up the hillside for his assault on the Temple, as well as the church-owned houses in the area

that Lundgren had intended to take and fill with the blood of whomever had the bad luck to be in them.

We then went back to the Kirtland Police Department for a short
meeting. When we left, each of us was even more curious, fascinated
and excited by the challenge than we had been when we arrived.

23

WHATSOEVER YE SOW

The road to the end of the prosecutions began. None of us could foresee when or where the road would end. We only knew that the end would come if we did what needed to be done. Steve LaTourette worked on balancing assignments for the prosecutions, on maintaining contact with all of the law agencies involved, and forming the theory of his case for Jeff's prosecution. In some ways his load had been lightened from an unexpected quarter. The attention of the media across the nation and around the world had been drawn to the bizarre story emerging from tiny Kirtland, Ohio. Both the Kirtland police and the prosecutor's office had been swamped with requests for information. The hounding had been persistent. But on January 16 Judge Jackson, at the request of J. Ross Haffey representing Ron Luff, had issued a gag order that no further statements be made to the press except on matters of procedure. As the facts of all the cases were so intimately intertwined, Steve interpreted the order to forbid public comment on any of the cases. So the need for dealing with the media was curtailed, which left much more time for proceeding with the substance of the prosecutions.

The Kirtland police were responsible for coordinating the largest murder investigation ever seen in Lake County, which had to strain the resources of the city and the police department. Andolsek was assigned sole investigating officer on the case, but he was also required to work his regular shift, including routine road patrol. He worked constantly, pursuing financial records and other records for all of the defendants, contacting anyone in the area or in Missouri who might have had contact with the defendants or the victims and who would be willing to give him a formal statement or talk about what they might know. The task was huge. A thorough investigation of the lives of all of the adults in the group was impossible for one man. Andolsek was haunted by the thought that he might miss something in the case that surely would be the biggest of his career. Steve and Karen Kowall consulted with Andolsek and Yarborough, suggesting approaches to the evidence and providing new leads from their conversations with Brand and Winship and their attorneys. They, too, felt the strain of attempting to manage a massive murder investigation, run an office and still handle the full-time work load that was unchanged.

Stress was relieved some for everyone by the undeniable excitement of the challenge. These cases were more visible, more complex and the most serious of any that were likely to be investigated and prosecuted almost anywhere. Karen Kowall, particularly, was excited. Steve La-Tourette was eager, angry and sad, all at once. Andolsek was excited, anxious, stretched taut. And Yarborough enjoyed the challenge and the satisfaction of *finally* seeing his old adversary exactly where he felt he should be. The rest of us were mostly amazed and confused, each trying to understand what had gone so horribly wrong with a group that was formed, presumably, to see God and His works.

At 9:00 on Saturday morning, March 10, we prosecutors met with Richard Brand in the grand jury room at the Lake County Courthouse. The grand jury room is small, congested and sparsely furnished. High-ceilinged, like most of the courthouse, the large windows contribute to a feeling of openness that belies the size of the room. Upholstered swivel chairs are bolted to the floor in two rising tiers for the grand jurors. On the floor in front of the tiers sit a short table and three to four chairs. A witness chair is on a riser at the end of the room farthest from the door. Richard, with his escort of deputies, wrists handcuffed and ankles manacled, sat at the table. He was flanked on one side by Steve and on the other by his Ohio attorney James Krivok, a small dapper man who just a few months before had been LaTourette's chief criminal assistant. We prosecutors were seated in the grand-jury chairs.

This was the first time that most of us had seen Richard. All of us had viewed his videotaped statement but only Steve and Karen Kowall had talked with him before that. Rick Collins and I had met Richard when he signed an affidavit immediately after his guilty plea in a holding cell off the courtroom, attesting that Damon had been at the farm on April 16 through April 18, 1989.

Dressed now in his two-piece navy blue jail uniform, Richard was clearly uneasy. He had trouble expressing himself without relying on quotations from the "three-in-one" (that one-volume compilation of the Book of Mormon, The Doctrines and Covenants, and the Bible) which he carried with him to the meeting. His voice was soft as he told a condensed version of the story of his relationship with the Lundgren family and how Jeff had manipulated his faith and the faith of the others in the group.

For several hours Richard talked and answered questions for the prosecutors. No one except Karen Kowall, Steve and Yarborough understood what Richard was talking about when he spoke of Moroni, Mormon, Lehi and Nephi. The names were alien, and the stories about them mystifying. While we felt Richard was telling much of the truth, we also believed that in some ways, perhaps in some significant ways, he was concealing parts of what he knew and that he might even be lying about some of the things he reported. Later, most of us came to feel that our assessment had been wrong. We believed that Richard was telling the truth, at least as he remembered it. It was clear that Richard believed that he was legally guilty of the crimes to which he had pled, but that he did not feel morally responsible. The reason for the murders, he continually insisted, was Jeffrey Lundgren.

When it was apparent that Richard was exhausted and that we prosecutors also wanted to leave, Steve ended the meeting. Richard, he said, would be available to assistants preparing for trial as often and as extensively as they needed to talk with him.

After the meeting Karen Lawson, Sandy Dray and I stayed for some time talking with Yarborough and Andolsek, trying to understand something about the RLDS, the LDS and the Book of Mormon, and how in the world the book and church doctrines could have been manipulated to lead to murder. Yarborough, from his background as a "backsliding" member of the local stake, could provide some answers but unfortunately we did not have enough knowledge at that time even to know which questions to ask.

It was clear to me that if I were going to understand what had happened sufficiently to respond intelligently to specific motions I would have to read the Book of Mormon. To a person who had essentially rejected organized religion decades before, this was not an attractive prospect. An understanding of what had taken place in the group obviously would demand time and dedication. My family, which had seen little of me while I had been finishing law school and studying for the bar exam, would again have to make do with less time. My husband Greg, a federal prosecutor, would again become Mr. Mom. But there was no choice.

In Lake County indicted cases are assigned randomly by lot to one of the three common pleas or trial-level judges. The cases against Alice Lundgren, Greg Winship, Sharon Bluntschly, Deborah Olivarez and, later, Damon Lundgren, were assigned to Judge Paul Mitrovich, a former county prosecutor well known for his stiff sentences and his demand that defendants who plead guilty in his court fully admit in open court their guilt for the crimes charged. Judge James Jackson, a red-haired, florid-faced man, was assigned the cases against Susan Luff, Dennis Patrick, and Tonya Patrick. Judge Jackson, as mentioned, was also the presiding judge when the cult defendants were arraigned, and so took Richard Brand's guilty plea and would be responsible for sentencing him. Later Daniel Kraft's and Kathryn Johnson's cases were also assigned to him. Judge Martin Parks, the youngest of the three judges in seniority, was assigned the case against Ron Luff and, later, the prime case against Jeff Lundgren.

Judge Mitrovich was and is known for his insistence that his docket move swiftly and that continuances, delays, be minimized. Trial dates for all the cases assigned to him were set soon after their assignment. The prosecutors knew that Greg Winship was almost certain to plead guilty. There was no time for Steve to assign prosecutors to prepare for a trial against him. On the other hand neither Bluntschly nor Olivarez appeared to accept that even though the murders were Jeff's idea and were carried out by him, they were liable in the eyes of the law for the result.

Each woman had been charged with five counts of conspiracy to commit aggravated murder and with five counts of complicity to commit aggravated murder. Each of the counts of conspiracy and complicity named one of the Averys as a victim. A charge of conspiracy accuses a defendant of having agreed with others to commit a crime, even though that defendant may not actually have done anything to further the crime other than the agreement itself. Complicity accuses a defendant of having actively assisted another in committing a crime. Each of the women was also charged with five counts of kidnapping. A charge of kidnapping accuses the defendant of having deprived another of his or her freedom to leave, by force or by deception, for the purpose of committing certain other crimes. A kidnapping charge does not require the sort of criminal behavior most people usually think of as kidnapping—that is, taking a person by force and holding that person for ransom.

Bluntschly and Olivarez still did not believe they were guilty of any of the crimes they were charged with because they were so sure that they wouldn't have done the things they did if they hadn't been so afraid of Jeff and if they hadn't believed his assurances that the killings were necessary in order for them to see God.

Ohio, in certain instances, recognizes duress, self-defense and insanity as viable defenses. Duress is an affirmative defense, in which the defendant claims that he or she did what they did because they were under immediate threat of death or great bodily harm. However, duress is not available as a defense of a homicide. Self-defense is available only when the killer was merely defending himself from the immediate threat of death from the victim. Legal insanity is another affirmative defense in which the defendant must admit that he or she did the acts of which accused but again says that he or she should be excused because they didn't know what they were doing or because they couldn't understand that what they were doing was wrong. Some states recognize another affirmative defense called diminished capacity; Ohio does not recognize this defense. In diminished capacity the defendant tries to demonstrate that he or she wasn't legally insane at the time of the crime, but did not have the ability, because of some factor outside their control, to actually form intent to do the crime.

If the defense of diminished capacity had been available in Ohio, it's likely that both Bluntschly and Olivarez would have chosen to try their cases. But since diminished capacity was not available to them, in order to win at trial they would have had to demonstrate either that they were completely unaware that the murders were being committed in the barn while they were in the house, or that they were not even physically present at the farm at the time of the killings and did not know that the murders were going to take place. It would be difficult, if not impossible, for the women to contradict anyone who was present at the farm that night and who could establish that they had to have been aware that Jeff planned to kill the Averys then—unless, for some reason, the State was unable to find that kind of testimony against them.

On April 25 Greg Winship pled guilty to five counts of murder, just as Richard Brand had done a month and a half earlier. It now seemed that the State should have available all the testimony it could possibly need against either woman. However, there was a potential problem that arose from the peculiar Ohio law.

The origin of the common-law rule of spousal privilege is lost in history, although some feminists tend to claim it arose from the ancient legal fiction that a man and his wife were one legal person and that that person was the man. The privilege requires that one spouse may not testify against another, even if the testifying spouse wants to do so, unless the spouse to be testified against allows the testimony. In April, 1989, Jeff had "married" Richard to Sharon and Greg to Debbie. If those marriages were found to be valid Richard would be unable to testify against Bluntschly, and Greg would be unable to testify against Olivarez—unless they agreed, which they wouldn't.

In most states there would be no question that the marriage ceremonies performed by Jeff were not valid. Ohio, however, is one of the few states to recognize common-law marriage, a marriage never officiated according to the statutes of Ohio or any other state or nation. First Bluntschly's attorney, Bob LaForce, then Olivarez's attorney, John Hurley, filed motions requesting that the testimony of the women's respective "spouses" be excluded because it was prohibited by the spousal privilege.

I filed a response in Bluntschly's case, repeated in Olivarez's case, denying that the "marriages" supposedly performed by Jeff fit the standards established by Ohio law for valid common-law marriages. A valid common-law marriage requires that the spouses actually announce to each other their respective intentions that from that time on they will be married, that it is their intention at that time to be married and that afterward it should be public knowledge that the two are cohabiting as spouses and they should be publicly acknowledged to be married. I argued that the marriages in question were concealed from everyone except the other members of the group, even from the families of the spouses, and that they were not publicly known to be cohabiting as spouses, so the marriages were not valid common-law marriages and the spousal privilege did not apply. Judge Mitrovich apparently agreed and decided that Richard and Greg would be permitted to testify. We then expected to make our cases against both women.

*   *   *

I admit I cried over some of the evidence, particularly the autopsy report for Karen Avery. The clothing Karen was wearing when she was murdered was similar to clothing my own daughter might have worn at that age. Exposure to much of the evidence was more emotionally draining than I had ever expected. My children—Ben, Meggan and Jon —were at that time fifteen, eleven and five, close in age to the Avery girls at the time of their deaths. It would be a lie to say I wasn't affected.

Rick Collins and Sandy Dray were assigned to prosecute Sharon Bluntschly. Her case, scheduled for early May, was the first set for trial. They were the first to interview Richard, and they had asked me to be present for the interview because of my knowledge of the evidence and of the case. We talked with Richard in the lawyer's room of the jail, a tiny concrete-floored room, six feet wide by eight feet long with a closed-circuit surveillance camera, a small window in the steel door and a telephone on the wall that could be used only to call a corrections officer. Two or three lightweight chairs and a small table were the only furnishings.

Richard was obviously uncomfortable, unsure about how he, a confessed murderer, would be treated by people whose job was to try to send criminals to prison. For our part, we were rather impressed with Richard as a person. He was handsome, bright, articulate, with an offbeat wit. He still frequently referred to his three-in-one for help in expressing himself and said that he spent almost all his time in his cell studying Scripture, trying to understand where he went wrong and to disprove the things that Jeff had said were true.

We prosecutors found it strange that Richard, who appeared to be a sensitive young man, could speak so coldly about the murders, at least until he was talking about Karen. He was somewhat distressed when he described his part in the six-year-old's execution, but even then he seemed to be strangely remote. Clearly he had convinced himself that Jeff was responsible for the entire experience and denied any personal liability.

It was also clear that Richard disliked Sharon and felt no ties or obligations to her as a spouse. At times he said he doubted that Sharon's child was his, figuring that Jeff could have been the father, although at other times he would say he was fairly sure that he was the girl's father.

Most of all, though, he felt sorry for himself. His engineering degree and his college education were completely wasted, he said, because he wouldn't be able to use them by the time he was released from prison. He had, he said, lost the only woman he had ever loved. His life was in ruins.

Richard described months of meetings in which the death of the Averys had been discussed specifically and by implication. He was certain that Sharon would have had to understand, just as the others did, that the Averys would eventually die. Also, according to Richard, when Jeff spoke to him outside the bedrooms on the afternoon of April 17, 1989, telling him that he would help in the barn that night, Sharon was close enough so that she must have heard and she had to have known what Jeff meant.

We interviewed Richard at the jail two or three times, then met on Saturday, April 21, 1990 in mid-morning in the conference room at the prosecutor's office with Yarborough and Andolsek to go over the evidence and decide how to proceed at trial. Karen Lawson also came to this meeting to learn the background. She had just returned to work after having convalesced for six weeks from back surgery and insertion of plates in her lower back. She was still in a great deal of pain.

The session we had was long and exhausting, lasting until late afternoon. We examined hundreds of photographs of the exhumation of the bodies and dozens of photographs of the autopsies. We tried to decide whether it was necessary to delve at all into the religious beliefs of the group in order to explain Bluntschly's involvement. The sheer volume of information was so overwhelming that the discussion was unfocused, jumping from one topic to another and often interrupted with the sort of black humor that is amusing only to cops and prosecutors, and even then only in context. We weren't able to develop a theory of the case that we felt would be comprehensible to the average juror and that would explain Bluntschly's actions and her motives.

This was not good. Each case should have its own theory; the lawyer should keep that theory in mind at all times in investigating and preparing the case and should present the case at trial following the theory. The theory of any case is simply a story that logically and reasonably explains all the evidence in the case. When people do incomprehensible things for reasons totally mysterious to most of us, the theory of the case is very difficult to develop and present. To explain to a jury how a woman could be involved in the murder of three children and their parents, wouldn't it be necessary to explain the religious beliefs on which that woman acted? But how could one explain beliefs that were so esoteric that they were not explicable except through the use of a system that required reading Scripture—not as written but inside and out and backward? Even with Richard's testimony, the trial was going to be extremely difficult.

Then Bluntschly accepted a plea bargain. She would plead guilty to five counts of conspiracy to commit aggravated murder. The remaining ten counts of her indictment would be held in abeyance pending her truthful testimony in the other trials. Sharon entered her plea on May 4.

Now, as prosecutors, we could interview Sharon. She spent several hours with us in the conference room telling her story of the Lundgrens. In some ways Sharon seemed remote from the events that had occurred around her. She had difficulty remembering dates and time frames and was much less certain than Richard had been about Jeff's teachings and the implications of his doctrines. She confirmed Richard's statements about the discussion in class relating to the deaths of the Averys. She cried when she talked about specific threats to herself and when she talked about Karen Avery being carried out to the barn. She denied having played video games with the Avery children on the night of the murders but did remember that Debbie Olivarez had stopped Karen when Karen tried to leave to find her mother.

We felt that Sharon was sincere, and that she, too, was caught in denial of her involvement in the murders. Sharon was also uneasy during the meeting, although she seemed to thaw somewhat when she realized that she was not going to be badly treated.

Debbie Olivarez accepted the same plea bargain as Sharon. Her guilty plea was entered on May 9.

All now seemed to be in place for Alice's trial.

24

A TIME OF TRIAL: ALICE

The problem with proving Alice guilty as charged was that she wasn't present when the murders occurred, not even at the farm when the Avery family were killed. She was at Makro buying picnic tables and candy. Her entire relationship with Jeff and with the group would have to be demonstrated to show her guilt.

From the beginning Alice had painted herself as an abused wife. Even while the group was still intact she had occasionally, in a pique, told one or another of the women stories of Jeff's brutality to her. None of the women had ever seen evidence of physical abuse, nor had they ever heard physically violent confrontations between the two, but Alice clearly felt that she could paint a credible picture of herself as a battered wife.

In January, Alice had waived extradition and voluntarily returned to Ohio, against Jeff's instructions. Once in Ohio, she proclaimed to her appointed attorneys and to her psychologist that, in many ways, she was happier in jail than she had ever been in her marriage because she didn't have to be afraid.

In the Lake County jail, Alice quickly brought her entire cell block under her control. Jail rumor had it that no one touched the newspaper on her range until Alice had seen it, that Alice did not have to do any of her own chores, that whatever Alice wanted, Alice got. There was even a persistent rumor that Alice was regularly invited to the office of the jail administrator, Helen Lukacs, for coffee and cookies.

When Steve inquired about that rumor, Lukacs denied it, but the jailhouse rumors said that the coffee breaks stopped after the inquiry.

One of the inmates who was on Alice's range for several weeks wrote a note to the prosecutors, claiming that Alice was bragging that she was going to be acquitted and get off scot-free, and that she would then write a book about her experiences that she intended to call *Glamours*. Alice was telling everyone, according to the note, that she was going to be rich from sales of the book and that she would buy a little white house for herself and her children where they would live happily ever after.

There was also a rumor that, when it became obvious that Debbie was going to be one of the star witnesses against Alice, Alice said, "When we get to Marysville [the Ohio women's prison], I'm going to kill that bitch."

Where Sharon was vague, Debbie was sharp. Where Sharon could not remember details, Debbie could remember almost everything with uncanny precision. Where Sharon was vulnerable, Debbie appeared to be strong. Several of us liked Debbie and were grateful for the wealth of detail in her information, but we could not understand how she, a mother and an apparently strong person, could have participated in the murder of children. Sandy and I, mothers ourselves, particularly could not comprehend how such a thing could have happened to Debbie and how she could have done what she did.

But whatever had happened, the facts that Richard and Sharon and Debbie and Greg remembered about Alice were beginning to make it plain that Alice had played a major role, in many ways second only to Jeff. Karen Lawson and Sandy and I came to feel that Alice bore a major role of the responsibility for the murders, if only because she was the only one who could have reasonably stopped them, and even if the only way to stop them was to blow up Jeff's scam in his face and tell the group the truth.

In keeping with Alice's theory of the case, her attorneys filed a motion requesting to be allowed to use the battered woman's syndrome in her defense. The Ohio Supreme Court, only a few months before, had ruled for the first time that the battered woman's syndrome was available as a matter of expert testimony when a woman had killed her spouse and was claiming that she had committed the murder out of fear and in self-defense. In the State's response, I argued that the battered woman's defense was available only to a woman who had killed her batterer, not to someone who had killed an innocent third party. The trial court ruled that testimony regarding the battered woman's syndrome was inadmissible.

Trial was scheduled for Monday, June 4. The final pretrial was set for May 23. On May 30, Mark Ziccarelli, attorney for the defendant, filed an affidavit of disqualification with the Chief Justice of the Ohio Supreme Court, seeking to disqualify Judge Mitrovich from serving as trial judge on the grounds that he was biased against the defendant. The judge denied any bias. According to Ohio law, once an affidavit of disqualification has been filed, the assigned trial judge loses all authority to proceed further with the case until the question of disqualification is resolved.

On June 15 the Ohio Supreme Court decided that Judge Mitrovich should not be disqualified. On June 22 Judge Mitrovich entered an order that trial would begin on July 24. This meant that Alice, the most difficult of the defendants to convict because, as mentioned, she was not physically present at the time of the murders, would be the first of the defendants to be tried.

While the legal maneuvering was taking place, we were interviewing witnesses and completing the theory of the case against Alice. From the interviews with the group members, including an interview with Keith Johnson, Sandy, Karen Lawson and I concluded that Alice had actually been Jeff's cheerleader, that she had been the glue that held the group together, and that Jeff could not have carried out any of his manipulations without her support.

Keith Johnson reported in his interview that on the evening of April 17, when Alice brought her two youngest children to the Patricks' apartment, she had had a conversation with him in which she had said, "The fog is blood red at the farm tonight."

Karen and Sandy very much wanted to be able to use that statement in Alice's trial, but they were not comfortable with using Johnson as a witness. He seemed to be unstable. One of the Kansas City ATF agents had reported that Johnson had said to him, "I've been thinking a lot about this whole thing. Maybe if Jeff isn't the prophet, I am." The agent asked Johnson if he really thought he was the prophet and he replied, "No, I guess not."

After the prosecutors as a group interviewed Johnson, he confided to Sandy that he wanted to warn her about what he intended to do that night. He said that since he was back in the area for a short time he was going to go to Chapin Forest, to the spot where Jeff had claimed that the treasury, including the Sword of Laban, was hidden. Johnson said that he was going to look under the rock where he believed the treasure to be. But he wanted the prosecutors to know that the treasure was guarded by an angel who would permit only God's prophet to come near the treasure. The angel would decapitate any unworthy person who attempted to uncover the treasure. Johnson said that since he was not the prophet, if the angel were there he would undoubtedly be killed. Even so, he said, he just had to know whether Jeff had lied about the treasure. If the treasure was not there, he would know that Jeff was not a prophet. If the treasure was there, then Jeff had been right and clearly he was a prophet. Johnson said that he was telling Sandy about his proposed expedition so that if he were found dead in the park the prosecutors would know that they were prosecuting God's prophet.

Johnson later also said to me that there were many times in the wilderness when he had thought about killing Jeff, that he wished now that he had killed Jeff when he had the chance. He hated the man, he said.

Sandy and Karen decided they could not risk putting Keith Johnson on the witness stand. They could not be sure what he would say this makes for a dangerous witness.

Sandy and I also visited the Cuyahoga County coroner's office to interview the pathologists who had done the autopsies of the Averys. Dr. Elizabeth Balraj and her assistants who had worked on the case, including Sharon Rosenberg, the trace-evidence specialist, were all present at the conference. We went over the evidence and the photographs with the pathologists and discussed what could and what could not be concluded from the observations the doctors had made. Sandy and I confirmed our understanding that Jeff had shot Dennis in the back, not in the heart, and had shot Cheryl and the girls in various places, not all in the head, as he had told the group in the wilderness.

We also learned that the victims, with the exception of those with head wounds, probably lived several minutes after they were shot, and would have been capable of movement and speech if they hadn't been bound and gagged. We learned that it was quite possible that the lime, which probably had been intended to hasten decomposition, may actually have retarded it, inasmuch as certain types of lime have that effect and the bodies were not as decomposed as one might have assumed they would be.

Even given the nature of their jobs and the number of corpses they had examined, the doctors seemed to be particularly upset by the obviously cold-blooded nature of the Averys' executions. Dr. Jiraki, who had examined Karen Avery's body, was clearly angry.

Sharon Rosenberg, a short, stocky woman with the face of a cherub and a prep-school accent, had examined the Averys' clothing for evidence. For the most part, the holes in the clothing, which Sharon called "defects," corresponded perfectly with the wounds the doctors had found. There were some anomalous holes, however, which she could not explain and which she felt must have been due to decomposition or wear. Sharon Rosenberg was certain that none of her findings contradicted in any way the observations of the pathologists.

Sharon warned us about the clothing. The odor, she explained, was quite strong because the clothing had been exposed to decaying flesh for such a long time and some shreds of flesh still clung to it. Also, she said, simply the fact that the clothing had been buried with five people increased fivefold any odor that clung to the garments. She took us down to the cooler in the cellar, which also contained racks of other clothing and a fresh corpse, to give us a brief exposure to the odor she had tried to describe. Exposure for only a few seconds was enough to convince us that Rosenberg had not exaggerated. It was also sufficient to convince Sandy that she wanted to bring the clothing into the courtroom to impress the jury with the reality of the deaths.

Hours were spent combing over evidence. At one point, defense attorneys and prosecutors examined the evidence that had been transported to Lake County from California, where it had been seized from the Lundgrens' motel room and storage locker and from the motel room that had been rented by Johnson and Kraft. The evidence was stored in the property room in the Lake County jail, where it took up several shelves and quite a bit of floor space.

The .50–caliber rifle in its case was a beautiful weapon, deadly and frightening to see. Cheryl Avery's trunk, packed full of Jeff's ammunition, survival manuals and at least a dozen knives, sat pushed up against one wall. In the trunk we also found a large purple banner, about three feet wide by two feet high. The banner was decorated with a spread-winged eagle, its talons extended, and a seven-pointed star. The banner was Jeff's battle flag, designed by Danny and made by Alice.

All five of us were amazed by the juxtaposition of incongruous items. The tools of death were side-by-side with religious books and tracts and with photograph albums portraying the Lundgrens as a "normal" American family. A school project signed by Kristen Lundgren said: "I love my Daddy."

Joe Gibson, Ziccarelli's partner and co-counsel, is tall and suave. His father, William Gibson, is Judge Mitrovich's bailiff. At one point Ziccarelli commented to no one in particular that he did not understand the reason for the murders. I said, trying to be clever, "The devil made him do it," and Gibson responded vehemently that he believed that that was exactly what had happened. He just could not explain Jeff to himself on any grounds except that the man was purely evil.

After an hour or so we left the evidence room and took the banner and a few other pieces of evidence with us. The battle flag would appear in all the trials.

July 24 finally arrived. The small courtroom, located in the basement of the courthouse, is attractive and modern in design. The walls are paneled in a dark-stained oak, with the bench, the jury box, the counsel tables, the bar and the visitors' pews in matching oak. Sandy and Karen had arranged with the judge and his bailiff that I would sit immediately behind the trial table in the spectators' seats since there was not room for three prosecutors and a police officer at the trial table. Karen and Sandy were tense but confident. They believed that Alice was guilty of all the crimes she had been charged with; they believed that they would be able to convince a jury that she was guilty.

Alice's physical appearance, when we first saw her, was a surprise. We had heard that she had lost weight, but we were unprepared for the extent of the change. According to jail rumor, she would eat her own meal, follow it with all the leftovers she could find, and then force herself to vomit. However she had achieved what she had done, Alice had shed almost half her bulk. She appeared thin and frail, dressed in a long black skirt and a blouse with a Peter Pan collar and a black bow. Her hair was cut short and curled and she wore oversize horn-rimmed glasses, giving her face a tentative, owlish appearance. Most of the time she was grim-faced, with the corners of her large, mobile mouth pulled down as far as they would go.

Judge Mitrovich insists that trials in his court proceed expeditiously, no wasted time, just as he expects his docket to move efficiently. He limited the voir-dire questioning and required that the attorneys not stray from his preapproved area of interrogation. Sandy conducted voir dire for the State, pacing back and forth in front of the jury box as is her habit in court. Gibson examined the jury for the defense, maintaining a cool, calm demeanor before the prospective jurors.

The jurors, including three alternates, were seated on the first day of the trial. The following morning, one of the jurors reported that she was too ill to go forward. She was excused and replaced with the first alternate.

After the juror was excused the jury was taken on a jury view of the crime scene, which had been requested by the State. The jurors were loaded onto a bus, accompanied only by the bus driver, who was not permitted to speak with them, and by the bailiff. Alice and her attorneys followed in a deputy sheriff's patrol car. Sandy and I rode in a second patrol car. Karen stayed behind to do final polishing on her opening statement. The bus and the patrol cars pulled into the parking lot of the Red Roof Inn, then into the parking lot of the Temple Visitors' Center. Finally the jury was taken to the farm, where they toured the house and the barn, individually approaching the pit along boards laid down to protect their shoes from the mud.

After the jury returned, opening statements were made and testimony began. In her opening statement Karen painted Alice as not only Jeff's cheerleader but the power behind the throne. She told the jury that the evidence would show that Alice was just as responsible for the deaths of the Averys as anyone else in the barn, even though she wasn't physically there.

For the defendant, Gibson naturally emphasized that Alice had not been present at the barn that night, that Jeff Lundgren was an evil man, that he was solely responsible for the murders of Dennis, Cheryl,

Trina, Becky and Karen Avery and that the only reason Alice was on trial was that she had the misfortune to be married to a monster.

The first witness for the State was Marlene Jennings, Cheryl Avery's best and only friend in Ohio. Mrs. Jennings, a Mormon housewife, had come to know Cheryl Avery because Karen Avery was the same age as Kate, the youngest of the Jennings' four children. The two children had met when the Averys lived in Kirtland, and their mothers had quickly become very good friends.

Marlene Jennings, a plain, quiet-spoken woman, described each of the Averys. She had known Cheryl Avery to be an ideal RLDS housewife, industrious, religious and submissive to her husband—not what Jeff and Alice had said. She told what she knew about the Averys' financial problems and mentioned the one time she had seen Jeff and Alice Lundgren at the Avery home. Apparently Jeff had been delivering dirty laundry to the Averys while Alice waited in the car! She also identified a family portrait of the Averys, taken in 1986, and a small snapshot she had taken of the family in their Kirtland home.

Sandy ended her direct examination of Marlene Jennings by asking her to tell about the last telephone contact she had had with the Averys, just a few days before their deaths, when Dennis had refused to call Cheryl to the phone. This was unusual behavior for the Averys and seemed to indicate that they were cutting their ties to anyone outside the group. Marlene Jennings finished by stating that she had not seen the Avery family since they suddenly disappeared in the spring of 1989. The defense had very few questions for Mrs. Jennings.

The State followed with the testimony of Deputy Ron Walters, who graphically described the scene at the barn as the bodies were being exhumed. As Karen led him step by step through January 4, Deputy Walters identified and described photographs of the excavation and evidence-gathering. At one particularly dramatic moment Karen asked Walters, who had just described the removal of Trina Avery's body from the pit, if there was anything more he remembered about that. Walters said that he could still vividly see a red liquid streaming from the body into the pit as the corpse was lifted free. That drew vigorous objections from the defense, which contended that it was overly gruesome and prejudicial. Those objects were overruled. Again, the defense had very few questions.

Next, Dr. William Downing testified that he had observed the scene in the barn, that he had requested that the Cuyahoga County coroner perform the autopsies while he observed, and that he had prepared the death certificates for the Averys. The defense had few questions.

Dr. Stanley Seligman, who had performed two of the autopsies, represented the Cuyahoga County pathologists. He described the autopsies one at a time, beginning with Karen's, and identified the photographs that illustrated each autopsy. The defense had no questions.

One photograph that the prosecutors had hoped to use was judged too inflammatory and prejudicial. It showed Cheryl Avery's face, the only face that had been identifiable. The tape had been removed and the face was fixed in what appeared to be a silent scream. The jury was not allowed to see it.

Sharon Rosenberg followed Dr. Seligman. The clothing, which had been stored for weeks in a freezer in the local funeral parlor, had been sprinkled with pink odor-retarding crystals by Chief Yarborough. The crystals, though, had little effect as Rosenberg pulled each piece of clothing out of the body bags they were stored in and described it and its evidentiary significance. Rosenberg and Sandy, who was examining her, wore plastic surgeons' gloves for handling the clothing. Karen held a tissue filled with Vicks Vaporub to her nose. She came near to having to leave the courtroom when she noticed that a lock of Cheryl Avery's hair still clung to the hood of her sweatshirt. The defense had no questions.

The State now followed with the testimony of Ron Andolsek, who was on the stand for some two hours. He described his interview with Alice the day following the murders, the exhumation of the bodies and the subsequent investigation. He identified numerous exhibits, many of which he had made himself, including a diagram of the farm and of the placement of the bodies as they were discovered in the pit. Andolsek was a calm, competent witness. He appeared thorough and unbiased, just the demeanor every prosecutor hopes that a testifying police officer will display. The defense had some questions for Andolsek, but there was really little he could say that would help or harm Alice.

Rick Van Haelst, looking cool and dapper, his voice musical, testified about his investigation and the subsequent arrest of the Lundgrens in San Diego. Karen asked Van Haelst to identify the videotaped statement Alice had given after her arrest, then the tape was played for the jury. For the first time, in a darkened courtroom on a television monitor positioned no more than six feet from the jury box, the jury saw Alice as she had looked more than six months earlier and heard her voice for the first time. She admitted that she had not believed that Jeff was a prophet for some time before the murders, and they heard her say that you would have to be stupid not to know what was going on. A sigh passed through the courtroom when the tape was finished.

On cross-examination the defense emphasized Alice's interest in seeing that her children would be cared for before she agreed to give her statement, and implied that she had been coerced into saying things she did not really mean through her anxiety for the well-being of her children. But even here the cross-examination was not vigorous, and it was becoming increasingly clear that everyone was waiting for Alice's co-defendants to testify.

They were not disappointed. Dressed in her navy-blue jail smock, pants and slippers, Debbie Olivarez took the stand first. As she limped into the courtroom to testify against her cousin's wife, her face was pale and drawn with physical pain from her back injury and, doubtless, with the stress of testifying.

Karen Lawson began by having Debbie introduce herself to the jury, then Debbie told about her lifelong acquaintance with Jeff, about first having met Alice in junior high school. Karen led Debbie to describe her life as it had been just before she came to Kirtland, and then asked her to talk about her first visit with Jeff and Alice in November of 1987, and her second visit in December of that year. While Debbie was describing the second visit, Karen asked her to tell about Alice's role in the group. Debbie replied:

> She was Jeff's wife. She was his confidante. He would say that many times before he taught classes he would talk to her about the things that he was going to teach, and she was mother . . .

During her testimony Debbie talked about the check for the proceeds from the sale of her house, which she had never seen but which Alice had endorsed. She told about Alice's instructing and chastising the women, and her warnings to them to be carnal, sensual and devilish. She described Alice's privileged life with the group, including the Red Lobster party trays, the lack of any responsibility for any sort of housework, the naps until noon and the antiquing sprees following a temper tantrum. She described the classes when Alice would be seated at Jeff's left hand when the murders of the Averys were discussed. Then a particularly telling exchange took place (referred to earlier):

Q. And every one of these classes you were in attendance?

A. Yes.

Q. Alice Lundgren was there?

A. Yes.

Q. How were the Averys going to die?

A. When it was first discussed, Jeff said he found out that in the Scriptures it is written that people are to be destroyed a certain way, men, women and children.

Q. How were men to be destroyed?

A. That they were to be cut in two.

Q. How were women to be destroyed?

A. That they were to be stripped and have their insides cut out.

Q. How were children to be destroyed?

A. They were to be picked up by the feet and dashed in the head.

Q. Dashed in the head?

A. Yes.

Q. What do you mean?

A. Picking them up by the feet and hitting them against the wall.

Q. Do you recall conversations concerning the death of Dennis, Cheryl, Trina, Rebecca and Karen Avery?

A. Yes, I do.

Q. Would you tell the ladies and gentlemen of the jury about those conversations?

A. One day Jeff and Alice and I were sitting in the kitchen, and Jeff said that he was still looking to see if that was the way that the Averys were to be destroyed. And he said that he wasn't sure about Becky because he didn't know whether to place her in the woman category or the child category.

Q. She was thirteen?

A. I thought she was approximately eleven.

Q. Okay. What, if anything, did the defendant Alice Lundgren say?

A. Alice said that if she—that it would depend on whether she had started her period or not, if she would be classified as a woman or a child.

Q. I'd like to call your attention to March of 1989. Do you have —did you have an occasion to be alone with Alice Lundgren at any time?

A. Yes, I did.

Q. Tell the ladies and gentlemen of the jury on what occasion that was?

A. Alice and I frequently went to the grocery store together. And one incident in particular, Alice and I went to a store, a grocery store in Chardon.

Q. What grocery store was that?

A. Giant Eagle.

Q. How did you get there?

A. We drove in the truck.

Q. Who drove?

A. Alice.

Q. What, if any, conversation did you have, and specifically, what did this defendant say to you?

A. At that time it wasn't the Averys that were just going to be destroyed, there would be ten people.

Q. Who were the ten?

A. The ten people were the Averys, Dennis, Tonya, and Molly Patrick, Richard Brand and Sharon Bluntschly.

Q. What did she say—Alice Lundgren say in that regard?

A. I was questioning what made Sharon and Richard different from Greg and myself. I said none of us are perfect and I don't understand what makes their sin different than my sin. How do—how am I supposed to know what makes us different, and how can I correct that? And she said that they were ripened in iniquity and they cannot change.

Q. What does that mean?

A. They were so sinful there was no help, no hope that they would change and repent.

Q. And this conversation was in March of 1989?

A. Yes.

Debbie also described Alice's visit to her bedroom on the morning of April 17, when Alice told her that five more people would be going to the wilderness, and she talked about their trip to the store that afternoon. Debbie remembered Alice and Jeff visiting the Averys to select which of their things the group would take to the wilderness.

She described the evening of April 17, 1989, when the Averys were led out to the barn one at a time. And she talked about Alice's telephone call, just minutes after Karen had left to go to her death. She described the class after the murders, told about the trip Alice, Jeff and Damon made to the Red Roof Inn. She told about Alice's decisions about the wilderness trip—made when Jeff wasn't able to control himself and the group.

Debbie then testified about the six months in the wilderness, and described Alice's peculiar role in preparing the women for the dance of Intercession:

One afternoon she had Susie, Kathy, Sharon and myself in the tent, and Tonya was there part of the time since at that time Tonya was Jeff's second wife.

And she instructed us about what we were supposed to do, how we were supposed to act, that women were created with—with three holes in which to be pierced whether that was orally, vaginally or anally. And she described how we needed to come in and take off our clothes, and that the underpants were to be the last thing off.

When we dressed they were to be the first thing put on.

And when the dance was over we were to lay on the floor with our faces down until we were told to rise.

Debbie identified the battle flag. She described Alice's rage and her physical attack on Jeff when she realized he was spending time with Kathy. She reported Alice's departure from Mack's Creek, which ended her direct examination.

The defense tried to imply that even if Debbie were telling the truth about some of her story, she was embroidering and exaggerating the part about Alice because she wanted to be sure she would receive as favorable a sentencing recommendation as possible from the State. The defense tried to get Debbie to admit that everyone, *including* Alice, was deathly and justifiably afraid of Jeff. They wanted Debbie to say that Alice was beaten and her life was threatened by Jeff. Debbie would not give them what they wanted.

During the recess following Debbie's testimony, Alice claimed to have been taken suddenly ill and court was recessed early for the day. The next morning Alice again claimed to be ill, but medication was administered and the nurse was ordered to remain with Alice at all times to observe her behavior. Alice quickly recovered and testimony resumed.

Debbie was followed by Sharon, who described her early life with the Lundgrens when she was, in effect, the family's maid. She talked about the classes on violence and death in which Alice would often be called on to explain some idea Jeff couldn't articulate. She also, like Debbie, described Alice's constant efforts to teach her to be carnal, sensual and devilish, and her participation in the disciplinary sessions:

Q. What, if any, classes did Alice Lundgren conduct?

A. Alice taught—from what I understood, her responsibility was to be over the women. And so she taught that to be a woman was to be submissive, was to be—to do the biddings of your husband.

Q. Did Alice ever give you any personal instructions?

A. Yeah.

Q. What were they?

A. She said that what was in men was what was in every woman. And what she wanted me to work on was being carnal, sensual and devilish. And that included a Tina Turner concert videotape that she had gotten for me specifically. And she had talked about, although she may not be the most beautiful woman in the world to look at, that what came—

Q. Who might not be the most beautiful woman in the world to look at?

A. Tina Turner.

Q. Please continue.

A. But it was what came from the inside, and how she moved, her body language. She—how she looked, how she spoke, and that was what I was to become like.

Q. Did Alice Lundgren follow these instructions herself?

A. That's a yes and a no. It kind of depended on the day. I think sometimes she was—she was that way. Other times her and Jeff fought.

Sharon described Alice's role in convincing the group that Jeff was a prophet:

Q. When did you first hear him be called a prophet?

A. I don't recall. I know that people from the outside of the group started to say how Jeff called himself a prophet. And he said, "But I'm not calling myself a prophet." But then it ended up being that he called himself a prophet and Alice said that he was a prophet.

Q. When, if ever, did you hear Alice call him a prophet?

A. There were times when she would say to us about believing who he is, that he is the prophet. And sometimes that was in a very—a very loving, kind way. And other times it was almost like, it was yelled in our faces, you know, "Believe who this man is."

Sharon also talked about letters she had written at Alice's instruction, following form letters that had been composed by Alice. She, too, described Alice's privileged lifestyle and her manipulation of Jeff. Sharon related conversations she had had with Jeff and Alice about the planned killing of the Averys:

After Jeff had described what he was going to do to the Averys in Madison, at one point he was upset with me. I wasn't doing something right, and he said, "Well, do you think I need to take you over with me so you can watch?" And I knew what that meant. That meant that I wouldn't be coming back. So that—that conversation was brought up later. And I remember one time Alice said, "Do you want to go over and watch what's being done to the Averys?" And it was like—it was in the living room, I remember, and her voice was high.

About Alice's role in the group, Sharon said that: "If Jeff wasn't around then he said at one point that Alice stood in his stead. Whatever she said you did, and you didn't question it. And if you questioned it and it got back to him, you'd hear about it."

Sharon talked about her memory of her trip to the bank with Alice on April 17, and nearly broke into tears when she repeated Alice's remark: "Tonight's the night for the Averys, and I've known for a long time that you and Richard would be in the pit with them."

She talked about the night the Averys were killed, and the remarkable class afterward. She told of the incident in which Jason nearly went to the barn while the bodies were being buried. She spoke of the wilderness, and of threats that revolved around the murders:

> The Averys were brought up several times. And I remember one time she said—it was on the picnic tables under the tarps outside, she had brought up the Averys. And she said, "Are you going to do what you're supposed to do?" In other words, get to see God. "Five people were killed. Are you going to—did that happen for nothing?"

When the women were preparing for the dance of Intercession, Sharon remembered that Alice said:

> "For all the suffering that he's gone through for you this is the least that you can do for him, to bring him a moment of joy, and put salve on the wound."

Sharon's story, similar to Debbie's, reinforced it, but it was also from her own individual experience.

Once more the defense attempted to show with Sharon, as it had with Debbie, that she was embroidering her story and that it would be much more accurate to say that Alice had been in a position no different than that of any other member of the group. Sharon, like Debbie, refused to agree.

Shar now told the story of her involvement with Alice and Jeff and her life with the group. Particularly, she talked about Alice's attempts to persuade her to stay when she had decided to leave and Alice's abusive participation in the session immediately before she left. The defense tried to show Shar to be a liar, but she stuck to her story.

*   *   *

The State called Dr. Phillip Bouffard, a handwriting expert from the Lake County forensic laboratory, to identify the endorsement on the back of the check for Debbie's house, the form letters to Richard's employer and Sharon's parents, and a sheet of instructions for the dance of Intercession as having been written by Alice. It then rested.

Now it was time for the defense.

The defendant's evidence took one day to present. Through character witnesses from the local RLDS the defense tried to show that the views Alice had adopted about religion and church teachings were not radical or even unusual. But one of Alice's witnesses made it plain that he was present only because he was subpoenaed and not because he had wanted to testify on her behalf.

Then Alice took the stand. She spoke softly but clearly, appearing almost demure and totally controlled. She denied that her role in the group had been a power one. She said that Jeff had always been a terrible husband, that he had been continually abusive and that he threatened her with a gun in their bedroom during their arguments but never spoke when he did it. That, she said, was why no one in the group understood that she lived in constant fear.

Alice called Jeff "a cold-blooded murderer" and said that she would have left him and turned him in to the authorities if it were not for their son Damon. She couldn't bear, she said, to turn in her son. She testified that after the murders Jeff had threatened her with a gun and she was too afraid for her life and the lives of her children to tell any one of the police or FBI agents about the murders the following day.

Alice swore that she did not really believe that Jeff would carry out the murders, that she did not know that the Averys would be killed the night of the seventeenth of April and that she had left the house to go to Makro that evening because Jeff had ordered her to do so. She also said that she had called the house before she returned because that was what Jeff had instructed her to do.

She went on to testify that she thought that all the talk about killing the Averys was just an Abraham/Isaac test of faith and that she didn't know that a pit was being dug in the barn. She said that none of the group members had told her what was happening.

When Mark Ziccarelli's direct examination of Alice was finished he returned to his chair from the podium. Before he was seated Sandy Dray was on her feet.

"Mrs. Lundgren, you're a liar! Aren't you?" She shouted the words. Alice denied that she had lied, but Sandy reminded her that she had already admitted that she had lied to the FBI and that some of her statements on the videotape had been lies according to her own testimony. Alice acknowledged that she had lied on those occasions but insisted that now she was telling the truth.

Sandy questioned her about the incriminating testimony that the former group members had given about her, and asked her if those people were lying. No, said Alice, they weren't lying, they were just mistaken. She refused to say that the things she had denied were true were deliberate lies, maintaining that the witnesses were "mistaken."

When asked about her efforts to help the women become more attractive to men by teaching them to be carnal, sensual and devilish, Alice denied that the Book of Mormon called such a state ultimate evil. She said such attributes were just those of a feminine woman. During this exchange Alice's dislike for and jealousy of Shar became apparent when she stated in a waspish tone that Shar did not need any such help. After realizing her mistake she quickly followed with the mild comment that Shar was a very attractive young lady.

Sandy pressed Alice hard about her alleged ignorance of the preparation of the pit and her claim that none of the group members had told her what Jeff was planning.

Sandy asked, "Are you telling us that no one ever said to you, "Holy schmoly, Mom, do you know what Dad's doing out in the barn?' " Alice said she hadn't been told.

Later, Sandy questioned Alice's assertion that she hadn't known what was going to happen as she was on her way to Makro that night. "So," she said, "you just said, 'I'm just on my way to Makro'?" as she duck-walked toward the courtroom door.

Sandy also brought up to Alice the letter she had written to her mother from jail that had been passed to the prosecution by the sheriff's department. In the letter Alice had said that her only hope was to convince the jury that she, too, was a victim of Jeff.

By the end of the cross-examination Alice's assertions were shown either to be false or ridiculous, but her composure never slipped. The defense presented one more witness, the service manager from the Honda dealership where Greg had had his Honda repaired on the seventeenth. Alice had testified that she had taken Greg to drop off his car at the dealership, and according to the time on the service order, if this were true, Alice could not have gone with Sharon to the bank as Sharon had testified.

The following day the State presented Greg Winship in rebuttal. Greg testified that Ron, not Alice, had taken him to the Honda dealership, then testified about the comments Alice had made to him when she had driven him to pick up his car that afternoon.

The defense concentrated on the fact that Greg was out on bond because his parents had been able to raise the money for his bail. The questions upset Greg; he felt they were unfair to the sacrifice his parents had made for him, but that didn't seem to influence the jury.

After a recess the State presented its closing argument. Sandy reviewed for the jury the testimony of the witnesses and, with the aid of charts outlining the elements of the offenses, pointed out how the testimony had shown that Alice was guilty beyond a reasonable doubt of all the charges. Sandy concluded by saying:

Common sense tells you that when [Alice] left that farm on April seventeenth she knew what was going to happen. She had a part to play. She played it. She did what she was supposed to do. And quite clearly, you see the evidence of what the other people were supposed to do.

She could have, with three of her natural children, these children that she was so concerned about, she could have gone to the Kirtland police station. She could have told them, "Stop this. Stop this hideous, awful, despicable, vile act that's going to happen."

But she didn't.

And she could have told the FBI, because she was safe on April eighteenth when she was sitting in the car with them, "My God, do you know what we did last night?" Not then, either.

And when she left Davis, West Virginia, after having a fight with Jeffrey Don Lundgren, not because he and she were murderers, but because she did not want to live in a polygamist relationship, ladies and gentlemen. She would tolerate his murders, but she would not tolerate his indiscretions with Tonya Patrick and with Kathy Johnson. And Kathy Johnson was the final straw.

Now, when she leaves Davis, West Virginia, do you think that decency, that concern for the dead bodies of the Avery family played any role in her considerations? She's free. She is away from this man that she is so afraid of, that she fears. She has three of her natural children with her. Does she go to the authorities? No.

And from that witness stand yesterday she told you that she never would have gone—she never would have told anyone that the Averys were lying in a pit in Kirtland, Ohio. She wouldn't have told anybody because she knew she was as much involved as Jeffrey Don Lundgren, as Damon Paul Lundgren, as Richard Eugene Brand, as Daniel David Kraft, as Ronald Boyd Luff, Deborah Olivarez, Sharon Bluntschly, Gregory Winship, and all the rest of them.

Ladies and gentlemen, we believe that the State of Ohio has carried its burden beyond a reasonable doubt.

This defendant, along with all the others, agreed that the Avery family would die, that they would die in the vile manner that you see before you today.

She promoted, she helped, she encouraged, and she did her job, and she is just as guilty as if she had been in the barn that night putting duct tape around Karen Avery's head, putting duct tape around the feet of Trina Avery, putting duct tape around the hands of Rebecca Avery, and of her parents, Dennis Avery and Cheryl Avery.

She is just as guilty of complicity. She is just as guilty of conspiracy. And she is just as guilty of kidnapping as if she had done those acts herself, and pulled the trigger herself.

I believe that when you examine all of the evidence and all of the testimony that you have had before you, that you have had to consider, you will also tell Alice Elizabeth Lundgren that she is a liar.

I believe that you will tell her that she is a liar by finding her guilty of all fifteen charges.

Thank you.

The defense argued that there was no real evidence that Alice was in any way responsible for the deaths of the Averys. They emphasized that she was not even present at the farm that night, and once again they claimed that the person truly responsible for these terrible crimes was Jeffrey Lundgren, whom they compared to Adolf Hitler. Once again they claimed that the only reason Alice Lundgren was on trial was because she was married to Jeffrey, that the entire trial had been about how bad Jeff was, and that the State's evidence did not even approach a showing that Alice was guilty of the charged crimes.

On rebuttal Karen said that if Jeffrey Lundgren was Adolf Hitler, then Alice Lundgren was the Angel of Death, Josef Mengele. She reminded the jurors of the testimony they had heard about the influence Alice had had over Jeff, and asked them to consider that if anyone could have prevented the murders, Alice could have. She could have stopped by the police station on her way to Makro and kept those children from being killed, and kept her own son from being a murderer.

The court instructed the jury on the law, and the jury retired to deliberate. No verdict was reached that day. Waiting for a verdict is easily the most stressful part of being a trial lawyer. At that point there's nothing more to be done no matter how many changes one might make in hindsight. The matter has been submitted to twelve strangers, who may or may not agree that one's side is in the right. Nerves are stretched near to the cracking point!

At mid-morning the following day the jury announced that they had reached a verdict. The attorneys and the defendant filed into the courtroom, spectators filled the rest of the benches. The eighteen-year-old forewoman of the jury handed the verdicts to the bailiff, who handed them to the judge. Judge Mitrovich examined each verdict form to be sure that it had been properly completed, then began to read. The first count was a guilty verdict. Georgia Kraft, Danny's mother, began slowly applauding. I was relieved and did not really listen to the verdicts on counts two through five since it seemed that they would also have to be guilty verdicts. Then count six was read, and it was also guilty. Another sigh of relief. Again, counts seven through ten were consistent with the verdict in count six. Count eleven was a guilty verdict, as were counts twelve, thirteen, fourteen and fifteen. It was a conviction on all counts!

Alice, incongruously, smiled and hugged her attorneys. The court ordered that a presentence report be completed by the probation department prior to sentencing, and adjourned. The prosecutors congratulated each other and Chief Yarborough, tears in our eyes. The first of the cult trials had been completed.

25

A TIME OF TRIAL: JEFF

While the attention of Lake County was riveted to accounts of Alice's trial in the local newspapers, and listeners were entranced by the daily live coverage of the testimony from the courtroom carried by the local radio station, legal dueling was also proceeding in Jeff's case.

Jeff had been returned to Lake County in mid-April from San Diego, where he had finally decided to abandon his fight against extradition. The California Supreme Court had turned down Damon's appeal of his extradition order just a few days before, and Jeff, Kathy and Danny had decided not to follow the same fruitless route.

The foursome had been confined in the San Diego County jail for four months and had made court appearances shackled together before the judge's bench. In March Jeff and Kathy had been seen to smile at each other and whisper, "I love you" before the bench.

In April it was time to return to the scene of the crime. The new Lake County sheriff, Patrick Walsh, who had been elected a little more than a year before, made the most of the opportunity. As each of the cult defendants had been brought to Lake County, Sheriff Walsh's handsome, dignified face had been prominent among those escorting the accused into the brand-new jail. In Jeff's case escort was provided to Ohio by Lieutenant Daniel Dunlap, who had been one of the excavators of the Averys' bodies three months earlier. Sheriff Walsh met the prisoner and his escort at the Cleveland airport.

The new jail, opened only months before, has nearly every security refinement available, including a sally port designed to allow patrol cars or other security vehicles carrying prisoners to enter the jail and to discharge their passengers without observation from the public. This precaution was made a part of the facility to assure against escape when a prisoner was arriving or leaving and that the prisoner himself would be secure from any attempt to harm him during transfer. In spite of the available facilities, each of the cult defendants, including Jeff, entered the jail through the lobby with Sheriff Walsh at his or her side.

The new jail is located on the street directly north of and parallel to the north side of the square in Painesville, where the Lake County courthouse sits. The jail is diagonally behind the courthouse.

On the day that Jeff arrived at the jail, a beautiful, warm spring day, almost a year to the day after he had murdered the Averys, county employees on their way home happened to be filing past. I was enjoying the spring weather and that on this day I was, for a change, actually going home on time. I wasn't aware that Jeff Lundgren was set to arrive at any moment. The scene was unique, with the deputies' cars lining the street and a crowd standing in front of and across the street from the jail. I'd known that Jeff was to be returned that day, and suddenly realized that I must have happened along at just the moment when he would arrive. As I got to the bottom of the driveway on the brink of the street a procession of patrol cars pulled up in front of the jail. Jeff, Kathy and Danny were escorted from the street into the jail.

The next morning a full-page color photograph of Jeff and Sheriff Walsh entering the jail appeared on the front page of the *News Herald*, Lake County's only daily newspaper, Jeff looking much as the public expected, hair shoulder-length and greasy and combed straight back, head lifted in an arrogant tilt, an enigmatic smirk on his lips. He appeared to notice the assembled crowd with mixed amusement and pleasure before disappearing into the jail.

The following Monday Lundgren was arraigned in Judge Parks's courtroom. As he sat waiting for his turn before the bench he surveyed the spectators with the same tilted head, sleepy eyes and slight smile he had worn a few days before. When his case was called he stood before the bench, flanked by his defense attorneys, Paul LaPlante and Charles Grieshammer, within a few feet of Steve LaTourette, the man who was seeking to have him executed, and entered a plea of not guilty. He was held without bail.

* * *

On March 23 the grand jury had indicted Kathy Johnson and Dennis and Tonya Patrick, each on one charge of conspiracy to commit aggravated murder, without death penalty specifications, based upon the plot to assault the Temple. Steve LaTourette and Karen Kowall had decided, based on interviews with the group members who were cooperating, that evidence to tie Kathy Johnson and Dennis and Tonya Patrick to the murders of the Averys might be too tenuous to assure a conviction. They had no doubt that all three group members were actively aware of the plans to kill the family but figured that since the three weren't present at the farm the night of the seventeenth and none of them had a special role or function in the group, as did Alice, it would make a conviction on murder charges chancy.

On April 25 the court ordered that the trial in *State of Ohio* v. *Jeffrey Don Lundgren* would begin on June 11, 1990. All motions were required to be filed no later than May 25, and all responses to motions should be filed within seven days after the motion being responded to.

On May 3 the State filed a motion requesting that the court restrict the time between the guilt and penalty phases of the trial, supposing that a penalty phase would be required, to one day. In Ohio, in a capital case, the State is not permitted to reintroduce during the penalty phase of the trial evidence regarding the murder or murders for which the defendant is being tried unless that evidence is also relevant to the aggravating circumstances. In a long delay between trial phases much of the horror of the crime may fade from the minds of the jurors, who are then confronted during the penalty-phase deliberation with *fresh* testimony from those who would try to excuse the defendant's conduct. We prosecutors hoped to keep the memories of the Averys green and very much alive in the minds of the jury deliberating the death penalty. The motion, however, was overruled as premature by Judge Parks.

In early May the defense requested discovery in the Temple-takeover case. "Discovery," as many laymen already know thanks to television and novels, is the process by which each side in a criminal or civil case is permitted to learn the evidence its opponent intends to use in support of his or her case. Criminal discovery includes a summary of relevant oral statements given by the defendant or any co-defendants to law enforcement officers, copies of written statements provided by the defendant or any co-defendants, names and addresses of all witnesses the State intends to call, copies of any books, reports or other documents the State may intend to use at trial, and an opportunity to inspect all evidence the State may intend to introduce at trial. Discovery from the defendant to the State is similar. In a criminal case, discovery is initiated by the request of the defendant, and must proceed from the State to the defendant, and then, at the State's request, from the defendant to the State. If the defendant does not request and receive discovery from the State, the State is not entitled to request or receive discovery from the defendant.

In Jeff's case the defense cleverly requested discovery in his Temple-takeover case, not in the aggravated murder case, hoping that the information provided on the takeover would be substantially the same as the state's information on the murders. It was the State's theory that the plot to assault the Kirtland Temple was still alive at the time the defendant was arrested in San Diego; Jeff had always maintained that when God appeared, the group would return to Kirtland and occupy the Temple. With the exception of the Avery autopsy reports and death certificates, and the videotaped statements of the other defendants, the discovery filed by the State in the Temple case provided the defense with almost complete information regarding the murder case without creating a defense responsibility to provide discovery to the State. We prosecutors did file motions with the court later, requesting that the court apply the spirit, not the letter, of the discovery rules and require the defense to provide discovery; the court overruled the motions.

Karen then devised an original technique for at least a partial solution to our problem. Ohio has a Public Records statute that permits any member of the public to request access to any record of any public agency that doesn't fall inside a tiny special class of exceptions to the statute. Police records, except those compiled for the purpose of litigation, are not protected under the Public Records statute. The majority of the investigative work a police department does on a criminal case is performed *before* charges are brought against anyone. So the courts have determined that, since investigative material wasn't specifically prepared for the trial of the person investigated, it wasn't compiled in anticipation of litigation and may be obtained by any member of the public who asks for it. Kowall thought that by extension any records of the Office of the Ohio Public Defender that are compiled in an investigation and not specifically intended to be used at trial should be open to the prosecutor.

I wrote a letter requesting the materials and sent it to the office of the Ohio public defender in Columbus. As we anticipated, the Ohio public defender refused to relinquish any of the requested materials. I then filed in the Ohio Supreme Court a request for a writ ordering the Ohio public defender to turn over the requested materials. What we got was a fast, indignant response from the Ohio public defender, who claimed he was the attorney for the defendant—clearly not true since the county public-defenders offices are completely separate from the Office of the Public Defender.

The Ohio public defender requested that the state Supreme Court rule that Jeff's trial could not begin until the court had had an opportunity to decide the question of the writ. As prosecutors we did not want the Lundgren cases delayed. Jeff's attorneys had been requesting continuances almost from the time his trial date had been set, contending that they could not possibly be prepared by July 9 even though the attorneys had been working on the case since early January. Most recently, on June 13, the court had grudgingly allowed the defense one more week, rescheduling the trial for July 16. Now it seemed that the defense might be able to use the Supreme Court to achieve what it had been unable to manage in the trial court. Steve LaTourette decided to withdraw the request for the writ and steel himself to deal with whatever surprises the defense might produce at trial. And the defense request was dismissed as moot.

At the beginning of July the defense filed a motion requesting that the court schedule a sixty-day recess between the guilt and the penalty phases of the trial. I suggested we reply by filing a notice of intent to represent all our evidence from the guilt phase during the penalty phase, the rationale being that all of the evidence was relevant to the aggravating circumstances attendant on mass murder and kidnapping.

The defense had also filed more than one motion requesting a change of venue, something only granted when pretrial publicity has been so extensive and biased that the trial judge decides it's impossible to seat an unbiased jury. One of the defendant's motions for a change of venue was accompanied by a report of a telephone survey of Lake

County residents made by a professor from Ohio University who performs such surveys regularly for the Ohio public defender. The survey concluded that not only did the vast majority of the population in Lake County know of the case, but most of them had determined that Lundgren was guilty and should be executed.

Steve LaTourette then assigned me to locate an expert in survey techniques who would be able to review the survey results and questions. I located a Dr. John Krosnick of the Department of Psychology at Ohio State University, who agreed to review the defense document. He submitted a twenty-two-page affidavit on the methods used in compiling and conducting the defense survey, concluding that the survey was "scientifically inadequate and potentially biased to such a degree that it is impossible to draw any meaningful conclusions" from it. So the motion for a change of venue was denied until at least an attempt had been made to seat a jury. We had won that round.

Earlier I had suggested that Richard Brand's testimony in Jeff's trial would be particularly effective if he were permitted to demonstrate for the jury, in an area marked on the courtroom floor with tape, what he had seen Jeff do the night he executed the Averys. Karen's notion was that Richard's testimony would be even more effective if it were given at the barn. A motion to that effect was filed but overruled. Steve LaTourette then decided to proceed with a tape outline of the pit on the courtroom floor. He arranged for Richard to be taken to the barn by Andolsek and a deputy sheriff to personally measure the pit in preparation for his testimony.

At the barn Richard was shown a .45–caliber handgun that had been recovered from Jeff's motel room in California and asked if he recognized the gun. When Richard said, "Sure, that's Damon's gun," the law officers' jaws dropped. Until that moment they had thought that the gun was the murder weapon and had not conducted ballistics tests because they had thought that the barrels of two of the .45s had been switched in the wilderness in an attempt to confuse the ballistics tests.

Jeff might well have sold the murder weapon in West Virginia, perhaps during one of his trips to the Elkins flea market. However, Sheriff Thompson had exhausted all his leads from the flea market several months earlier without locating a .45–caliber handgun. With this latest news Thompson went to the local media, asking them to publicize that the murder weapon had not been found and requesting that any citizen who believed he might have the possible murder weapon contact the sheriff. Within twenty-four hours both the murder weapon, a .45–caliber Colt Combat Elite, silver with a blue slide, and a second .45–caliber Colt, a Gold Cup, had been turned over to Thompson. Neither owner wanted his gun returned. Thompson discovered that Jeff had sold the guns at a local pawnshop the day before he left West Virginia for the last time. The pawnshop owner told the sheriff that he had been waiting for him to come around about the guns, that he had known that the sheriff would show up sooner or later.

Rick Kent, who had helped unearth Jeff's victims several months earlier, went to Davis with Andolsek and Yarborough to retrieve the weapons. When he tested the Combat Elite there was no doubt that it was the murder weapon. The test slugs fired from it matched exactly those recovered from the bodies of the Averys, except for two bullets that were too corroded to compare. The murder weapon had finally been located.

On July 12, with the defendant's pretrial time almost expired, R. Paul LaPlante, the defendant's chief counsel, informed the court that the defense was not prepared to go to trial on July 16 and that he personally refused to appear in court for the trial. Judge Parks found LaPlante in contempt and sentenced him to serve ten days in the Lake County jail, suspending all but eight hours of the sentence and ordering him to report to the jail at 8:30 A.M. on July 16, the following Monday. The judge also reset the trial for August 13.

LaPlante immediately hired a local attorney, David Freed, to represent him in his contempt case. Freed filed a motion with the local court of appeals to stay the jail sentence until it could review whether or not the contempt order was proper. The court of appeals would not grant the stay without the consent of the prosecutor, to be given at an on-the-record hearing to be conducted the following day in Warren, Ohio, where the court has its offices. I was sent to Warren to represent the State before the court of appeals. Steve LaTourette had been placed in the uncomfortable position of attempting to enforce an order that would place his friend and former boss in jail. He took the position that he would take with any other attorney under similar circumstances: the court's order should be upheld and the attorney should be jailed, but it was only fair to allow the order to be held in abeyance until the court of appeals had been able to review the order to determine whether or not it was valid. The stay was granted.

All of us expected the defense attorneys to raise the issue of "duress" as a major part of their strategies. We expected that Jeff would say that he was under duress from God to commit the murders. Even though duress was not supposed to be admissible as a defense of murder, having it raised was a potential problem. A motion asking the court to prohibit mention of evidence that was improper was the answer. We agreed that the motion should be filed in Damon's case and in Ron Luff's case. Now we felt the motion should be filed in Jeff's case. He should be prohibited from ever presenting so-called evidence that he killed the Averys because God would strike him dead if he didn't do it. We filed and the motion was granted. It's difficult to be sure, but it would seem that the action probably affected the trial strategy of the defense.

The defense had found they needed to bring in witnesses from out of state for the penalty hearing. More delay. A motion was filed requesting a delay of five days between the guilt and penalty phases to allow them to obtain subpoenas through channels for these out-of-state witnesses. The State opposed the motion but the request was granted and the records regarding the subpoenas were sealed so that we prosecutors would not be able to learn in advance who the defense was calling as witnesses.

Finally, the waiting was over. August 13 arrived, and with it the first day of jury selection. Judge Parks's courtroom, the largest and most impressive in the courthouse, was surrounded and invaded by hordes of media. A makeshift, roofless hut of plywood and concrete blocks was constructed in the marble corridor immediately outside the courtroom door to house the technicians and monitors for the reporters who couldn't find room in the courtroom itself.

Jeff Lundgren appeared in an ill-fitting tan tweed sports jacket and tan slacks, his shoulder-length thinning hair combed straight back, his tall, muscular body padded with a layer of fat. He would sit there in court, day after day, in a wooden swivel chair, that suggestion of a smirk on his face, alternately rocking back and forth or taking notes.

Voir dire, jury selection, in a capital case is different than in other felony trials. The basic purpose is the same—to assure so far as possible that both sides feel that the jury deciding the case is as nearly impartial as any more-or-less random group of other people. In a capital case, though, another question arises: does the prospective juror have an objection to the death penalty that is so strong as to prevent that juror from voting to impose the death penalty if it were required by law? A jury sifted by that standard is called death-qualified and, under the procedure followed in most courts, is then passed on to the next phase of jury selection, which is the common voir dire conducted in other felony trials. Death-qualification itself can take weeks since many common-pleas judges allow each juror to be questioned about the death penalty individually. The seemingly endless process is extreme for both the jurors waiting in a featureless room with more than a dozen other people they've never met before, and for the attorneys, asking the same questions over and over to an eternal line of faces. When a jury is eventually seated in a capital case the participants tend to feel a great sense of relief, almost as if they've passed through a hazing ritual designed to eliminate all but the hardiest.

A capital trial itself can be hugely time-consuming. From the beginning of jury selection to the return of the jury's verdict often takes six weeks or more. Jury selection alone may take over two weeks. For the attorneys such a trial can become a grueling test of physical endurance, as well as demanding the last reserves of emotional and mental stamina. The jury, too, are under unusual strain. Jobs and families must be largely abandoned for more than a month while they sit for most of every day listening to testimony that ranges from the technical and boring to the macabre and sometimes heartbreaking. They are forbidden by the judge to discuss what they are hearing and seeing with anyone, even each other, so they're not even allowed the emotional catharsis of sharing feelings with other human beings. Still, the jurors can come to feel unusually close to each other under these conditions, but interpersonal tensions that might otherwise not arise, or be overlooked if they did, can become a real problem.

The judge, who sometimes must make instantaneous decisions on complex legal issues, is also under real pressure, both from being exposed for the first time to the testimony and other evidence the jury are hearing, and from the consciousness that it is his or her job to assure that the trial is properly conducted—if it isn't, it may all have to be repeated later, or worse, an innocent person may be convicted.

Probably the most and—surprising though it may seem—least

stressed person in the room is the defendant. The defendant is on trial for his or her life. Enough said about the stress inherent in *that*. But the defendant also probably knows that even if convicted and sentenced to death any actual carrying out of the sentence is still problematic or at least ten years in the future. Appeals of death-penalty convictions are drawn out to such an extent that, for example, no convicted murderer has yet been executed in Ohio pursuant to the current statute, which became effective in October, 1981.

Voir dire lasted until August 22, when the twelve jurors and three alternates were sworn. The newly seated jurors were then taken on a jury view, just as the jury had been for Alice's trial. The prosecutors had filed a motion requesting that the jury view take place after dark, to give the jurors an accurate picture of the scene at the time the killings took place, but that request had been denied and the jury view took place in the afternoon.

The next day opening statements were made. Steve LaTourette presented for the State. One of Steve's major strengths as a trial lawyer is that his nice-guy persona comes across in the courtroom. He began with Jeff's statement to Debbie Olivarez that death stinks, then apologized to the jury for being forced to bring the stink of death into the courtroom.

Charles Grieshammer, co-counsel for the defendant, then rose to make his opening statement. Grieshammer's first words stunned the courtroom. He admitted that Jeff had, indeed, shot and killed all five of the Averys, but asked the jury to listen carefully to the evidence and to withhold their judgment until all the evidence had been presented.

The State went first. Donna Bailey, Cheryl Avery's mother, had been asked if she would testify so as to make the Averys living human beings for the jury, as Marlene Jennings had done in Alice's trial. Mrs. Bailey, understandably, refused, so that we started with Larry Scott, who told about his contacts with Keith Johnson. Then the jury heard about the discovery and exhumation of the Averys' bodies from Lieutenant Dunlap, Andolsek and Dr. Downing. Dr. Balraj represented the Cuyahoga County coroner's office. A diminutive, precise, intense individual, she was an excellent witness, always prepared and effective. Somehow, a large-caliber bullet looked even larger when pinched between Dr. Balraj's delicate fingers. After Dr. Balraj described the autopsy of each victim, she stepped down from the witness stand and stood directly in front of the jury, where she used the autopsy photographs to better explain her testimony.

Dr. Balraj was followed by Sharon Rosenberg, who once again described and displayed the Averys' clothing. Karen Kowall, who examined Sharon and assisted her with the clothing, carried Vicks Vaporub in a tissue that she frequently raised to her nose. The jury and even the defense attorneys leaned away as far as possible from the clothing.

Rick Van Haelst was next. He testified about his coordination of the arrests of Jeff and the others in San Diego and about the warrants for the searches of the motel rooms and the storage locker.

Scott Parkhurst and Lanny Royer, ATF special agents at the time assigned to the San Diego post, had taken part in the searches of the motel rooms and the storage locker, and Parkhurst had taken the seized evidence to Lake County in a private airplane. The two agents identified an arsenal that included two semi-automatic rifles, several other rifles, the .50–caliber rifle and several handguns, both revolvers and pistols. There were also four cases of ammunition loaded in heavy wooden boxes with thick Plexiglas covers bolted to the tops.

When Lanny Royer, who stands well over six feet, lifted the .50–caliber rifle from its case, the spectators were clearly impressed by the size of the man and the size of the weapon. Cross-examination of these ATF agents was negligible.

Now came the portion of the case everyone had been waiting for. It was time for the group members themselves to testify, to talk about Jeff Lundgren and their lives with him and the execution-murders of the Averys.

Sharon testified first because she had been the first group member recruited in Kirtland. She repeated the story of her background and her arrival in Kirtland that she had told during Alice's trial, and she talked about the militarism in the group, the plans to take over the Temple. Karen then questioned her about the Averys and their money:

A. Yes. There was an amount of money that Dennis and Cheryl had been living on and at one point Jeff was saying that he wanted that money from Dennis. I found out it was ten thousand dollars and he subsequently got it.

Q. When you say that he "subsequently got it," what do you recall occurring at this particular time in terms of how Jeff Lundgren acquired that money?

A. I remember I was in the living room of their home on Chillicothe, and Dennis came in the house and Alice was there and he had asked for Jeff and wanted to know where Jeff was and he was not home and so Dennis did not give it to Alice but he left to come back later. And Alice was very offended by that and Jeff said, "If you give it to Alice, it's the same as giving it to me," and so later on Dennis did come back and it was my understanding that Jeff received the money.

Q. How did you learn that Jeff had received the money at that particular time?

A. He said so.

Q. He told you at that particular time he had received money from Dennis Avery?

A. Yes. He was upset that Dennis hadn't given it to Alice in the first place and went right out, he said, and started spending it, buying a lot of things.

Sharon further testified:

He said that the Averys would never change. I remember him saying that it was too bad that because of the parents the children also would have to be killed, because the parents were bringing them up wrong and they were turning out like their parents were. . . .

Sharon gave her testimony calmly and straightforwardly. This was the first time she had seen Jeff since she had left the group the previous December, but mostly she did not look at him. Her direct examination, in which she covered basically the same topics and incidents related in Alice's trial, was lengthy and exhausting.

The cross-examination was even more so. Paul LaPlante seemed to have a great deal of difficulty with Sharon because her tendency to be very literal in her perceptions and responses frustrated his usual technique of asking oblique questions that implied more than they said.

Debbie Olivarez followed Sharon to the stand. Her limp was even more pronounced as she entered the courtroom than it had been for Alice's trial. Unlike Sharon, she looked directly at Jeff as she took the stand, then seemed to ignore his presence for the remainder of her testimony.

Debbie's testimony was also much like what she had given in Alice's trial, particularly with regard to the events before April 17, 1989. Here is Debbie's description of a conversation she and Jeff had had in the wilderness:

Q. Now, during that time period after you had moved to the second campsite, do you recall having a conversation with Jeff Lundgren about the killings of the Averys?

A. Yes. I was preparing a meal one day and he came up and described to me how he had killed each one of the people. He said—I mean I knew that each one was taken in one by one. He said that they were taped. Their feet bound and their hands bound, their mouths covered. He said that all of the— Cheryl and the girls' eyes had been covered, but not Dennis's because when he killed Dennis he wanted him to see who his judge was. He told me that he had shot Dennis in the heart once and that Cheryl and the girls had been shot in the head.

Q. Did he indicate to you at that time when he shot the girls whether or not there were any reactions from any of the girls during the course of the killing?

A. He told me that when he shot Trina, that she said "ouch" and he shot her a second time.

Q. Now, at that particular time, Debbie, did he make any statements to you concerning the fact that he had killed these people?

A. Yes. He said, "Death stinks. But," he said, "I am going to have to get used to it," because he had talked about that the Scriptures said he had to kill 10,000 people by his own hand. He said, "Now I am down to 9,995."

On cross-examination of both Sharon and Debbie the defense tried to establish that the group had really been no different from early Christian or Mormon groups in which everyone contributed to the common good. The defense counsel also wanted the women to say that Jeff truly believed everything that he taught, and that he directed his life according to the Scriptures. Neither woman would agree that any of these was the case.

The defense also wanted the jury to hear that Jeff spent hours poring over his Scripture, wanted them to conclude that Jeff actually had governed his own life and those of his followers by adherence to the dictates of his interpretations of the holy books. Neither woman was willing to say that in her opinion Jeff actually believed in the truth of all the instructions he claimed to have gleaned from Scripture.

Richard Brant next took the stand. Handsome and clean-cut, his appearance and demeanor were a marked contrast to the navy-blue jail uniform he wore, as well as to the bearing and appearance of the defendant, smirking and rocking at the trial table. The first part of Richard's testimony paralleled the women's. Then he gave a detailed account of the events in the barn on the night the Averys were killed. Perhaps the most dramatic testimony of the whole trial occurred when Richard was describing what he had seen Jeff do when he killed the Averys. Steve and Yarborough created a rectangle, using gray duct tape, on the courtroom floor, exactly the size of the Averys' grave. Then, as Richard described each of the victims being lowered into the grave, he took the position inside the rectangle that he had last seen that person assume in life. Steve, Colt .45 Combat Elite in hand, stood outside the rectangle as Richard described what he remembered Jeff had done, and acted out Richard's account of Jeff's actions that night.

Richard also said he remembered something Jeff had said on the eighteenth of April after the FBI and the Kirtland Police Department had left the farm. Richard testified:

> He said it was good that he had killed the Averys because they would not have been able to hold up under the questioning or the pressure that the FBI applied.

On cross-examination, the defense again tried to establish that no matter how bad Jeff's actions seemed in the light of hindsight, and no matter how much it might seem that Jeff had misled his followers, Jeff was really only acting as he believed the Scriptures told him he must, and so was living his life by what he believed to be the Word of God. Richard confirmed Sharon's and Debbie's testimony that they couldn't tell what Jeff believed.

On redirect examination Steve questioned Richard on his current belief about Jeff and his teachings:

Q. Richard, on cross-examination you were asked a number of questions about your beliefs as to this defendant being a prophet of God back in 1987, '88 and '89, and if I understand your testimony correctly you said that you believed in fact he was?

A. Correct.

Q. Did you still have that same belief and understanding today?

A. No, sir.

Q. Could you please turn to the ladies and gentlemen of the jury and indicate what has occurred that has caused you to change the perspective that Jeffrey Don Lundgren was once a prophet and you don't believe so today?

A. From the very beginning he was always relating the dreams, visions he had. Since that time I have gone back over and tried to recall things that he told me that he said he saw that would occur, and in each instance I have come up with a conclusion that he lied to me. That those things never can happen, never will happen, which lead me to conclude that he never saw anything to begin with. His teachings from when I first moved up here have turned one hundred eighty degrees. When I first moved up here—I'll give you an example.

Mr. Grieshammer: Objection to the narrative testimony.

The Court: Overruled.

Q. Please give us an example, Mr. Brand.

A. Alice Lundgren, his wife, was always to be with him. They were one. They were inseparable. She would make it with him. By the time we got to Chilhowee, Missouri, in October of 1989, he is saying, "Well, I don't know if she is going to be with me or not. In fact, if she tries to commit suicide I am just going to let her do it."

So his teachings over the course of time have gone one hundred eighty degrees. I have gone back since I have had the time to spend in my jail cell to go over the things he taught, reviewed it to get a fresh new perspective. Things he taught I find out in my opinion to be total lies, total contradictions to what he was teaching in 1989. I find nowhere where it says it takes the death of five people in order to have, indeed to receive, power. In my opinion he has been a liar from the beginning.

Rick Kent was the State's final witness. He used enlarged photographs to illustrate that the fatal bullets were fired from Jeff's .45. Kent also described rounds of ammunition that had been found in Jeff's National City motel room and in the storage locker. Kent had examined them closely and determined that some were tracers and others armor-piercing rounds—both used solely for military purposes, he pointed out, never for hunting.

The State rested.

The defense presented no witnesses, including Jeff Lundgren, which only mildly surprised the prosecutors. After all, if Jeff were allowed to testify by the defense, he would then be open to cross-examination. Not an attractive prospect, considering his attitude and the fact that his responsibility for the killings had been admitted at the beginning of the trial.

In closing argument Karen told the jury that the State had conclusively proved every element of every charge against the defendant. She concluded:

Ladies and gentlemen, in this particular case, the evidence is clear. It is undisputed. What the evidence shows is that on April 17, 1989, this man by himself planned the cold, calculated murder of the Dennis Avery family. He got the members of his group together, told them what they were going to do, planned it out and carried it into execution.

Ladies and gentlemen, I ask when you consider the evidence in this case and you consider the elements of the charges, I feel that when you consider that evidence you will find there more than ample evidence to meet each of the elements in this particular case.

I would ask you, when you go to the jury room, don't waste time considering facts, details, because they are very clear in terms of the evidence in this case. I'd ask you to come back with a quick verdict in this case. I'd ask you to come back and tell this man that he cannot hide behind this Book anymore. I'd like you to tell this man that you see him for what he really is. That he is nothing more than a killer of three children, the killer of five innocent people whose only mistake in life was that they trusted him.

Ladies and gentlemen, I'd ask you when you consider the facts rely on your commonsense and the physical evidence. I believe when you do that you will find that all of these counts have been proved beyond a reasonable doubt and also that each specification has also been proved beyond a reasonable doubt.

In addition with the kidnapping counts as well, and I will ask you to return verdicts on the aggravated murder counts, the first specification, the second specification and the kidnapping counts of guilty, and come back and tell this man he is guilty.

Thank you very much.

For the defense, Grieshammer in his closing attacked the State's case, saying that it was inflammatory and offensive and created a "circus-like" atmosphere. On rebuttal close, Steve LaTourette attacked the defense for its characterization of the evidence, saying that he would not apologize for its offensive nature because it was not the State that was responsible for the nature of the proof, it was the defendant. The prosecutor finished by reading Deuteronomy 13:1–5:

If there arise among you a prophet, or a dreamer of dreams, and giveth thee a sign or a wonder,

And the sign or the wonder come to pass, whereof he spoke unto thee, saying, Let us go after other gods, which thou hast not known, and let us serve them;

Thou shalt not harken unto the words of that prophet or that dreamer of dreams: for the Lord your God proveth you, to know whether ye love the Lord your God with all your heart and with all your soul.

Ye shall walk after the Lord your God, and fear him and keep his commandments, and obey his voice, and ye shall serve him, and cleave unto him.

And that prophet, or that dreamer of dreams, shall be put to death; because he hath spoken to turn *you* away from the Lord your God, which brought you out of the land of Egypt, and redeemed you out of the house of bondage, to thrust thee out of the way which the Lord thy God commanded thee to walk in. So shalt thou put the evil away from the midst of thee.

Steve suggested that those lines should apply to the false prophet Jeffrey Lundgren. He showed his feelings of deep anger, open and on his sleeve—which stood before the jury in stark contrast to the man on trial.

On August 29 the jury were instructed and retired to deliberate. They returned in just slightly more than two hours with guilty verdicts on all counts.

The task was half done.

In the sentencing phase of a capital trial, the penalty phase or the mitigation phase, the State argues that the aggravating circumstances of the murder outweigh beyond a reasonable doubt any mitigating factor that might be demonstrated by the defendant. Defense attorneys present testimony designed to paint a picture of the defendant as a person apart from the crime, including testimony from the defendant's family, from psychologists and social workers, hoping that the jury won't be able to sentence someone they feel they *know* as a person to die in the electric chair. Sometimes this tactic works.

The penalty phase of the Jeff Lundgren trial began on September 17. The defense presented testimony from Jeff's aunt and uncle; from his father's sister and his mother's brother, both of whom testified that he had been an obedient and responsible child whose parents had been cold and overly strict. Jeff's aunt and uncle were followed by a woman who described herself as Jeff's only high school friend, and then by a woman who had been a member of Jeff's religious study group in Independence.

Keith Johnson and Kevin Currie both testified on Jeff's behalf. Keith was obviously indignant that he had not been called by the State, and Kevin—almost perversely—still described himself as Jeff's friend although he had acknowledged in his testimony that he had left Kirtland because he was afraid that Jeff was going to kill him. Both men testified that they believed that Jeff believed the things that he taught were true and that they thought that Jeff thought God had instructed him to kill the Averys.

Dr. Nancy Schmidtgoessling, a psychologist who had tested and interviewed Jeff Lundgren, testified that she believed that Jeff was delusional, although not actually, or legally, insane. She said that he had grandiose ideas and an inflated sense of his own importance, and that he believed all the things that he had taught.

So she joined Kevin and Keith in her conclusion.

On the third day of the penalty hearing Jeff stood to make the unsworn statement that capital defendants are privileged to make under Ohio law. He spoke for an entire day, apparently using the notes he had made during the trial. His surprisingly high-pitched, rather soft voice droned on and on, hour after hour. He explained, he justified, he denied, except he did not deny killing Dennis, Cheryl, Trina, Rebecca and Karen Avery. Dennis was a false prophet, he said, and so had to be killed, and his family was necessarily doomed with him. He maintained as always that he was required by God to kill the Averys.

The State presented three rebuttal witnesses, Bishop Stobaugh, Shar Olsen Sprague, and Jeff's supervisor at Our Lady of the Ozarks Hospital. Closing arguments and the court's instruction were given at the end of the morning on the fourth day. The jury retired to deliberate just before noon and asked that lunch be brought in to the jury room so they could deliberate while they ate. Just two-and-a-half hours after they had left the courtroom the jury returned. Their recommendation: that Jeff Lundgren be sentenced to death five times over.

Jeff's only visible reaction to the verdict was the abrupt loss of his smirk, and a momentary pause in the constant back-and-forth rocking of his chair as the first verdict was announced.

The prosecutors were surprised only by the speed with which the verdict was returned. Jeff had all but assured the verdict himself when he gave his statement, saying in effect: "I did it, I'm glad I did it, and I'll do it again if you give me the chance."

But even though we had worked long and hard for the verdict, there was no elation. Relief and satisfaction, yes, but no one felt the desire to celebrate a death-penalty verdict. Even for this man. I was shaken. I had never experienced anything approaching the solemnity of an occasion in which a group of twelve people tell another human being that his actions have been so terrible that he no longer deserves to live.

26

A TIME OF TRIAL: DAMON

Joe Gurley, surprised—but pleased—because of past strained relations with LaTourette, to have been asked to join the prosecution team, knew right away which of the defendants he wanted to prosecute. Damon Lundgren, he believed, would be the most challenging to prosecute and would yield the greatest personal triumph if he could persuade a jury to impose the death penalty—after all, he figured, a jury would likely be sympathetic to Damon because he had been reared by Jeff and Alice and so would be inclined to give him the benefit of the doubt when it came time to impose sentence.

Gurley himself believed that Damon was guilty, and dangerous because of the parental training he had received. But he also believed that many other criminals and murderers had had even less opportunity to rescue themselves from their backgrounds than had this son from a middle-class background. The death penalty was appropriate and effective as a deterrent, too, or it would be if swiftly imposed and carried out, and he definitely felt that it would be appropriate in this particular case.

Gurley was also pleased to be working with Dave Joyce, whom La-Tourette had also asked to prosecute Damon. Joyce readily acknowledged Gurley's greater experience in prosecuting homicides and invited Gurley to assume the de facto lead-counsel position.

* * *

Damon had been returned to Lake County in early April of 1990 by the Lake County sheriff's department. His extradition procedures in California had proceeded more quickly than those of the other defendants held in San Diego. In the last week of March I was informed by the assistant attorney general in San Diego, who was handling all the cases of the cult defendants, that the decision of the California Supreme Court regarding Damon's extradition appeal would be received at any moment. The attorney advised that Lake County arrange to pick up Damon immediately when the decision was received, if it was favorable, because the next appeal would be to the federal court system in California, which had recently denied an extradition petition in an extraordinary decision whose effects on the Lundgren defendants could not be anticipated.

Early in the first week of April I was notified that Damon was available to be transported to Lake County immediately and I informed the sheriff's department. Oddly, there seemed to be no great excitement about removing Damon from California. No deputy left for San Diego on Tuesday, no one was scheduled to leave on Wednesday. By Wednesday both the attorney in California and I were getting upset. Steve LaTourette contacted the sheriff's department and explained the problem forcefully and in detail. Lieutenant Green was then sent to San Diego on Thursday, April 4, where he arrested Damon and returned with him to Lake County. According to rumor, the delay had occurred because Sheriff Walsh had wanted to be on hand for the transportation but had needed to be in Lake County for an extended meeting at the same time. He had, it seemed, decided to delay transporting Damon until the meeting was done. Fortunately nothing had occurred to block Damon's return before the sheriff realized the extent of the problem.

Once Damon was returned to Lake County, the question of Albert Purola, a prominent Lake County defense attorney, being appointed his counsel created some misgivings within the prosecution. We were aware that Purola had been consulted by Alice's San Diego court-appointed attorney about strategy in Alice's case before Alice waived extradition, so Purola had been at least briefly associated with the defense of one of Damon's co-defendants. Also, a controversy had arisen in Ron Luff's case a few months earlier when Judge Parks had granted a restraining order restricting contacts of attorneys and law-enforcement officers with representatives of the media. The media challenged Judge Parks's order in the Supreme Court of Ohio, where

Judge Parks was represented by Albert Purola. We knew that Purola and Luff's attorney had conferred about strategy. So while Purola was not actually involved with representation of Luff, there was the likelihood of the appearance of impropriety. And we worried that might make us vulnerable to a reversal on appeal if Damon were convicted.

Steve told me to prepare a motion requesting that Judge Mitrovich not appoint Purola to represent Damon. The matter was presented to the court but the motion was never filed because the court required that Damon sign a waiver indicating that he had been informed of the potential conflict of interest and that he personally wanted Purola to represent him in spite of the potential conflict. On May 15 Mitrovich appointed Purola to represent Damon, and also appointed Charles Cichocki, a young attorney from Chardon, the county seat of Geauga County, who had at one time been a Lake County assistant public defender.

While this rather arcane legal maneuvering was going on, Damon was drumming up some support on his own in the Kirtland community. Although he had been something of a loner in high school, the young people who knew him there as well as his few friends just could not believe that Damon would be voluntarily involved in the murders of five people. Several of the young people from Kirtland High School visited with Damon in jail and a number of girls exchanged letters with him.

At Kirtland schools Damon had complained about his father's strictness and had even said that he hated his father. Now his new-found supporters put this together with the fact that he had been quiet and inoffensive to support the belief that Damon must be unfairly charged and was being unjustly prosecuted. They seemed to overlook that it's a rare high-school student who does *not* express dislike for his or her parents and believes that he or she is being persecuted by rules that are too strict and demands that are too harsh. Also, that an individual who is inoffensive in a group where he feels powerless may be very different when he believes himself invulnerable to attack.

Some in the Kirtland community believed that Alice had been battered and even felt sympathy for her, but at the same time believed that she should have done something to prevent her husband's slaughter of innocent children. Many never believed her tales of abuse. But a great many Kirtlanders did believe that Damon was not at all responsible for the murders and became vocal in his support.

*   *   *

On June 7 Judge Mitrovich filed an order setting the trial in Damon's case for September 4, 1990. Gurley did not like the trial date, figuring that having Damon's trial after Alice's and Jeff's would make it very difficult to convince a jury to impose the death penalty. The sympathy factor, he thought, would be reinforced by the testimony about his parents that the public would hear at the other trials. Gurley remained certain, though, that he would be able to convict Damon of aggravated murder, partly because of the specific technique he uses for trials in which the jury's sympathy is likely to be with the defendant. In those cases, he says, he doesn't try to persuade the jury to like him or to be comfortable with a guilty verdict. Instead he strives constantly to remind the jury of their *duty* and of the oath they took to judge fairly and impartially. He stresses that the *law* requires them to reach a verdict that they might resist if they were permitted to judge with their hearts instead of their heads. He tries to force such juries to vote guilty even though they're angry with him for doing so.

Gurley also has a rigid sense of right and wrong, and draws a very clear line between the criminal and the average citizen. For him, anyone who would commit a crime becomes something different, apart. Anyone whom he defines as a criminal is less than human and needn't be treated as a human being. He brought this attitude to his interviews with the group members, accustomed as he was to dealing with snitches who would testify against their alleged friends. First he interviewed Debbie, whom he felt to be blasé about her involvement in the killings. He would not accept her explanation that she had spoken about the murders so many times by then that it carried very little impact for her, and he let her know in no uncertain terms that he was the boss in this situation and that he did not like her because she was a murderer. Gurley also intimidated Richard Brand. He wanted his witnesses to know that he was in control and he wanted witnesses who had already been found guilty of a crime to look as if they were afraid of him. I suggested to Joe that Debbie and Richard were stronger people than Sharon and Greg. If he used that technique with Sharon and Greg he might end up with no testimony at all from them. The other prosecutors said pretty much the same thing and Joe Gurley did modify his approach some.

*   *   *

The prosecutors hoped to have another witness from the group available for Damon's trial—Susie Luff. She had been scheduled to begin trial in Judge Jackson's courtroom in early August. Rick Collins and Tom Lobe had been preparing for that trial, and Andolsek was trying to track down the history of the .50–caliber rifle for Susie's trial.

After Alice was convicted on all fifteen counts of her indictment, however, both Susie and her attorney, Louis Turi, apparently began to worry that she might easily be convicted as well, even though Susie still maintained that she hadn't known about the plans to kill the Averys. In hopes of arranging a guilty plea from Susie, Steve LaTourette agreed to allow her lawyer, Turi, to talk with Debbie about the testimony she would be able to give about Susie's prior knowledge. Debbie gave him Susie being bored in the house the week before the seventeenth and her offer to help the men with the rocks from the pond and her expeditions to carry lemonade to the men working in the pit.

LaTourette got what he wanted. On August 3 Susie entered a guilty plea to five counts of conspiracy to commit aggravated murder. She received exactly the same deal that Sharon and Debbie had previously received. The complicity counts and the kidnapping counts were held in abeyance pending her full cooperation and her truthful testimony. After her plea, though, Susie continued to maintain ignorance, even though the prosecutors were all certain that she was lying. With two small children at home and a husband who might still be sentenced to the electric chair, Susie was not about to go out of her way to help the State against Damon. She was allowed to return to Independence, where she had been living with her parents and her children since she had been released on bond several months before. Steve LaTourette had not even opposed a reduction in Susie's bond out of sympathy for her children—near the ages of his own—who might well never see their father again and who would mostly have to grow up without their mother.

In pretrial strategy sessions Gurley and Joyce had decided that the defense was going to rely on a claim of duress, that Damon had provided minimal assistance with the murders and then only out of great fear of his father. At my suggestion the State filed its motion to prevent the use of such a defense, not only during the guilt phase of the trial but also in mitigation. I argued that while the statute specifically listed duress as a mitigating factor in sentencing, Damon's situation did not fit the legal definition of duress and testimony regarding his claimed fear of his father should not be admissible. The court did grant the motion with regard to the guilt phase of the trial, but denied it with regard to the penalty phase.

Judge Mitrovich thought that individual voir dire to death-qualify a jury was unnecessarily time-consuming and that there was no need for death qualification to be done first. Approximately seventy-five prospective jurors were summoned to Judge Mitrovich's courtroom on the morning of September 4 for the beginning of jury selection in Damon's trial. Since only forty people could occupy the courtroom at one time, the remainder of the prospective jurors were told to sit across the hall in the media room. The jurors watched the voir dire on closed-circuit monitors as it progressed in the courtroom across the hall. They were also instructed to remember any questions asked of the jurors in the courtroom to which they might have responded and to remember any questions they might have.

In the courtroom the prospective jurors were seated on the spectators' benches rather than in the jury box as the attorneys questioned them. The attorneys first examined the jurors about their general qualifications for jury service, as they would in any other felony trial. After some thirty jurors had been qualified in the general voir-dire process, the death qualification began. Damon, a slight blonde young man of average height, just turned nineteen, sat between his attorneys, wearing, not surprisingly, an anxious expression.

Gurley and Joyce of our team were somewhat frustrated with the process, having as they were some difficulty in picking jurors who they felt would be favorable regarding both guilt and the death penalty.

On September 11, one week after jury selection began, the jury was sworn in and taken on a jury view of the house and barn at 8671 Chardon Road, with stops at the Red Roof Inn and the Kirtland Temple, just as two juries before them had been. The jury view was followed with opening statements; Joyce provided the one for the State with a recital of the facts that the two prosecutors intended to demonstrate as the trial progressed. The opening statement from the defense asserted that Damon had played a minimal role in the killings and that he had been unaware that they were to occur until just before the men went out to the barn.

Again, the State began with the testimony of Marlene Jennings describing the Avery family as she knew them. Shar then described her experience with the Lundgrens. Cross-examination of both women was relatively brief.

The State called a friend of Damon to testify about his activities at school, particularly the fact that at the time of the deaths of the Averys Damon was involved in a school project about religious cults. The State also called Michelle Cassidy, a college student and clerk at a local convenience market, who testified that in the spring of 1989 Damon and Richard Brand had visited the market, looking for lime. She particularly remembered the incident because she had known Damon and was embarrassed that she at first thought he and his friend were asking for a type of citrus fruit. A neighbor of the Lundgrens from Kirtland also testified that she heard gunshots the night of April 17, 1989.

The ATF agents from San Diego who had arrested the Lundgren family and searched their motel room and storage locker also testified. James Allison, the agent who had arrested Damon, testified that Damon had said to him, "I didn't do the actual shooting."

Then the prosecutors began to have trouble. Andolsek was sitting at the trial table with them as the representatives of the State. But he, Gurley and Joyce were not comfortable with each other, and the discomfort was evident when it became time for Andolsek to testify. Joyce was doing the direct examination, and it was obvious that the two just were not communicating. Andolsek didn't seem to understand what points Joyce was trying to make and what he wanted Andolsek to talk about. Joyce felt that Andolsek was being uncooperative and wasn't volunteering information that he had provided in the two previous trials. Andolsek's testimony, which the prosecutors had calculated would take approximately two hours, took only half an hour, and their entire witness schedule was in shambles.

Earlier that morning, at Gurley's request, I had been on the telephone with George Arruda, one of the FBI agents who had interviewed Damon on the morning after the Avery deaths. Arruda had originally been scheduled to testify the next day but because the trial was proceeding much more rapidly than the prosecutors had anticipated, I had asked Arruda to be available that afternoon. At the noon recess I called to ask him to come to court immediately to testify when court reconvened in the afternoon. Arruda, although somewhat upset by the lack of opportunity to prepare, was willing to come but insisted that he would have to go home to change into a suit. An FBI agent, he said, couldn't testify in casual attire. FBI sartorial prescriptions being what they were, obviously Arruda would not be available to testify at the beginning of the afternoon.

I then called Patti Galupo, who had been out in the field chasing defendants through weeds and over fences. She came directly to court and borrowed a jacket from one of the assistant prosecutors. Rick Kent was also summoned to appear as soon as he could make it.

That afternoon, while Gurley and Joyce presented testimony in court, I sat in the snack bar down the hall with the witnesses who had already arrived, including Rick Van Haelst, who had just flown in, and Larry Scott. As each witness arrived I sent a note into the courtroom to Gurley, letting him know who would be available to testify next, the order determined by who showed up when.

In fact, witness-scheduling was a problem for the State during the whole guilt phase of Damon's trial. Greg Winship testified at the last moment, and his final preparation was done by Karen Kowall from Joyce's notes because there had been no opportunity for Joyce to meet with Greg as planned. From my perspective, the entire trial was a frantic scramble. When the State rested on Friday, September 14, I was relieved that part was over but also worried about the verdict. I believed that the evidence had not been convincing enough about Damon's prior knowledge of his father's plans and his wholehearted participation in the plans and activities of the group.

That afternoon the defense presented its evidence, consisting primarily of the defendant's testimony. Damon testified for several hours, claiming that he had known nothing of his father's teachings regarding the deaths of the Avery family because he had not been required to attend classes regularly. He denied having helped to rig the light in the pit room in the barn. Indeed, he denied knowing about the pit. He also claimed that he had not been aware of the plan to assault the Temple and that he had had very little contact with the firearms in the home.

Damon went on to say that he was first aware of the plan to kill the Averys after dinner on the night of April 17, 1989, when the men assembled in his bedroom to be instructed in the plan about the murders. He claimed that he was so shocked and horrified by the conversation that he couldn't even speak and that he was too afraid of his father to make any protest. He had participated to a very limited extent because he was so afraid not to.

Damon said that he had been unable to force himself to help subdue and tape Dennis Avery to any significant extent. He was, he said, only capable of forcing himself to run his thumb briefly over the tape that someone else had put over Dennis's mouth. He testified that when he ran his thumb over the tape, Dennis looked directly into his eyes and that it was a horrible experience.

After Dennis's death, said Damon, he was so upset that he couldn't go on, couldn't participate any further in his father's plans, and was only able to sit on the steps leading to the second floor of the barn and cry. He denied that he had been reassigned as a lookout.

Gurley was relentless in his cross-examination. Customarily, in cross-examining a defendant, Gurley would attempt to force the defendant to say that witnesses whose testimony had directly incriminated the defendant were lying. Just before Damon took the witness stand the defense attorneys requested that the court not permit Gurley to question Damon in this manner. The court granted the motion. Gurley then completely reversed his usual tactic. He led Damon to relate all of the ways in which he agreed with the statements of the previous witnesses, particularly Debbie, Richard and Greg, and then emphasized that the only statements Damon maintained were lies were those in which witnesses had implicated him as a criminal. The prosecutors enjoyed that cross-examination.

Closing arguments were given, the jury was instructed and deliberation began on Monday, September 17, the same day that proceedings began in the penalty phase of Jeff's trial. Deliberations continued all that day and all the following day. Finally the jury returned with a verdict at approximately 8:00 P.M. on September 18. They found Damon Lundgren guilty of kidnapping and aggravated murder with death-penalty specifications in the deaths of Dennis, Trina, Becky and Karen Avery. He was acquitted in the death of Cheryl Avery. The prosecutors speculated that the jury must have believed that Damon was too upset during Cheryl's murder to participate, but that he had recovered in time to assist with the killings of the girls. Their interpretation was confirmed by a juror after the penalty phase of the trial was over. The jury were then instructed to return for the penalty phase of the trial on the following Monday.

* * *

On the twenty-fourth of September the defense filed thirteen motions relating to the conduct of the penalty phase of the trial. The motions were all overruled. When the trial began again the State moved to incorporate all the evidence from the guilt phase of the trial. The motion was granted. The defense then proceeded to present witnesses.

Keith Johnson, Kevin Currie, Susan Luff and Dale Luffman all testified for the defense. The defense also called several people who had known Damon at Kirtland High School. All of the witnesses testified that Damon was an innocuous young man; all testified that Damon's involvement with any criminal activities was solely the result of his family background, and that, in their opinions, he had no proclivity for such activity on his own. Dale Luffman, in fact, stated that he would like his sons to grow up to be just like Damon! Cross-examination of these witnesses was limited. Damon also provided an unsworn statement in which he claimed again that he had had no advance knowledge of the murders and that he did not participate to any significant extent. He said that he was sorry for what had happened and that he had done what he had done only because he was afraid of his father.

The defense rested on Tuesday. On Wednesday closing arguments were presented, the jury was instructed and retired to deliberate. Later that same day the jury returned with their sentencing verdict. The jury recommended that Damon be sentenced to twenty years to life for each count of aggravated murder, the minimum possible sentence for aggravated murder.

Damon's life had been spared.

27

A TIME OF TRIAL: RON

Ron Luff, Jeff's second in command, intimidated the other group members and slavishly followed Jeff's orders. Ron Luff willingly subjected his own wife and young children to the persecution endured in the wilderness by all the members of the group except the Lundgrens themselves. Ron Luff cold-bloodedly led each one of the Averys to the barn to their deaths, giving six-year-old Karen a piggy-back ride and tickling her to distract her as he lowered her into the pit. Ron Luff was aloof and indifferent as he described his role in Lundgren's group and his pivotal role, "second in command," on the night that Jeff Lundgren joined the roll of mass murderers. Ron Luff appeared to be a monster second only to Jeffrey Lundgren, and Steve LaTourette wanted to prosecute this monster himself.

Steve also wanted co-counsel to bear some of the load of the lengthy, complex prosecution, particularly since he himself would be chief counsel on two and possibly three more capital cases in the upcoming calendar year. Using a suggestion of Karen Lawson, Steve picked Joe Delguyd to assist with the Luff case. Karen, who had hoped to try one of the capital cases herself in spite of her personal opposition to the death penalty, was disappointed when she was not offered the opportunity to sit with LaTourette on Luff's case. Actually, she had intended to suggest that Delguyd be employed as a special prosecutor in one of the other cases.

*   *   *

Ron Luff, who like the others, except for Richard and Greg, could not afford to hire an attorney to represent him, was appointed counsel by the court. The judge chose J. Ross Haffey, a flamboyant, well-known Cleveland defense attorney, and Haffey's associate, Richard Morrisson, a quiet, scholarly man in his late thirties.

Haffey, short, bald, portly, and Delguyd, short, trim, handsome, had been paired on opposite sides in many capital cases in Cleveland. Haffey, who apparently believed that extreme assertiveness, some would say bordering on insolence, was his most effective technique in dealing with opposing attorneys and judges, fired his opening salvo shortly after he had been asked to represent Ron Luff at his arraignment and before he had been officially appointed to represent him for trial.

On January 16, the day of Ron's arraignment, Haffey filed a motion to remove the county prosecutor from Ron's case and requested that the court punish Steve LaTourette. Haffey based his motion on comments that Steve had made to the press during the twelve days since the five corpses had been discovered in the Kirtland barn. Haffey also requested that all members of the court staff, the prosecutor, the prosecutor's staff, and all law-enforcement personnel be prohibited from speaking with the media about Ron Luff's case. Haffey asserted that if such an order were not issued it would be impossible for Luff to receive a fair trial in Lake County.

Judge Jackson temporarily granted the motion for a protective order and required that no further statements about Ron Luff's case be provided to the media other than statements regarding matters of public record, such as the time and place of hearings and other court proceedings. The order was intended to be effective only until the matter could be reviewed by the judge to whom the case was ultimately assigned. The court also postponed hearing the request for removal and sanctions until the matter could be heard by the assigned judge.

Meanwhile another problem had been created in the Luff case. On the same day that the judge had issued his order regarding the news media, Haffey had filed a request for notice of evidence to be used at trial, pursuant to Criminal Rule 12. A Rule 12 request for notice is akin to, but not identical to, a Rule 16 request for discovery. In answer to a Rule 12 request the State need only list in very general terms the evidence to be used. No specific information regarding any particular piece of evidence need be given. For example, the State may tell the defense that it has in its possession statements made by the defendant and/or his co-defendants and that it intends to use those statements during the trial, but it's not required to tell the defense what was said in those statements. On the other hand, a discovery request pursuant to Rule 16 requires that the State turn over a copy of a written statement provided by a defendant and a summary of any oral statement made to a law-enforcement officer by the defendant.

Unfortunately, for whatever reason, Haffey's request for a Rule 12 notice, which was filed at approximately the same time as the other defense counsels were filing their Rule 16 requests for discovery, was misinterpreted by the prosecutors as a Rule 16 request. Full initial discovery was provided, with no obligation on the part of the defendant to provide reciprocal discovery as would occur with a Rule 16 request. I discovered the error when I was preparing the much more extensive supplementary discovery, but by then it was too late. Discovery had been supplied, and the State never did receive discovery from the defendant in spite of later motions I filed attempting to persuade the court that discovery should be required.

The investigation, arrests and impending trials of the "cult" members had, as mentioned, generated extensive local television coverage, including the syndicated national tabloid news broadcast "A Current Affair." On January 30 Haffey had filed a motion requesting that the court order the three local television stations and "A Current Affair" to preserve all news and commentary tapes, including out-takes, about the deaths of the Dennis Avery family from January 5 until the trial date in Ron's case. The motion was granted on February 6.

On February 7 Haffey filed on behalf of his client a waiver of speedy trial until October 10, 1990. Every criminal defendant is entitled to a quick resolution of the charges against him. Some states, of which Ohio is one, have enacted laws that set strict time limits within which an accused person must be brought to trial. In Ohio the speedy-trial statute requires that a person accused of committing a felony must be brought to trial within 270 days after indictment. If the accused is incarcerated, each day of jail time counts as three days. So if, say, a person is indicted for a crime and can't meet the bail set by the court, that person must be tried within ninety days of indictment. Of course the defendant may decide to request or agree that more time may pass before his trial, or he might file motions that delay the time while the court is considering them. The State, with the consent of the court, or the court itself, may also delay the trial but only for a relatively short time and only for a very good reason.

In Ron's case, Haffey waived time—that is, agreed that speedy-trial time would not be counted until October 11. Haffey's timetable for Ron's trial seemed to be aimed in several directions at once. The most important aspect of the delay, as in the case of Damon's defense, was that the trial would likely occur after Jeff's. Such an outcome seemed more than likely as both trials were to be heard by Judge Parks, who already had indicated that he didn't intend to allow extended delays at the requests of the defendants in his capital cases. The fact that Haffey could pretty much count on Jeff's trial to precede Ron's allowed the defense counsel two advantages that he wouldn't otherwise have had. First, Lake County would have been exposed to the testimony in Jeff's trial and maybe in several others. The community would be thoroughly familiar with the allegations about Jeff's complete control of the group and his instigation of the murders. Undoubtedly Haffey thought that there was a good chance that public sympathy would be swayed toward compassion for those who had been victimized by Jeff, and that that public sympathy would cause a jury to be less likely to sentence Ron to death, or, indeed, less likely even to convict him.

If, on the other hand, it became clear during voir dire that the publicity had not had the desired effect and that Lake County was in a hanging mood, then the fact that several trials of the cultists had already occurred in Lake County should make a change-of-venue motion more likely to succeed. If so, Haffey and his client could try their luck in another part of Ohio where the prospective jurors were not as likely to have decided that anyone involved with the murders of three children should automatically receive the death penalty.

Also, J. Ross Haffey was a candidate for election to the Ohio Supreme Court in November. An October trial date in a case likely to receive statewide attention could not help but be a boost to his campaign.

Delguyd was eager to do battle with Haffey. The two had been less than friendly rivals in Cleveland courtrooms. Delguyd could barely wait to resume the war. The relationship between the two men was well-summarized by a story Delguyd enjoyed telling at every opportunity. According to Delguyd, one of the cases that he tried with Haffey was proceeding in the expected manner, with frequent objections and interruptions, leading to conferences among the judge and the attorneys at the bench. During one such conference, says Delguyd, Haffey turned to him and said loudly enough for the jury to hear, "Hey, Joe, how do you get your hair to stand up like that?" Delguyd responded, "I don't know, Ross. I guess it's 'cause there's a lot of it. How do you get your belly to hang out like that?" Delguyd says that the jury was delighted by the exchange.

Delguyd's eagerness would also cause some problems in the case. He was convinced that Ron should also have been indicted for robbery of Dennis Avery, because he rifled the dead man's pockets for the motel room keys and removed Dennis's wallet and papers. He felt that a robbery count and a robbery specification added to the aggravated murder count involving Dennis Avery would provide a much stronger death-penalty case. Delguyd wanted to be able to remind the jury during the penalty stage about Luff's callous treatment of the corpse of a man whose death he had been instrumental in causing.

Steve LaTourette, Karen Kowall and I felt that a reindictment was not worth the risks. We were already aware that Haffey was a tough, some might say even ruthless, adversary who took full advantage of any oversight, and we believed that the fewer unnecessary moves made, the better off the case would be.

But Delguyd prevailed. Ron was reindicted in mid-August, this time charged with one count of robbery in addition to the other fifteen counts, and with one more aggravating circumstance.

Haffey promptly went into action. At Luff's arraignment on the new charges Haffey filed a not-guilty-by-reason-of-insanity (NGRI) plea in both cases. With such a plea the accused must admit doing the things he is accused of but then must demonstrate that he should not be held criminally responsible because he was not rational enough at the time to intend to commit a criminal act. Without the required degree of criminal intent, the crime does not exist. In a trial in which the defendant pleads NGRI, the focus of the evidence shifts from proving that a crime occurred and that the defendant committed the crime to proving that the defendant was or was not legally sane at the time the crime was committed. So a defendant who intends to use a NGRI defense must inform the State at the time of the arraignment or soon thereafter, or he will not be permitted to use that defense.

None of the cult defendants had as yet pled NGRI, even though the acts in question were so illogical, and some of the other conduct of the group members was so bizarre that the prosecutors had wondered why at least one of them had not entered such a plea. The answer may have been in the extremely strict standards set by the law in determining legal insanity. In Ohio a person claiming to be legally insane for purposes of a criminal trial must show that, because of a mental disease or defect, he either did not know at the time that his act was wrong.

The law defines a mental defect as damage to the cognitive function, as from brain injury or congenital mental retardation. Mental disease is generally defined as a condition of the mind that impairs reason to the extent that the sufferer is not in contact with reality. Every member of the Lundgren group, except for Damon and Alice, claimed that at the time the Averys were killed he or she did not believe that killing the Averys was wrong. This belief, however, was the result of a belief system at odds with the laws and morality of the social system of the majority of the United States. It was not the result of a mental disease or defect. For purposes of the law, each member of the group had made a conscious, rational choice at some time to follow Jeff Lundgren, and every unfortunate consequence that followed that rational choice was caused by that choice and by the choice to continue to follow Jeff no matter how deviant his path. Nothing that any of the group members had done indicated insanity as defined by the law.

Haffey, however, had now shifted the focus in Ron's case. Earlier he hadn't filled an NGRI plea, perhaps because his client would not allow him to do so. Ron had always been adamant that he did not want to be imprisoned for the rest of his life. He wanted people either to understand what he had done and let him go or execute him. With that point of view it wouldn't be surprising if he refused to cooperate with a NGRI plea. However, by August Ron had been in jail for eight months. He had seen Jeff put on trial for his life, he had seen Alice convicted of all the charges against her, he had seen his friends plead guilty, knowing that they would be sent to prison, and he knew that his wife had pled guilty and might well face prison. At this point there was little doubt that the State would prove each charge against him and that the minimum he would face was twenty years of prison time before he was eligible for parole. It now seemed the only chance he had was to attempt an NGRI plea and hope that the jury's sympathies would be with him.

But if Ron had not been reindicted, he never would have had the chance to enter the NGRI plea. The deadline for an insanity plea in the first case had long since passed. Only the second indictment arguably reopened the opportunity for the NGRI plea. Steve LaTourette's task had been significantly complicated.

A second complication also resulted from the reindictment. Usually when a second indictment is handed down relating to the same incident for which an individual has already been charged but charging additional crimes, the second case and the first case are merged through a State motion to consolidate. After the merger the surviving case contains parts of both indictments, and the initial indictment will be dismissed so that no possibility of confusion regarding charges or trial obligations remains. In this case, since Ron had been reindicted in the second indictment on all of the original charges with the simple addition of the robbery charges, the entire first indictment was dismissed.

Again, the prosecutors were head to head with an unexpected problem. One of the more esoteric ramifications of the speedy-trial statute is its treatment of subsequent charges concerning a criminal incident for which the offender had previously been charged. In such situations, the law requires that the later charges are subject to the speedy-trial limitations of the original charges. So if only one week had remained in which to try Ron Luff on his original indictment when that indictment was dismissed, then he would have had to be tried on his second indictment within that week or the second indictment would have been dismissed.

The problem with speedy trial and the second indictment was much more serious. Haffey had discovered recent case law indicating that the waiver of speedy-trial time on Ron's first case did not apply to his second case. Therefore, speedy-trial time had elapsed on the second case before it was even indicted, and when the first indictment was dismissed, according to Haffey's interpretation, the State was left with *no* charges.

The prosecutors argued that the statutory interpretation advanced by Haffey should apply only to the new charges, not to the charges that were identical to those on which the speedy-trial time had been waived. Judge Parks agreed with the State. The new indictment was permitted to stand, but the robbery charge and the robbery aggravating circumstance were removed from the charges. So after all that, the State was left with a new indictment identical to the old but with a new defense plea of not guilty by reason of insanity.

As the October 10 trial time approached, both Steve LaTourette and Delguyd were putting together their last-minute preparations. Witness interviews were done on weekends and into the evenings. I was there to help with preparation of the witnesses and of the evidence and to suggest areas each witness would cover. One Saturday shortly before jury selection was scheduled to begin, Steve had been scheduled to meet with Greg Winship to review evidence and testimony but was unexpectedly called away, so he asked me to review the necessary items with Greg, making sure that Greg could identify all the things he would be expected to recognize. During our meeting Greg said he never had seen all of the physical evidence in the cases and wondered if he could see it now. Greg and I sat on opposite sides of the conference table for more than an hour while he examined every item of evidence the State had used. Several times his eyes filled with tears, particularly when he looked at the autopsy photographs and the photos of the exhumation of the bodies. It was then that Greg suddenly remembered standing by the pit after Becky had been shot and hearing her struggle to breathe. When he was done with it all, Greg looked up, his face frozen in creases, and said, "Thank you. Now maybe I can start to put all this behind me."

I said nothing to that

A third prosecutor was chosen to sit at the trial table in Ron's case. She was Ariana Tarighati, a young woman who had been hired when Steve LaTourette assumed office to set the appellate division of the office to rights and had moved on to major felonies in common-pleas court. She was pleased and excited to be helping try an aggravated-murder case.

With her in place, the painfully slow process of jury selection began on October 10. As prosecutors and defense counsel questioned one after another of the prospective jurors, it became increasingly clear that a large number of the panel had been exposed to significant amounts of information and misinformation about the cult prosecutions. Could an impartial jury be seated?

After two weeks of jury selection, just before the finally selected panel was to be sworn in, Haffey renewed his motion for a change of venue. The prosecutors, not really happy with the jury that had been selected, decided not to oppose the motion. Judge Parks excused the jurors who had been selected and declared that the motion for a change of venue would be granted. Now it was the responsibility of the court to locate a new site for the trial.

The suspense over Judge Parks's decision ended when the judge announced that Ron Luff's trial would be moved to the Lucas County Courthouse in Toledo, and that the trial would begin on November 26, the Monday after Thanksgiving.

At about the same time, some suspense was ended in another case. On November 5 Danny Kraft pled guilty to five counts of aggravated murder without death-penalty specifications and to five counts of kidnapping. Danny, who still believed in Jeff, had been persuaded to plead when Jeff, for his own mysterious reasons, agreed to talk with Danny and to explain to him that it would be all right to enter such a plea and that it would not be a betrayal of Jeff, his god. The plea allowed Danny to escape exposure to the death penalty but to risk twenty years in prison before parole eligibility on each of the aggravated-murder charges.

After the plea Judge Jackson immediately began a sentencing hearing. The first and major player at the hearing was Danny himself, who made an unsworn statement lasting one entire court day. Danny explained chiasm and his belief in Jeff and Jeff's teachings in detail. In the two days that followed, Danny's parents and Shar also testified about this talented, seemingly gentle man they had known. A psychiatrist and expert in cult-exit counseling also testified about the treatment Danny apparently needed. At the end of the testimony Judge Jackson sentenced Danny to serve twenty years on each of counts one through five, concurrently with each other, and terms of ten to twenty-five years on each of counts six through ten. The terms on counts six and seven were to be served concurrently with each other and concurrently with the terms on counts one through five, and the terms on counts eight, nine and ten were to be served *consecutively* with each other and consecutively with those on the first five counts.

Just a few weeks earlier Dennis and Tonya Patrick had pled guilty to

reduced charges of obstruction of justice. Each was placed on probation for eighteen months and allowed to return to Independence.

Steve LaTourette was now faced with putting together a trial team
which could function long distance. The office of the Lucas County
prosecutor was helpful in arranging for facilities for the Lake County
prosecutor during his indefinite stay in Toledo. Steve decided that
secretarial help was essential and decided that his personal secretary,
Kathy Dalton, would be needed in Toledo at least part of the time.
Then came the question of who would sit second chair in the trial
itself.

Sandra Dray and Karen Lawson were leaving the prosecutor's office
at the end of the year. When Steve was first elected they had committed themselves to his staff for one year so that he could be assured that
sex cases and important drug cases would be properly prosecuted.
When the cult cases had come up at the beginning of 1990 both
women had been interested in becoming involved in their prosecution
and both had also known that the staff would be strained to the breaking point with the murder cases. They did not want to abandon the
office just as their help was particularly needed. Now, though, they
felt they could no longer sacrifice their private practice. They had told
Steve their decision in September, and the hole that their imminent
departure would leave in his staff was one of the major considerations
in determining the allocation of available attorneys during the Luff
trial.

Joe Delguyd was well aware that the county commissioners were
not likely to be favorably inclined toward adding the fees for a special
prosecutor to the exceptional expenses needed to provide for attorneys
and a judge and their staffs for weeks out of town, plus the expenses of
bringing in witnesses from all over the country. Delguyd stepped
aside, although he very much would have liked to see the case
through to its conclusion.

LaTourette picked Tarighati as his second-chair counsel for Toledo,
but on November 16 she was injured in a severe auto accident and
there was no chance she would be able to travel to Toledo and spend
weeks in a high-profile murder trial.

With Lawson, Dray and Tarighati gone, Steve was stumped. He
didn't believe he should hire a special prosecutor but he also couldn't
afford to deprive his already threadbare staff of one more assistant.

Finally he decided to try the case himself with the aid of Vince Culotta, a law clerk and new attorney who had been admitted to the bar only weeks earlier. It was settled—LaTourette, Culotta and Yarborough would be the full-time trial team in Toledo. They would drive the three and a half hours from Lake County to Toledo every Sunday evening and would reverse their trip every Friday evening. Kathy Dalton would be in Toledo two or three days a week during jury selection and every day during testimony. Witnesses and evidence would be transported by William "Pete" Mason, investigator for the prosecutor's office and ex-deputy sheriff. Toledo in November and December is icy and gray. The trial team would be separated from their families for most of the holidays, but everyone wanted to put the cult trials behind them.

Preparing for the trial that was originally scheduled to begin on October 10, Steve now faced the question: which group members should he call to testify against Ron? Richard and Sharon and Debbie and Greg had been eager to testify against Jeff and Alice, and they hadn't been reluctant to testify in Damon's trial. Greg, in fact, had been disappointed he was not called in Jeff's case. All now said they felt that Jeff and Alice were evil and they believed that all three Lundgrens were dangerous.

But Ron was different. Each apparently could see himself or herself in Ron's shoes. Richard had said that his best friend in the group was Greg but that he believed that he was most like Ron.

There were other considerations more significant to LaTourette than the personal difficulty Ron's friends might have in testifying at his trial. Steve wanted the best, toughest witness he had available, one who had the best chance of resisting the battering he or she was likely to experience from defense counsel. He did not want to put Richard Brand on the witness stand in Ron Luff's trial. Richard would be the best witness to Ron's actions the night the Averys were killed, but Richard had been directly involved in the murders and had had almost as significant a role as Ron's. Richard had accepted a plea bargain that considerably lessened the possible punishment he could suffer, while Ron would be on trial for his life. Steve did not want the jury to be faced with the contrast between the possible fates of the two men.

So Steve devised a simple strategy. He would call Debbie to the stand because she seemed to be the brightest, most articulate and stable of his available witnesses. Debbie also has an extraordinary memory, which allows her to recall events in detail and to locate those events accurately by date. Debbie, then, was the ideal witness to describe the functioning of the group.

Then Steve would let Ron be a witness against himself about his behavior the night he led the Averys to their deaths. He would play Ron's videotaped confession for the jury and allow them to hear for themselves Ron's emotionless minute-by-minute description of the murders. There could be, he decided, no better witness to the events in the barn that terrible night.

November 26 arrived. Ron's trial began with much less attention in Toledo than it had received in Lake County. The trial was assigned to a small courtroom on the fourth floor of the marble-walled Lucas County Courthouse. The prosecutors were provided with a conference room down the hall from the courtroom for evidence and witnesses. The courtroom itself had recently been remodeled. The interior was certainly more contemporary in design than other, larger courtrooms on the same floor, and definitely more contemporary than the courthouse itself. The courtroom provided seating for only eighteen spectators; each observer was provided with a molded plastic chair bolted to the floor. Every day one of the spectator's chairs was occupied by Ron's mother. Occasionally his father was also present.

Jury selection proceeded slowly. After two weeks both sides declared themselves to be satisfied, and the jurors were sworn in. Then during the worst snowstorm of the winter the jurors were loaded on a bus and brought to Lake County for a jury view, shown what the previous three juries had been shown but without the lifelong familiarity with the area shared by the others.

Testimony began the following day. The trial proceeded pretty much as Steve had planned. Ron, who was much thinner and paler than he appeared in his video, sat each day at the trial table between his attorneys, looking at the floor. Haffey later commented to one of the prosecutors that he had instructed Ron to sit just that way at all times. Lieutenant Dunlap, Ron Andolsek, Dr. Balraj, Sharon Rosenberg, Rick Van Haelst, Lanny Royer, and Scott Parkhurst testified, just as they had in the previous trials.

Then it was time for Debbie to take the stand. Steve asked that I accompany Debbie to Toledo, both to be a companion and to be on hand to suggest any areas of Debbie's possible testimony that might be useful to him and that he might have overlooked. Debbie was recovering from back surgery she'd had several weeks earlier. The surgery, the same which Karen Lawson had had earlier that year, was necessary because of the deterioration that had occurred in her condition since her back injury more than a year before. At the time of the trip to Toledo she was in considerable pain.

At first Steve LaTourette intended that Debbie and I stay hidden in our motel rooms since the prosecutors and the defense attorneys were staying in the same motel and he didn't want Haffey and Morrisson to know that Debbie would testify the following day. Eventually he decided, however, that such a restriction was probably unnecessary— after all, defense counsel was probably thoroughly prepared for each of the group members.

As Debbie was sitting with Steve, Vince Culotta and me in a lobby of the motel the evening of our arrival to prepare for her testimony the next morning, Haffey and Morrisson walked by. Morrisson recognized Debbie and pointed her out to Haffey. Haffey then approached the group and in his usual manner tried to bully Debbie into talking to him. She refused, although she was upset and confused. Later Morrisson returned with a subpoena with which he tried to serve Debbie, apparently in an attempt to upset her again.

The next day Debbie took the stand after Rick Kent and once again testified on direct examination about her involvement with Jeff, but this time she talked about Ron's role as second in command. She told about his involvement in the "sessions," and his loyalty to Jeff, no matter what Jeff's demands, and no matter how difficult those demands were for Ron to accept. Through it all it was clear that Debbie had no hostility toward the defendant.

When Haffey began his cross-examination he immediately attacked Debbie for her supposed privileges as a prosecution witness, pointing out that he had spotted her in the motel cocktail lounge the night before. He tried to confuse her by suggesting that she was legally married to Greg Winship. Off and on throughout her testimony he would refer to her as Mrs. Winship. But his primary point was to emphasize that the doctrines taught by Jeff, while bizarre, were logical extensions of the doctrines of the RLDS church and that the group members not only completely believed Jeff's teachings but believed him when he taught that killing the Averys was morally correct.

Debbie's cross-examination was not finished on Friday. That evening Mason drove Debbie, Rick Kent and me back to Lake County while LaTourette traveled to Columbus, where he thought he was to present awards at a meeting of the state prosecutor's association to Lawson and Dray for their prosecution of Alice. As everyone else knew, Dray and Lawson had received their awards earlier, and LaTourette was to be honored as the Prosecutor of the Year for his performance to date in handling the cult trials.

Debbie and I went back to Toledo on Sunday evening, and Debbie finished her testimony on Monday morning. The State rested the same day.

Most of the defense rested on the position that Ron was insane. However, the defense's expert witness, Dr. Kurt Bertschinger of the Lake County Court Psychiatric Clinic, could not testify that Ron suffered from a mental disease or defect. The essence of the doctor's testimony was that Ron believed at the time of the killings that the murders were morally right even though he knew that they were legally wrong. This, Haffey attempted to argue, demonstrated that Ron did not appreciate the quality or significance of his acts, a portion of the legal test for insanity.

Haffey also called Alice and Jeff Lundgren to the stand to testify on Ron's behalf. Jeff exercised his Fifth Amendment right to refuse to testify, but Alice once again took the stand to tell how Jeff was a terrible man who controlled and bullied those around him, including herself. Both Susie and Ron Luff testified. Susie talked about the changes in Ron's personality after he became a follower of Jeff and about Ron's unshakable belief in Jeff's teachings. Ron, himself, testified relatively briefly, saying that he felt he was just following orders and that the murders were all Jeff's fault. But there was also that videotaped confession.

After the defense rested, closing arguments were presented and the jury was instructed and left to deliberate. The wait for the verdict was excruciating. The trial team was exhausted. Steve and Vince had worked for hours every night after a full day in court, preparing for the next day's legal arguments and testimony. They had lived for weeks away from home and their families. They were drained. Yarborough, the insomniac, had lived virtually on chewing tobacco and nerves.

The jury, some of them in tears, returned a verdict of guilty on all counts. It was the week before Christmas. The penalty section of the trial was scheduled to begin after the New Year.

*   *   *

The penalty portion of the defense was presented mostly by Morrisson, Haffey having insisted that he had lost credibility with the jury by presenting a losing case to them in the guilt portion of the trial. Ron's mother testified, remembering Ron as a boy and as a youth, and the defense flew in from out of state two experts in cult psychology to testify about the effects of leaders like Jeff Lundgren on the free will of their followers. Ron delivered a long unsworn statement attempting to explain his involvement with Jeff and his willingness to assist in murder. By the end of the week the jury had returned with its recommendation: twenty years to life on counts one and two, and thirty years to life on counts three, four, and five. Apparently, the jury felt that Ron was excused from some guilt for the deaths of Cheryl and Dennis Avery because the two voluntarily participated in Jeff's group and put themselves at risk. Judge Parks immediately followed the jury's recommendation with regard to the aggravated murder counts, making the sentences consecutive, and then imposed sentences of ten years apiece for Counts Six, Seven, Eight, Nine, and Ten, and caused them to run consecutively with the sentences on the first five counts. Ron Luff, the man who had said he wanted to be executed or be set free, was sentenced to spend at least 150 years in prison before being eligible for parole. A lifelong sentence.

Early in January Kathy Johnson, accompanied by her infant daughter Rasia, pled guilty to obstruction of justice before Judge Jackson. Sentencing was delayed pending a presentence report to be prepared by the probation department.

The cult trials, which had dominated the news and the courts in Lake County for almost exactly a year, were finally done.

EPILOGUE

BROKEN HEARTS AND CONTRITE SPIRITS?

In the RLDS and in the Mormon faith a truly repentant sinner is one who has a broken heart and a contrite spirit. Jeffrey Lundgren referred to this indirectly when he said at the penalty phase of his trial that Dennis Avery had been a sinful man because he, Jeff, could not break his heart. The macabre saga of Jeff and Alice Lundgren and those who followed them is one of broken hearts, but at this writing there are few contrite spirits.

Alice is not contrite, and whether or not she has a heart to break is open to question. Alice was sentenced by Judge Mitrovich on August 29, the day that Jeff was found guilty of aggravated murder and kidnapping of the Averys. Alice was sentenced on ten of the fifteen charges she was found guilty of. The court and the attorneys agreed that complicity to commit aggravated murder and conspiracy to commit aggravated murder are allied offenses of similar import—in effect, that they are the same crime in this particular situation. The court was permitted to sentence on only one of the allied offenses, and the prosecutors were to choose which charges they preferred for sentencing. Alice was convicted of five counts of conspiracy and five counts of complicity. Each of the counts named one of the Averys as victim. However, legally, a conspiracy to commit related criminal acts can only occur once. The conspiracy was to kill all five of the Averys, not a conspiracy to kill each of them separately, not five separate conspiracies to kill them. Even though Alice had been charged with five counts

of conspiracy she only could be sentenced for one count since techni-
cally there had been only one conspiracy.

Since complicity involves assisting in some act, while conspiracy
involves simply agreeing that the act shall occur, it's possible to be
guilty of five *complicity* charges in the case of these murders while
being guilty of only one *conspiracy*. So the sentence that Alice faced
could have been for one conspiracy and five kidnappings, or for five
complicities and five kidnappings. She was sentenced to twenty years
in prison for each count of complicity to commit aggravated murder,
and ten to twenty-five years for each count of kidnapping. All of the
sentences are to be served *consecutively*. Alice's minimum sentence,
then, is 150 years; she is eligible for parole in about one hundred
years.

At the time of Alice's sentencing, Chief Deputy Warren Goodwin
asked Karen Lawson to advise him whether it was permissible for Alice
to make a statement to the media after her court appearance. Goodwin
said that he had reviewed the statement and that it would take no
more than five minutes for Alice to read it. Lawson told Goodwin that
neither she nor the prosecutor's office could advise him as to how the
sheriff's department should handle its prisoners. It was up to him.

After court Alice, flanked by the chief deputy and by the jail administrator, talked to the press in the hallway outside Judge Mitrovich's
courtroom. This is how she was quoted by the local newspaper, the
News Herald:

> "My name is Alice Elizabeth Lundgren. I am not Josef Mengele and I am
> not the angel of death. I am the mother of four.
> "We are all in this place today to hear the sentence imposed by the
> court for conviction of criminal activity. I was found guilty for a crime
> committed that I had no knowledge would occur and was carried out by
> others when I was not present nor aware of their activities. This whole
> process has not been so much about law or justice or truth; it has been
> about political fame and fortune. The tragedy of the loss of Dennis and
> Cheryl and Trina and Becky and Karen is still being perpetuated.
> "The Avery family were warm, living individuals, not graphic displays
> of evidence. We are all aware of the tabloid mentality of motions that
> have been filed concerning privileged attorney-client information trying
> to be opened by court order or requests for nighttime jury views or on-

site testimony as though it would somehow add to the comprehension of the heinousness of this crime.

"No amount of theatrics is needed to impress the average person with the ugliness of what occurred. Let us remember that this crime did not come to the knowledge of authorities out of guilt or remorse over the loss of five human lives. It came to light out of vengeance, an act of anger as the result of a man now rejecting his once-accepted belief of polygamy.

"Keith Johnson willingly turned over his wife of nearly twelve years and the mother of his four sons out of his acceptance of a concept that he professed belief in. When that belief waned and his personal anger overcame him, then he went to the authorities. It was revenge, not morality that was his motivation. Why could he draw the map to locate bodies? Because he dug the grave, along with another man who had charges dropped against him, claiming he was not involved.

"The graphic and emotionally chilling testimony that was offered in court came from individuals who were present and had full knowledge of events as they were occurring. They could not testify as to my direct involvement because there was none. They did offer conflicting and unsubstantiated stories of my alleged knowledge. Testimony in my trial of statements I allegedly made have now been attributed as statements of Jeff Lundgren. Plea bargains were granted to a total of five individuals to obtain a conviction of the bigger fish, plea bargains that were allowed for the three women who laughed at the opportunity to save the lives of Cheryl, Trina, Becky and Karen. They're going to serve very little prison time if anything for saving themselves rather than the children.

"During the process of my trial an extraordinary amount of testimony centered on insignificant issues. Whether or not I ate from the party platter from Red Lobster does not make me aware of what's going on and the conduct of Jeff Lundgren on the night of April 17. Testimony pertaining to certain bizarre sexual rituals, no matter how personally painful or humiliating that activity was, has nothing to do with the death of Dennis and Cheryl and Trina and Becky and Karen, and I found it offensive to their memory.

"What testimony was allowed was designed to shed as little light on the truth as possible. It was not allowed that the jury see a videotape of ATF agents speaking to the media in January where I, too, was numbered on the list and had been discussed how I too would be killed most mercifully. It was never allowed that the jury have a professional explanation of the battered women's syndrome and how that affects a victim's behavior. Instead of a jury being educated in the self-defense mechanisms a battered woman uses, they were left to believe that the classic defense mechanisms they witnessed were cold, calculating and callously indifferent behavior. Had they been allowed to be educated they would have recognized a classic example of a defensive posture taken by a woman who learned a long time ago that you cannot outmuscle or physically outmaneuver an attacker, that instead the only tool you have to work with is your mind.

"The departure of expected courtroom decorum displayed by the prosecutor as she screamed and shouted in my face, 'Holy schmoly, Mom,' and 'Mrs. Lundgren, you're a liar,' gave the jury a perfect example of a woman realizing that she'd exchanged batterers. But because the jury was uneducated in this perception, it was misinterpreted. The angel, as I was depicted, would never have encouraged Cheryl to take Becky to Lake County Mental Health because of Becky's anorexia. The angel of death does not write letters of information for her children's psychiatrists and deprogrammer, only to have them stolen by the prosecutor's office as evidence at her own trial, and yet not allowed to read such evidence as it was self-serving. 'The angel of death' does not buy Christmas gifts for a little girl who likes rainbows that later appear as evidence of her last clothing.

"No matter how much pain and destruction [garbled by crying] from my life, no matter how tragic the deaths of Dennis and Cheryl and Trina and Becky and Karen, that does not, nor ever could it have been reason for me to accept the suggestion of 'Alice should have blown his brains out' as was offered in closing remarks. I found it ironic that the suggestion of aggravated murder was an acceptable course of action to have prevented aggravated murder. That would have made me equal to Jeff Lundgren, which could never be because I'm not a cold-blooded murderer. He is.

"There are a great many lessons to be learned in this experience, not the least of which is that justice and fairness are not necessarily equal. I commend the fifteen people who accepted the arduous responsibility of deciding my fate in that courtroom. I wish they'd been allowed to know all there is to know in relationship to evidence. However, they did the best they could, given what they were allowed to know.

"My life has taken on a whole new definition over the past several months. In a very real sense I have known more freedom within the walls of Lake County jail than I have known for years. I want to thank the sheriff's department and especially the correctional officers that have been my good fortune to interact with over these last several months. They have treated me with fairness and human dignity, which is a new and refreshing experience as compared to the dynamics of the group I came out of.

"Although I do not know specifically the day-to-day life I will see in prison, I do know that I will use the experience afforded me to grow and improve from day to day. My sympathy and desire for a healing process to begin goes out to the families of all that have been profoundly affected by the actions of April 17.

"I hope that although it shall never be forgotten, I hope that the lessons learned can bring peace and healing to this community and to all who have been profoundly affected by this tragedy."

As Alice spoke Sandy Dray, Karen Lawson and I listened in the background. Karen and Sandy became so incensed that others in the corridor escorted them out of the area to avoid a scene. Alice actually went on for some twenty minutes, exculpating herself and blaming everyone else, mentioned and unmentioned, available and unavailable. There was no evidence of a contrite spirit on that day.

After her sentencing Alice asked to visit Jeff but was refused by the authorities. She did not ask to be permitted to visit her son Damon. One can only speculate why.

Alice is now serving her sentence in the Marysville prison for women. She is working in the admissions center, where she processed Kathy Johnson, Susie Luff and Sharon Bluntschly into the institution. Sharon was assigned a job in the same office, and when there were protests that the cult defendants should not have contact with one another, it was Sharon, not Alice, who was moved to a less desirable job. Alice was, it would seem, still taking care of Alice.

Alice's case is currently on appeal, and she apparently has reconsidered her desire to see Jeff. In April, 1991, she filed for divorce. Jeff let it be known that if a divorce was what she wanted he would not oppose it.

In her petition Alice cited irreconcilable differences and imprisonment. According to her appellate lawyer, he and Alice are hoping that the divorce will help her appeal. Somehow that seems unlikely.

Jeff Lundgren—sentenced to death five times over and to the maximum of five consecutive ten-to-twenty-five-year terms for the kidnappings. Several of the jurors who sat on Jeff's case and voted for the death penalty came back for Jeff's sentencing. Judge Parks set the execution for April 17, 1991. That date has, of course, since been delayed because of the appeal filed on Jeff's behalf. His actual execution is not likely to occur for at least a decade, unless recent U.S. Supreme Court decisions speed up the process by limiting appeals.

Meanwhile, if a governor should decide that Jeff really was just deluded and actually did believe that God told him to kill, it is even possible that he will be granted clemency and the sentence of death commuted to life imprisonment. As I sat in the courtroom that day of Jeff's sentencing it occurred to me that of all of us present, he was the one most likely to be alive ten years from now. He will without question be carefully cared for and not permitted to succumb to accidents. Which of the rest of us can say the same?

It is a terrible thing to hear another person sentenced to die. I believe in the death penalty and I believe that if anyone ever deserved the death penalty, Jeff Lundgren does. And yet hearing the actual death sentence pronounced, brought tears to my eyes.

Jeff Lundgren has never shown any evidence of a broken heart or a contrite spirit. More, he is dangerous, and he is evil, and no civilized society that is obliged to protect itself from evil should allow him to survive.

Damon, sentenced to the maximum available penalty, will serve four consecutive terms of twenty years actual incarceration for counts one, three, four and five of his conviction, and four consecutive sentences of ten to twenty-five years for the kidnapping convictions, the latter to run consecutively to the other four sentences. Damon Lundgren, son of Jeff, will be eligible for parole in approximately one hundred ten years.

After Damon's trial his supporters in Kirtland raised a noisy outcry about the supposed unfairness of the trial and about Joe Gurley, the special prosecutor, who was lead counsel in the case. There was also protest over the sentence, Damon's supporters apparently feeling that he had suffered enough.

Those good citizens of Kirtland failed to appreciate that Damon too is dangerous. In spite of his protestations to the contrary, Damon is truly his parents' son. Some may suggest that Damon just had the bad luck to draw the parents he did, to be raised by them. Many people are reared by those who probably should never have been parents, and some of these people turn out badly and some do not. In any case, unfortunate parenting is not a defense. Whether or not Damon might have been a civilized person had he had a different father is *now* irrelevant. The clock cannot be turned back, and the public is safer with Damon Lundgren where he is.

*   *   *

In the course of my research for these cases I came across a book entitled *Combating Cult Mind Control*, by Steven Hassan. Mr. Hassan, who was once a Moonie, now calls himself an "exit counselor" and has written his book, he says, to warn others about the hazards of cults. Many of the techniques cited by Hassan as means of controlling the minds and behaviors of cult recruits were used by Alice and Jeff. Interestingly enough, Alice was responsible for at least as many of the mind-control behaviors used by the pair as was Jeff.

Did one or the other or both read a book or books on the subject? We know that Jeff studied Sun Tzu's *The Art of War*, which has some brief passages dealing with manipulation of one's troops and one's enemy. Did Jeff delve even further into Chinese military lore and discover texts on the brainwashing techniques used in the Korean conflict? Or did this ungodly couple stumble through trial and error, beginning in Independence, onto techniques that worked so well for them? It's unlikely that we will ever know.

What we *do* know is that Jeff and Alice were a lethal pair. Alice's ability to manipulate and her need for control meshed perfectly with Jeff's narcissism and grandiosity. Do I think that the pair began their misadventures anticipating murder somewhere down the line? No. Jeff is lazy but bright and thinks of himself as an inherently superior person, while at the same time harboring—and denying—some very large suspicions that he actually does not measure up. Jeff is exactly the sort who would be expected to engage in the petty thievery and marital infidelities that mark his background. Alice is, on the evidence, an amazingly effective manipulator. Both Shar and Sharon said, at different times, even knowing now how much Alice had exploited them during their time with the group, that they both *miss* her. Yes, Alice is extraordinary. In a face-to-face situation she can convince most people of almost anything. Only those who know the truth are able to resist her, yet even some of them, it seems, are still vulnerable.

Alice lies constantly, and often gratuitously. A small example: She has told Marlene Jennings that she is learning to knit in prison. Actually, Alice has known how to knit for years. Alice is terribly good at what she chooses to do. Unfortunately she lost whatever scruples she might once have had, which allowed her to manipulate people, literally, to death.

I do not think that Jeff ever believed his own lies, ever actually thought that he was a prophet. Nor do I believe Alice ever believed he was a prophet. Such belief was reinforced for me by Jeff's seeking the protection of the Fifth Amendment at Ron's trial and by the consistency of the other group members' statements about Alice. If Jeff really believed he was a prophet, God's chosen, why would he need to rely on mere man's protection against telling the whole truth? And a woman who so blatantly lied to others about her husband's supposed divinity, while laughing at those same people for their belief, never herself believed.

I believe the Averys died because they got in Jeff's way, and because he did not like them. His so-called religious reasons—the Scriptures according to Jeff—were a smokescreen for the group. I think, in particular, that Jeff killed them because he was really afraid they would upset his applecart by demanding their money too loudly and too *publicly.* Why did he think he could get away with it? Because the absolute power his followers had turned over to him had warped his perception of what he could do with impunity. He had no idea at the time he shot Dennis, Cheryl, Trina, Becky and Karen that anyone outside his group knew anything about what he was doing or planning. With his sense of power, of overweening self-importance, he believed that he had been able to conceal all of his deadly plans from the local authorities. The notion that the Kirtland police and the FBI were in any way suspicious of his activities simply didn't occur.

Debbie has suggested that her cousin Jeff shot the Averys with different kinds of bullets in different areas of their bodies because he was experimenting with the effects of ammunition on the human body. Despite his boasting to the contrary to the group, Jeff had never killed anyone, nor had he ever seen anyone killed. I believe Jeff fully intended to carry out at least a portion of the planned assault on the Kirtland Temple. Had the FBI and the Kirtland Police Department not arrived at the farm on the morning of April 18, I think that Jeff would have led an assault on the Temple within the next week. The killing of the Averys had proved—as intended, I believe—to all of his followers that he was lethal, that they would have to do as he said without question or they would die. I think that Jeff intended to kill the people living in the Temple area, as he had described so many times, and at the last minute to cancel the actual takeover of the Temple itself, claiming that God was not pleased with some aspect of the operation. He would *then* have taken his already prepared group into the wilderness, where they would have disappeared.

I believe that Alice did not want Jeff to carry out this plan. She was much too happy with a life in which she had no work to do and had no worries about unpaid bills or a wandering husband. Alice had not been blind to the fact that things had gone so well for so long. She was well aware that there was a good chance that Jeff would eventually be caught if he actually went ahead and killed someone. But she was not willing to alert the group in order to stop the murders. I also think it was Alice's plan, not Jeff's, that she be gone from the farm that night. I think she believed that if she were not present at the time of the murders, she would not be held legally responsible if and when Jeff was eventually caught. She could have prevented the deaths of the Averys if she had been willing to forego her role as queen bee; she was not willing to do so.

To put it simply: Jeff couldn't have done it without Alice, and Alice wouldn't have done it without Jeff.

Many people have said to me that Jeff's followers must just have been "weak-minded" folk and/or in some other fundamental way radically different from the rest of us. I don't believe it. Jeff's followers are, in many respects, like countless others who consider themselves quite sane and decent. I participated in nearly every interview that any of the prosecutors conducted with members of the group, and in the process, as well as later, I think I came to know something of Sharon, Richard, Debbie, Greg and Shar beyond their involvement in the group. They are bright people. They may even be described as loving people with much to give—perhaps too much—who first of all and in the beginning genuinely, I believe, wanted to do right and serve God on earth. They were also well-educated for the most part, not untutored and inarticulate.

What they shared at the time they came to fall under Jeff Lundgren's spell was a personal emotional crisis that made each uniquely vulnerable to a strong, overbearing personality that seemed, at first blush, not implausible in his claims.

Every group member, except for Danny Kraft, had been trained to believe that one may be acceptable in the sight of God and the church only by living one's life exactly according to the church's dictates. Into this mix—volatile as a uranium pile—came someone who was apparently holy and who pronounced himself ready and able to relieve each follower of his and her overwhelmingly burdensome concerns—all in exchange for their humble obedience, which was not considered a sacrifice of importance. Freedom from what seemed unacceptable responsibility, even if for a short while, with the opportunity to work for the greater good of mankind, seemed well worth any sacrifice. So each of Jeff's followers freely gave away his or her free will and by the time they wanted it back it was too late.

I am no psychiatrist, but I suggest that each of us has had the experience of being emotionally vulnerable—whether we admit it or not, are aware of it or not—of feeling that life just can demand *too much.* Each of us has been vulnerable to the same kind—if not degree —of temptation that forever twisted the lives of the group members, their families, their victims and their victims' families. Anyone in any unguarded moment of their lives can become susceptible to the sort of manipulation practiced so expertly by Jeff and Alice Lundgren. And there are many people who use the same or similar techniques in a relationship to manage a destructive advantage over the other party not so different from the advantage Jeff and Alice came to exercise over their victims. Such exploiters don't physically kill their victims, but they can leave wrecked lives and minds in their wakes. The tale of the Lundgrens and their group is an extreme example, a worst-case scenario, a nightmare come to life, but it should be understood to involve the dynamics not so unusual in the lives of so-called sane and reasonable people. It may be simplistic to say so, but basic to a defense is to hold ourselves accountable and responsible for our own life-decisions.

At the end of January, Greg, Sharon, Debbie, Richard, Susie and Kathy received their prison sentences. Debbie, Sharon and Susie were given the stiffest sentences their plea bargains would permit: incarceration for seven to twenty-five years. All three will be eligible for parole in approximately four and a half years, although no one really expects that they will be released at the first eligibility. Sharon and Susie were taken to prison immediately. Debbie was given a stay of execution on her sentence to permit her back to heal completely. She reported to jail on May 3, 1991.

Greg was sentenced to twenty years to life, consecutively for each murder count. Under Ohio sentencing statutes, however, he will be eligible for parole in about fourteen years. Richard received fifteen years to life for each murder, in terms to be concurrent. He will be eligible for parole in approximately ten years, although, again, it's unlikely he will be released when he is first eligible.

Kathy Johnson was sentenced to Marysville for one year by Judge Jackson, with no credit for her time served in California. Kathy continues to believe that Jeff is the god of this earth and that he will walk out of his prison to her when the time is right. She says she loves him. Apparently Kathy intends to return to her mother's home when she is released from prison, where she will live with her daughter. Kathy's sons are living with Keith on his father's farm. Kathy has not seen them since the group dissolved and she chose to go with Jeff. Keith is unemployed. According to sources from Missouri, he spends whatever money he has on religious books rather than on clothing and food for his children. Keith is divorcing Kathy.

I have said earlier that members of the Lundgren group hardly fit expected stereotypes. Richard is an attractive man with a pleasant personality and a quick wit; Sharon is a gentle woman who is often in her own world but even so seems kind and considerate; Greg is a sensitive person, meticulous, with a nice sense of humor; and Debbie is bright, often rather jolly, assertive and earthy. Not one of them seems vicious or vindictive.

On the other hand, though all demonstrate broken hearts, only Greg and Debbie seem contrite. Each of the others, to at least some degree, seems to cling to the belief that he or she did nothing really wrong. Having given all else to Jeff, they apparently have also given him the blame.

Since Debbie's release from jail on bond in September, 1990, so that she could have her back surgery, she and Ron Andolsek have seen a great deal of each other. They take their relationship one day at a time, not knowing if it will survive their separation but each grateful for the other's companionship now.

Marlene Jennings has gained a new friend. According to her, while she was testifying in Alice's trial she had a religious experience, a revelation from God that Alice was innocent. Consequently, Mrs. Jennings now believes that an innocent person has been sent to prison and that she is solely responsible for that injustice. She now corresponds regularly with Alice, helps to make her life more comfortable in any way that she can and acts as an advocate for Alice on the outside. Currently Mrs. Jennings is attempting to help Alice retrieve some of the furnishings and belongings from the farm.

The big losers? The Avery and Bailey families have lost the children of two generations. Dennis and Cheryl Avery will have no descendants. Dennis and Cheryl stubbornly insisted on following a man who rejected their devotion and finished by sacrificing not only their money and their home but their lives and the lives of their children. The dream that they pursued led them to subject themselves to a leader who hated them. We can speculate, but no one will ever know the lack that they must have felt in their lives to have pursued Jeff and Alice with such devotion. Indeed, the Averys were unique in the group in that they were the pursuers rather than the pursued.

The friends and relatives of the group members have, of course, suffered and will continue to suffer. The group members have lost large portions of their lives, and their families have lost their companionship and dreams for the future. But the big losers, second only to the Averys, are the children of those in prison. Debbie Olivarez has not seen her children since her arrest and may not see them all of the time she is in prison. Kathy Johnson's sons have been separated from her since December of 1989, and no one, except Keith, knows when they will see their mother again. Matthew and Amy Luff have lost their father forever, and their mother for at least four years. Dawn Bluntschly will not live with her mother again, at least until she has started school. Jason, Kristen and Caleb Lundgren have lost their parents, their older brother, and any chance to take pride in their heritage. Who knows if any of them will be able to survive what has happened, let alone become productive, reasonably well-adjusted adults?

Trina, Becky and Karen Avery lost their futures. Trina, the quiet student, eager to learn; Becky, the active child, good at needlework; and sweet Karen, with the large brown eyes and the heart-lifting smile —all buried with their parents in Missouri. Those with the biggest futures were the biggest losers.

INDEX